A LIGURIAN KITCHEN

RECIPES AND TALES *from* THE ITALIAN RIVIERA

the HIPPOCRENE Cookbook Library

Afghan Food & Cookery

African Cooking, Best of Regional

Albanian Cooking, Best of

Alps, Cuisines of the

Aprovecho: A Mexican-American Border Cookbook

Argentina Cooks!, Exp. Ed.

Austrian Cuisine, Best of, Exp. Ed.

Bolivian Kitchen, My Mother's

Brazil: A Culinary Journey

Burma, Flavors of

Cajun Women, Cooking with

Calabria, Cucina di

Caucasus Mountains, Cuisines of the

Chile, Tasting

Colombian Cooking, Secrets of

Croatian Cooking, Best of, Exp. Ed.

Czech Cooking, Best of, Exp. Ed.

Danube, All Along The, Exp. Ed.

Dutch Cooking, Art of, Exp. Ed.

Estonian Tastes and Traditions

Egyptian Cooking

Filipino Food, Fine

Finnish Cooking, Best of

French Caribbean Cuisine

French Fashion, Cooking in the (Bilingual)

Germany, Spoonfuls of

Greek Cooking, Regional

Greek Cuisine, The Best of, Exp. Ed.

Gypsy Feast

Haiti, Taste of

Havana Cookbook, Old (Bilingual)

Hungarian Cookbook, Exp. Ed.

Icelandic Food & Cookery

India, Flavorful

Indian Spice Kitchen, The, Exp. Ed.

International Dictionary of Gastronomy

Irish-Style, Feasting Galore

Italian Cuisine, Treasury of (Bilingual)

Japanese Home Cooking

Jewish-Iraqi Cuisine, Mama Nazima's

Korean Cuisine, Best of

Laotian Cooking, Simple

Latvia, Taste of

Lithuanian Cooking, Art of

Macau, Taste of

Malta, Taste of, Exp. Ed.

Middle Eastern Kitchen, The

Mongolian Cooking, Imperial

Nepal, Taste of

New Hampshire: from Farm to Kitchen

New Jersey Cookbook, Farms and Foods of the Garden State:

Norway, Tastes and Tales of

Persian Cooking, Art of

Pied Noir Cookbook: French Sephardic Cuisine

Piemontese, Cucina: Cooking from Italy's Piedmont

Poland's Gourmet Cuisine

Polish Cooking, Best of, Exp. Ed.

Polish Country Kitchen Cookbook

Polish Cuisine, Treasury of (Bilingual)

Polish Heritage Cookery, Ill. Ed.

Polish Traditions, Old

Portuguese Encounters, Cuisines of, Exp. Ed

Pyrenees, Tastes of

Quebec, Taste of

Rhine, All Along The

Romania, Taste of, Exp. Ed.

Russian Cooking, Best of, Exp. Ed.

Scandinavian Cooking, Best of

Scotland, Traditional Food From

Scottish-Irish Pub and Hearth Cookbook

Sephardic Israeli Cuisine

Sicilian Feasts

Slovenia, Flavors of

Smorgasbord Cooking, Best of

South American Cookery, Art of

South Indian Cooking, Healthy

Spanish Family Cookbook, Rev. Ed.

Sri Lanka, Exotic Tastes of

Swedish Kitchen, A

Swiss Cookbook, The

Syria, Taste of

Taiwanese Cuisine, Best of

Thai Cuisine, Best of, Regional

Trinidad and Tobago, Sweet Hands: Island Cooking from

Turkish Cuisine, Taste of

Tuscan Kitchen, Tastes from a

Ukrainian Cuisine, Best of, Exp. Ed.

Uzbek Cooking, Art of

Warsaw Cookbook, Old

Vietnamese Kitchen, A

A LIGURIAN KITCHEN

RECIPES AND TALES *from* THE ITALIAN RIVIERA

LAURA GIANNATEMPO

photographs by **MICHAEL PIAZZA**

HIPPOCRENE BOOKS

NEW YORK

This is a work of memory, and memory, for better and worse, has its idio-syncracies, its whims, sometimes a whole mind of its own, especially in the young. In a few rare cases I have compressed, combined, or modified the flow of events for the sake of narrative continuity. In others — equally rare — I have changed names or omitted details at the request of participants.

Jacket and book design by Brad Rickman.
Photography by Michael Piazza.

For more information, address:

HIPPOCRENE BOOKS, INC.
171 Madison Avenue
New York, NY 10016

ISBN 0-7818-1171-6
Cataloging-in-Publication Data available from the Library of Congress.
Printed in the United States of America.

ACKNOWLEDGMENTS

A big, heartfelt thank you to all the people who helped make this book possible:

My parents, Rosanna and Piero, who raised me to appreciate good food and good things in life, and who have so graciously accepted the fact that their only child moved so far away from them. Your lively and generous spirits flavor every page of this book, and every day of my life. I miss you.

Silvana, Franco, and Marco Guerci, my vivacious Ligurian family, for keeping the doors of their beautiful homes always open to me and for allowing me to experience Liguria and its food in all their magnificence over the past twenty years. This book simply wouldn't be without you.

Paolo Rondelli at Terre Bianche Agriturismo near Dolceacqua for his warm hospitality and wonderful food.

Titta Moltedo in Recco for telling me everything I wanted to know about *focaccia al formaggio*.

Walter De Batte in Riomaggiore for a long, enlightening chat about wine in Liguria and beyond.

Angela Scipioni at the Cenobio dei Dogi Hotel and Restaurant in Camogli for graciously sharing one of the restaurant's recipes.

My mother-in-law, Sandy Putnam, and Brian O'Donnell for the frequent use of their big Maine kitchen, for their enthusiasm about my food, and for their bravery in eating everything I've ever made (good and bad).

My sister-in-law, Stacy Rickman, for testing some of the recipes and her husband, Matt, for tasting them—the ones without fish, anyway.

My friend and colleague Anne McBride, who first believed I could write a cookbook and whose advice has been generous and indispensable.

Iris Bass and Rajni George at Hippocrene Books for their faith and enthusiasm.

Everyone at Fish Tales, my local fishmonger in Brooklyn, for accommodating my many requests.

My instructors at the Institute of Culinary Education for turning me into a pro.

La Ladrona, Il Bianchetto, Angiolina, and all the other wonderful people in Bonassola who provided such a vivid backdrop to my family's summer vacations.

My dear friend and the photographer of this book, Michael Piazza, for his beautiful, inspired photography (it wouldn't look half as good without your magic touch), for testing some of the recipes, and for tasting many, many others.

My husband, Brad Rickman, for his unwavering support and patience throughout this project, for tasting every single dish over and over and giving me precious advice, for his gorgeous work on the book design, and for being such a wonderful companion through life. I love you.

for my parents, ROSANNA & PIERO

Osservare tra i frondi il palpitare
lontano di scaglie di mare
mentre si levan tremuli scricchi
di cicale dai calvi picchi

Observe between branches
the far-off throb of sea scales
while cicadas' wavering screaks
rise from the bald peaks

—Eugenio Montale, *Ossi di Seppia* (1925)

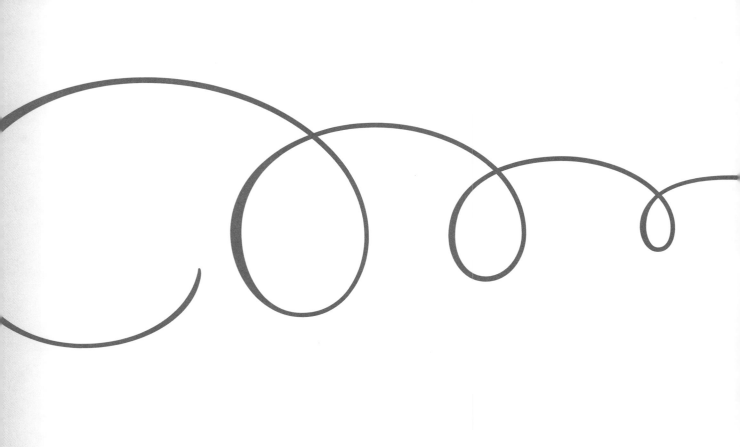

Contents

...

leggermente c...

olio extra vergi...

cchiai di pe...

di più) e qui...

...nde lo sto...

pulito taglia...

Far insaporir...

...n bicchier...

*M*orning is my favorite time of the day in Bonassola, a sleepy seaside village on the eastern coast of Liguria—that narrow strip of beautiful coastal land in the northwest of Italy known as the Italian Riviera. When I wake up there's usually coffee brewing on the stove in the small *moka* espresso maker, my mother and my aunt Silvana already moving about the kitchen making breakfast for the family.

Milk is warming in a small pot next to the coffee and there's water boiling in case someone wants tea. Silvana opens a packet of Mulino Bianco cookies for my cousin Marco, while my mother arranges homemade jam and *fette biscottate*—crunchy slices of crackerlike white bread—on a small plate. But the best part is when Franco, my uncle, rides up the steep lane to the house on his *motorino* scooter carrying the newspaper and a large, fresh slice of plain focaccia wrapped in white paper, still warm from the oven. Already, the morning bears the promise of superb food.

Still half-asleep, I open the house's French windows, sit in a taupe lawn chair on the roofed veranda, and take it all in: the flamboyant hot pink bougainvillea clashing spectacularly with the softer, sage-toned olive trees of the terraced landscape, the deep blue waters of the bay beneath, and the fragrant, iodine-charged Mediterranean breeze. Slowly, I begin to wake up. I take a bite of the deliciously salty, oil-doused focaccia, sip my *caffè latte*, and browse the headlines of *La Repubblica*, the newspaper I read when I'm in Italy. When I imagine paradise, it looks like this.

For me—a girl from foggy-in-winter, hazy-in-summer Torino in the northwestern corner of Italy, not too far from the Alps—Liguria has always been a strip of eternal sunshine; a fabulous place where temperatures never fall below floral-dress-flutteringin-the-breeze level, where an endless stretch of blue sea flickers in dazzling sunlight, and where food has a special sensuous quality—particularly when your meals are relished in a front row seat to the Mediterranean.

This tiny area of the world has a special place in my heart. It evokes memories of lively, overcrowded beaches, of pointless but wildly entertaining small talk under large sun umbrellas, of hours spent soaking up the warm Ligurian sun in a state of bronzed bliss, of inspiring walks amidst the lushly scented *macchia mediterranea* (the "Mediterranean stain," a figurative reference to the local vegetation)—and, most of all, of delicious and spectacularly boisterous outdoor meals with family and friends.

For as long as I can remember, I've spent the better part of my summers in the small town of Bonassola, near the all-too-well-known Cinque Terre. But while those five famous villages lose much of their allure in the summer—when they're inundated by herds of jolly, loud tourists who cram the impossibly narrow streets in the old town centers, eat up all the gelato and focaccia, and turn these traditionally quiet fishing communities into local branches of New York City—Bonassola has managed to retain a "local" kind of charm and, with that, a slow-paced calmness reminiscent of another era. So much so that if you're a thrill-seeking twenty-something looking for a little adventure, Bonassola is probably not where you want to end up.

In summertime, the population almost doubles as people from nearby Genova and the big cities of Milano and Torino drive to their vacation homes. But it's always the same bunch of people, really, and they all know each other or of each other. So in the dog days of summer, Bonassola clings anachronistically to a comfortable provincialism, a decidedly small-town vibe varnished with only the thinnest layer of city-folk chic.

My uncle Franco, a pure-bred Ligurian, is a gregariously funny and charismatic guy—and quite the gourmand. In Bonassola he'll only buy focaccia in two places: Bianchetto's, owned by an old baker who owes his nickname (bianchetto means "little white") both to his white hair and to the fact that he's constantly covered with flour; and La Ladrona—not the store's actual name, but one my uncle insists on using in honor of the old spinster who owns it. *La ladrona* means "the big thief" and it's Franco's contention that, when she can get away with it, she'll conveniently *forget* to hand back part of your change. (Her focaccia is by far the most expensive in town—another good reason for her epithet—but, by some accounts, it's also the best.) Despite his abhorrence for alarm clocks when on vacation, Franco is adamant about personally picking the seafood that will end up on the table that night. And so he rises bright and early, dons his summer uniform of shorts, T-shirt, and flip-flops, hops on the *motorino*—forgoing the helmet, of course; it's summer, and we're in Italy after all—and dashes through tight, meandering roads up the hill and down again to the fresh fish market in nearby Levanto.

Silvana, his wife of thirty years, is still amused by her husband's whims. She is from Piemonte, like me, but she's lived in Liguria for most of her life, and she can (and better!) whip up a flawless seafood salad or a plate of exquisite *trofie al pesto* like any native. I've spent many an afternoon in the kitchen with her and my mother, chopping onions and tomatoes, stirring a fragrant fish soup, or roasting *branzino* for one of many extraordinary dinner parties on the terrace. This book is about those afternoons spent in our Ligurian kitchen.

Much has changed in my life since I first started spending my summers in Bonassola in 1983. I moved across an ocean and a continent, leaving my native Italy to adopt a new language and a new culture; I married an American man and moved yet again from laid-back San Francisco to that relentless, energy-instilling throb that is New York City; I gave up a career to embark on a food-centered exploration of the world and of myself. But Bonassola has remained my *punto fermo*, my anchor—a place I can go back to every year knowing that not much has changed, knowing that no matter what has occurred in the rest of the world or in my own life, I can always rely on those serene mornings nibbling on focaccia and sipping *caffè latte*, on those spectacular late-night dinners hosted by my comically buoyant uncle with his motley—if not always fascinating—clique of friends, and on the soothing comfort of helping Silvana and my mother in the kitchen while bantering about the latest fashion or the neighbor's affair with the hunky, and much younger, lifeguard. It's a place where I reconnect with myself, with my past, and with the kind of slower, simpler way of life that's so elusive in my frenetic urban present. I take walks. I go to the beach. I swim in the energizing waters of the Mediterranean. I eat honest, uncomplicated, and infinitely satisfying food at a pace that feels just right—*normal*, I dare say.

Before you start cooking

The food of Liguria is, to me, among the freshest, most vibrant, and tasty of all of Italy. It's mostly *cucina povera*, the cooking of the poor, extremely simple and unpretentious, made with marvelous ingenuity and boundless creativity from the scant ingredients offered by a parsimonious soil.

The Mediterranean Sea blessed Ligurians with an abundance of delicious fish, but the *entroterra*—the inland—wasn't as merciful. The soil here is dry and unevenly fertile, and the mountainous terrain has always prevented the kind of sweeping crops that stretch across the northern Padana plains. Centuries ago, peasants were forced to build terracelike strips of land, called *fasce* or *terrazze*, stone after stone, to create a level surface that would allow them to squeeze something out of this ruthless land of precipitous hills diving right into the sea. Modern irrigation systems and fertilizers have made life much easier today, but previous generations had to make do with what they had. And they became extremely resourceful in order to make the most of their soil and still bring meals of abundant flavor to the table.

Liguria's food is truly a mirror of its land. The scarcity of artisanal Ligurian cheese or butter can be traced to a lack of adequate pasture land for cows and other animals. Peasants kept a few goats or sheep in their backyards alongside chickens and rabbits, but that's about it. Likewise, the lavish use of a remarkable variety of wild herbs—from unrecognizable weeds and borage leaves to wild rosemary, marjoram, and basil—derived from a need to take full advantage of everything the land so grudgingly bestowed.

Ligurian cooking is perhaps best known for its fish. Regional kitchen traditions certainly draw on the impressive local bounty, but they also bring copious amounts of vegetables into play, make sumptuous use of aromatic herbs, and want you to drizzle the amazingly fruity Ligurian olive oil on every possible dish.

Because the cuisine is so simple—because no butter or cream or rich meat stocks come to the rescue to give dishes a strong backbone—Ligurian cooks rely on the best-quality ingredients they can lay their hands on, especially in the selection of herbs and vegetables. And so should you. Growing your own would be ideal, but since few of us can do that, including myself (I live in a 650-square-foot apartment in Brooklyn), try seeking out a farmers' market near you; you'll be surprised at the difference it makes. At the very least, buy your produce at the local health food store or at one that sells fresh, preferably organic goods.

As for fish, get to know your fishmonger or the fish guy (or gal) at the grocery store. That way, they'll give you the very best fish. Because—did I forget to mention?—you should use the absolute freshest fish on the market. Check the eyes; if they're filmy and opaque, the fish is a few days old and past its prime. Check the gills; are they slimy and nasty? You probably don't want to eat that fish. Don't be afraid to ask the fishmonger to show you the merchandise before he or she cleans and cuts it.

The recipes in this book don't add up to an encyclopedia of Ligurian cuisine. It's not my intention to present you with a comprehensive collection of dishes from the region. Instead, I want to take you on a more intimate, personal journey through that extraordinary marriage of land and sea that is Ligurian cuisine—where virtually everything that grows in the sun between this slender and harsh strip of land and its gorgeous waters will sooner or later end up in the pan. So I've chosen recipes that have meaning to me and reflect my own very special relationship with Liguria. While there certainly are a few traditional dishes, I've left out a number of time-honored recipes, such as *cima alla genovese* (a long list of giblets and offal stuffed into a veal's belly) or *cappon magro* (a towering salad that can easily take eight hours to make), either because I've never made them myself or because they're far too time-consuming to make, besides the obvious challenge of finding all the ingredients. Almost no one, even among Ligurians, makes them at home anymore; and if they do, it's only for a very special occasion.

Instead, I've introduced a few recipes that may not be typically Ligurian, but that incarnate the spirit of Ligurian cooking, using emblematic regional ingredients or preparations that any Ligurian could've come up with. These are either dishes my family makes, dishes I tasted in restaurants in the area, or things I've concocted while spending time with my family in Bonassola. They are inspired by Liguria—by its approach to cooking as well as its ingredients and, most important, by its spirit. To me, they are just as Ligurian as the others.

But most of all, this is a book that should inspire *you* to cook. I don't want it to be some lofty catalog of traditional cuisine with ingredients no one can find or recipes no one will ever dream of making, gathering dust on some forgotten shelf. I want it to be used for weeknight cooking as well as for special occasions; there are recipes in it for both.

Before you start cooking, there are a few important things to keep in mind. First and foremost, always use high-quality, fruity extra-virgin olive oil. It doesn't have to be from Liguria (although that wouldn't hurt), but it should be extra-virgin. This means no heat or chemicals were used in extracting the oil, thus preserving its flavor, quality, and nutritional properties.

When I ask for parsley in a recipe, I always mean flat-leaf parsley, also known as "Italian parsley." Some ingredients and preparations, you'll notice, are somewhat recurrent. Ligurian cooking uses abundant amounts of basil, marjoram, bitter greens, garlic, and tomatoes, as well as dried mushrooms and day-old white bread. When I ask for peeled and seeded tomatoes, that means cooked for about one minute in boiling water, then shocked in ice water and peeled. I use kosher salt unless otherwise indicated. When there's an alternative, it's generally sea salt. While it's not absolutely indispensable, you may want to invest in a mortar and pestle. Many of the dishes—the sauces in particular—were traditionally made with one, and I think they have a richer, more intense flavor when this simple kitchen tool is in the picture. That said, I use a blender or a food processor all the time, particularly when I'm in a bit of a rush. So if you have the time, indulge in making your pesto the slow way, but if it's six o'clock and you have to put dinner on the table, the food will scarcely be less delicious if you use a few power tools. If you don't have bread that's a few days old, use fresh bread instead; just bake it in a hot oven for at least ten minutes first.

Many of the recipes in this book are fairly quick and can be prepared in less than forty minutes. Clearly, when fresh pasta making or kneading dough for focaccia are involved, things take a little longer. But don't be discouraged. You can reserve these dishes for a lazy Sunday afternoon or a special occasion. You can also make pasta or focaccia dough in advance, freeze it, and have it ready on demand.

One last thing before you begin cooking. Remember that Italians are not in the habit of following recipes. When I ask my mother or aunt for a recipe, they generally give me a measurement for the main ingredient—say, one kilo of sea bass. The rest is a pinch of this, a drop of that, a glass of this. (*Yes, but what size glass?*) It's basically left to me to figure it out. This is because, once you get a hang of a few basic techniques and methods, you can start improvising and getting creative. And that's what I hope you'll do. Don't get hung up on exact measurements (unless it's for a cake). Experiment with different herbs, spices, and combinations once you're confident with a dish. That's when you really start having fun!

THE *real* LIGURIA

When my mother woke me up early on an impossibly muggy July morning in 1983 and instructed me to pack a few things for a weekend at the beach, I had no idea this seemingly mundane trip would have such a permanent impact on my life.

"We're going to visit Silvana and Franco," she announced.

Aunt Silvana is my mother's first cousin. So she's really not my aunt, but the two are so close—they even look alike—that the family has long considered them siblings. *Sorelle materasso*, the mattress sisters, is what Silvana's husband, Franco, calls them, for a laugh. He's yet to tell me why.

Silvana and Franco had rented a house in a small Ligurian town I'd never heard of. And they were raving about it. They were so enamored that they bought a *terreno*, a piece of land on the hills just behind the town, and were making plans to build a vacation home there.

"It's not like the *ponente*," said Franco on the phone, alluding to the tourist-trodden western coast of Liguria. "Here it's peaceful and quiet. The *real* Liguria, free from the assaults of *crucchi* and *inglesi*." He meant the German and English tourists who'd bought vacation homes in Liguria and, at least according to Franco, set about depriving that part of the region of its authenticity. Bonassola, on the other hand, was charming and foreigner-free, and so close to those stunningly picturesque and largely undiscovered little villages of the Cinque Terre. He couldn't have known, at the time, that the Cinque Terre would also fall under siege one day, just as much as the *ponente*.

We needed to see this wonderful place, my mother decided. My father, a calm, taciturn kind of guy who'd rather spend eight hours in his attic studio fidgeting with some odd piece of electronic equipment of his own fabrication than face Franco's ebullient talk, gave in reluctantly. We were going to Bonassola.

To this day, whenever we travel to visit family or friends, my mother feels the urge to pack all sorts of food supplies to take to our hosts. The day before, she embarks on an expedition to the market, where she buys cases of seasonal fruits and vegetables. She crams paper towels, cookies, olive oil, and wine in the trunk and the back of her tiny car. "I'm a guest," she says in defense of this habit. "I don't want to impose. It's impolite to show up empty-handed and assume they'll pay for everything you eat." Yes, I tell her, but wouldn't a cake or a bottle of wine do? No one ever shows up with a trunk full of goodies when they pay *us* a visit. To be completely honest, I'm never sure whether our hosts are thankful or terribly offended by the insinuation that we'll all starve to death if my mother doesn't bring food.

That morning in July 1983 was no exception. We packed the car with a small suitcase and the habitual cargo of leafy greens, apricots, peaches, and cookies and headed for the *autostrada*, direction La Spezia. The *autostrada*, for the record, is the infamous Italian highway, where speed limits are mere suggestions and people drive as if they're always late for an extremely important appointment. It doesn't help that my calm, quiet father turns into a maniac behind the wheel.

Just off the Carrodano exit, a few tortuous miles inland from Bonassola, the road changed dramatically. It's not that it got less treacherous, just that the thrill was of a different kind. It wound, turned, twisted, and climbed up the hill, one lane in each direction, barely wide enough for two cars, with the rocky hill on one side and a hair-raising cliff on the other. My father charged every curve at seventy miles an hour, but I was too absorbed by what I saw outside the windows to be terrified.

To reach Bonassola, you have to cross Levanto, the neighboring town. This means you go up and down a soaring hill not once, but twice. During this roller-coaster ride, you drive by minuscule villages that are nothing more than isolated clusters of colorful houses built literally on top of each other, cascading down the hillsides, almost suspended in the Ligurian *macchia* of glistening olive trees, fragrant broom and linden trees, and desertlike shrubbery of agaves and acacias. Lavaggiorosso, Lerici, and Montale (like Nobel poet laureate Eugenio Montale, who was from the region) are some of the heroic villages that seep across the inland hills.

We veered around another hairpin turn on the top of the second hill past Levanto and began to descend toward Bonassola. It was from this lofty viewpoint that I caught my first glimpse of the town. It was stunning; a perfect half-moon bay of turquoise waters turning deep blue further away from the coast; a sliver of white beach patched with round, bright blue and green sun umbrellas; and soft, pastel-colored houses huddled around the ubiquitous Italian church with its towering *campanile* (bell tower). I noticed an ancient crumbling structure with a big clock overlooking the beach—an old sighting tower, I later learned.

As it turned out, the house Silvana and Franco had rented in Bonassola wasn't "downtown." It was, sure enough, up the hill—another hill, that is. You reached it by following Bonassola's absurdly narrow main road through a few more hairpin turns upward. Even my dad was forced to reduce the speed and once even to come to a screeching halt when a perky Ape—a tiny three-wheeled flatbed preferred by local farmers—came zooming down, invisible until it nearly crashed into our car. Later, we learned the local practice of honking wildly before each turn so you didn't have to bother slowing down.

My relatives' house was at via Roma 99. A rather promising address, I thought. But when we arrived, we found nothing but two garage doors painted bright azure and a black, locked gate door that lead to a narrow concrete stairway, ascending into what appeared to be the Ligurian wilderness. Where was the house? There were no cell phones in 1983. My father called for help the old-fashioned Italian way: a couple of ferociously loud honks. A few minutes later, we saw Silvana coming excitedly down the stairs.

"*Ciao, come state? Avete fatto buon viaggio?*" she asked cheerily, inquiring about our trip.

We followed her back up the stairs, which wound their way through a perpendicular Mediterranean jungle thick with silver-green olive trees, small lemon groves, rose bushes and geraniums, and vibrant little wild flowers. Finally, toward the top, I spied the house. It was built in the old Ligurian style. The washed out, pale yellow paint was peeling off in several spots and each window, equipped with large, deep green shutters, was framed by a thick, white chip-pocked trim.

After a good climb, we arrived at a waist-high iron gate that led into a spacious L-shaped terrace. (I would go up these stairs many times in the years that followed, always taking them after I'd climbed the old stone steps up the hill from the beach, often under a sweltering summer sun.) Later, I would come to think of the terrace as the best part of that old house. It was spacious and airy. Behind it were the stones of the *fascia* at the rear of the house, draped in cascading bougainvilleas and white and pink oleander trees. The rest was wide open to the lush *macchia* and to that wonderful blotch of cobalt that was the Mediterranean sea.

"Are you hungry?" asked Silvana. It was lunchtime, and I admit my stomach was growling.

We followed her to the narrower part of the terrace under a vine trellis covered with leafy *arrampicanti*, climbing plants that created a pleasantly cool shade—a much welcome shelter from the blazing midday sun. This is where Silvana and Franco had lunch every day and, though I didn't know it then, it was where I would savor countless Ligurian meals. The table had been set with the rental house's unique collection of scruffy, hand-me-down dinnerware: a faded plastic-lined, cherry-patterned tablecloth ("for the outdoors," Silvana quickly pointed out with a smirk), old mismatched plates that each seemed to be chipped in some place, and worn out Picardie-style glasses—quite fashionable today but so démodé in the eighties. Two cold, sweaty bottles towered at the center of the table: chilled white wine and *acqua minerale*.

Silvana had prepared authentic *pesto alla genovese* with green beans and potatoes, using the small, sweet-scented local basil leaves from the *terreno*. The pesto had a uniquely light green color, a luxuriously creamy texture, and a delicate, yet rich and deeply satisfying flavor. Paired with fresh homemade *trofie* pasta bought from La Ladrona in town, Silvana's pesto was exquisite. I had never tasted anything quite like it. Was it in any way related to that thick, bottle green amalgam my mother called pesto? I didn't think so. But, to be fair, the blame lay not with my mother's culinary skills—she's quite a good cook, especially in her own element of Piedmontese cuisine. The trouble was that she used store-bought basil from Torino, the very thought of which makes Ligurians cringe. Real *pesto alla genovese* is made exclusively with the sweet, light-colored basil from Prà, an area on the hills behind Genova. Traditionally, the ingredients—basil, pine nuts, garlic, pecorino and Parmigiano cheeses—are ground together with a mortar and pestle—although many Ligurians, including the members of my family, have learned to appreciate the advantages of a food processor when making their regional specialty.

After the pesto came a large blue-rimmed bowl sporting the inevitable chip, filled with deep red chunks of perfectly ripe tomatoes, thin slices of onions, and a handful of chopped basil leaves, dressed simply with salt and abundant fruity olive oil. The tomatoes were from the *terreno* as well, Franco announced with the pride of a budding weekend farmer. Next year, he told us, the olive oil would be from the *terreno*, too, as they were hoping to have their first olive harvest.

One bite of these juicy red tomatoes and I knew I was in for another revelatory gastronomic experience. They were beyond tasty; they were sweet, fruity almost, with just a hint of acidity, firm yet bursting with flavorful juice. Every bite was an explosion of Mediterranean sunshine in my mouth. And that wasn't the end of it. The best part came after the tomatoes were gone, when big chunks of freshly baked bread found their way to the fragrant blend of olive oil and tomato juices left on the bottom of the plate, for what is one of the pinnacles of Italian culinary civilization: *la scarpetta*. The word means "little shoe," but it has nothing to do with Manolo Blahniks. Rather, it refers to the simple act of wiping your plate clean of tasty sauces and condiments with a piece of crusty bread. Few things in life get any better. Who cares how chipped or antediluvian your dinnerware is when this is what you're eating? A simple but perfect meal with a killer view of the Mediterranean and a soft sea breeze gently shaking your hair—what more could anyone ask for?

I think of that day every time I have utterly tasteless, mealy, shamefully under-ripe supermarket tomatoes in New York. Eat them raw with just a little salt and olive oil and you'll have the worst meal in your life. It's hard to believe they're even remotely related to the delicious fruit I had in Bonassola. The only thing that comes close are the colorful heirloom tomatoes you find at farmers' markets for the price of small diamonds. But they're worth it, especially if you're after the sheer perfection of Italy's simplest dishes. Italian food is all about shopping, someone once told me.

The owner of the old rental house was an elderly widow, Angiolina, who had lived all her life just down the road in an ancient, crumbling stone house that looked abandoned. Angiolina was seventy-something, and she'd never traveled any farther than Levanto—the slightly larger, adjacent town dubbed "the metropolis" by outsiders from the big cities who scoffed at the local folks' narrow-mindedness. She was a rough type, with spiky gray hair barely tamed beneath a knotted handkerchief, heavily-lined leathery skin burnished by years of hard labor in this unforgiving agricultural land, and the inevitable shapeless, dark-colored, shin-length wraparound dress every respectable country woman past her prime must wear in this part of the world. My own grandmother had a rather unimpressive collection of these outfits, which are to Italy's elderly women what polyester pants, gaudy shirts, and white sneakers are to Florida retirees.

Angiolina was quiet and aloof, but you could hear her loud and clear when she had something to say. And despite her moderate wealth—due in no small part to those same scoffing city folk, who paid exorbitant sums to spend summers in her plain old house—she was rather thrifty, a quality she shared with many old-school Ligurians.

We were just about ready to put the finishing touch to our lunch under the vine trellis with a bowl brimming with ripe apricots and plums (hauled by my mother from Torino), when we heard a female voice holler at the terrace gate.

"*Permesso?*" the voice inquired as a frail, slightly hunched old woman made her way past the gate. And there she was: Angiolina, in person, precariously toting a large tray covered with aluminum foil. Did she really climb the stairs with that? The tray was full of what I soon came to know as her legendary *verdure ripiene*: zucchini, peppers, and eggplant stuffed with ground meat, mortadella, Parmigiano, pine nuts, and aromatic herbs roasted in the oven until soft and oozing with caramelized goodness. Angiolina's *verdure ripiene* were considered by many to be the best in town. These sure lived up to their reputation—slightly browned and crisp on the outside, with a moist and flavorful heart. She'd baked too many, she said. Did she come too late? We had time. In fact, I could've continued eating forever. Meals have a tendency to stretch for hours in Bonassola, as they always do when the company is good and the food is sincere, uncomplicated, and expertly prepared with the best and the freshest the land—and sea—have to offer.

SMALL PLATES & SNACKS

antipasti e stuzzichini

Quick Oyster Gratin

Ostriche Ripiene

Like all respectable coastal folks, Ligurians love their oysters. I love oysters too, but eating them raw makes me a little nervous—unless I have absolute confidence in the chef or the fishmonger. This is a great way to enjoy the briny lusciousness of oysters without fret. And you get to choose how you want to present them. In their shells, with the oohs and aahs de rigueur, or as a gratin, which may look less impressive but is equally appetizing. This recipe will serve three large oysters per person, enough for an appetizer. Double the amount of oysters, along with the other ingredients, if you'd like to serve it as a main course.

SERVES 4

12 large or 24 small oysters

4 salted anchovies

1 tablespoon finely chopped parsley

2 small cloves garlic, finely chopped (about 1 tablespoon)

1 small yellow onion, very finely chopped (about 1 cup)

½ cup homemade bread crumbs (see recipe page 211)

4 tablespoons extra-virgin olive oil

Salt

Freshly ground black pepper

1 teaspoon freshly squeezed lemon juice (optional)

Preheat the oven to 400°F.

Clean the oyster shells and shuck the oysters with an oyster knife, reserving 1 tablespoon of the liquid and the shells, if you plan on using them. Pat the shucked oysters dry with a paper towel.

Rinse the salted anchovies under cold running water to remove excess salt and chop them very finely.

In a large bowl, mix together the oysters with anchovies, parsley, garlic, onion, and half the bread crumbs. Add 2 tablespoons of olive oil, a pinch of salt (be careful not to oversalt, as the anchovies are already salted), and a grind or two of pepper. Mix everything very well so the oysters are nicely coated with the other ingredients.

FIRST PRESENTATION OPTION **Oysters in a shell.** Lay each oyster in a reserved half shell, making sure to spoon some of the other ingredients in with each oyster (use shells that are clean and whole). Place the shells in a large rimmed baking sheet, sprinkle evenly with the remaining bread crumbs, drizzle with the remaining oil, and bake for 10 to 15 minutes, depending on the size of the oysters. Drizzle, if you wish, with the lemon juice before serving.

SECOND PRESENTATION OPTION **Gratin-style.** Place the oyster mixture in a baking pan large enough for one snug layer of oysters. Sprinkle evenly with the remaining bread crumbs, drizzle with the remaining oil, and bake for 10 to 15 minutes, depending on the size of the oysters. Drizzle, if you wish, with the lemon juice before serving.

Smoked Swordfish with Baby Arugula, Extra-Virgin Olive Oil, and White Pepper

Pesce Spada Affumicato con la Rucola

I had this dish at a fabulous restaurant in Camogli and was an instant convert. It may not be traditional, but it's everywhere these days in Liguria and beyond. It's quick, easy, and fresh—perfect for a hot weather day, when the last thing you want to do is get close to hot burners. You'll find smoked swordfish in specialty stores or online (see Sources). If you have a hard time tracking it down, you can replace it with another kind of smoked fish: salmon, of course, but also trout or albacore tuna.

SERVES 4

12 ounces smoked swordfish

⅓ cup fruity extra-virgin olive oil, plus more as needed

1½ teaspoons freshly squeezed lemon juice

Salt

Freshly ground white pepper

2 cups baby or coarsely chopped regular-size arugula (about 2 ounces)

Cut the smoked fish in paper-thin slices (or as thinly as you can), and arrange them on a serving platter or on four individual plates. Don't worry if the slices are not even or if the fish breaks apart as you cut it. It may not be picture perfect, but it'll still be delicious.

In a small bowl, whisk together the olive oil and the lemon juice until you obtain a light emulsion. Add salt and pepper to taste, but don't oversalt, as smoked fish is usually quite salty. Toss half the dressing with the arugula in a bowl and pour the rest over the fish.

Top the smoked fish slices with the dressed arugula, sprinkle with extra pepper, if you like, and serve. Feel free to drizzle a little more olive oil over the entire dish if you feel it's too dry.

Potato Fritters with Marjoram and White Truffle Oil

Cuculli di Patate

These tasty little fritters make great finger food, perfect to dip in rémoulade or tartar sauce or salsa verde (see recipe page 51). And they're quite easy to prepare. They can be made and breaded ahead, refrigerated or frozen, and dipped into the frying oil when you're ready to serve them.

Speaking of frying oil, Ligurians have always fried with olive oil because that's what was readily available. Today many people in Italy use vegetable oils, like canola oil, because they're lighter and less expensive. But I still prefer olive oil for frying because it imparts great flavor—and, contrary to what some people say, I don't think it makes for heavier fried foods. You can also use a blend of olive oil and vegetable oil.

SERVES 6 TO 8

1 pound russet potatoes

3 tablespoons pine nuts

4 tablespoons (½ stick) unsalted butter, cut into 1-tablespoon chunks, at room temperature

3 tablespoons finely chopped marjoram

1½ cups finely grated Parmigiano-Reggiano

1 ½ teaspoons white truffle oil

Salt

Freshly ground black pepper

4 large eggs

½ cup unbleached all-purpose flour

1 cup homemade bread crumbs (see recipe page 211)

At least 6 cups extra-virgin or virgin olive oil or a blend of canola and olive oil, for frying

Bring a large pot of water to a boil, drop in the whole, unpeeled potatoes, and cook them for about 25 minutes, or until fork tender.

While the potatoes are boiling, mash the pine nuts with a mortar and pestle, or in a small food processor (such as a Cuisinart MiniPrep).

Drain the potatoes, peel them (use latex gloves or a kitchen towel to protect your hands from the heat), and pass them through a ricer or food mill into a large bowl, as you would do to make potato puree.

Add the pine nuts, butter, marjoram, Parmigiano, and truffle oil to the bowl of pureed potatoes. Mix with a wooden spoon, and season with salt and pepper to taste. Add 2 of the eggs, stirring well to incorporate them.

With this mixture, form little spheres (*cucculi*) shaped like small walnuts, rolling the potato mixture between the palms of your hands. Set them aside.

Beat the remaining eggs and pour them into a shallow bowl. Put the flour and bread crumbs in separate plates or shallow bowls. Bread the cuculli in batches by coating them in the flour first. Then dip them in the beaten eggs and coat them with the bread crumbs. Set them aside on a clean surface or a large baking sheet.

Pour the oil into a large saucepan and bring it to frying temperature, 365°F, over medium-high heat. If you don't have a thermometer, dip one fritter in the oil. If it starts fizzing, the oil is ready. Fry the cuculli in batches for 1 to 2 minutes, or until golden brown on the surface. Take them out of the oil with a spider (a flat-disked strainer) or a slotted spoon and transfer them to a plate lined with paper towels to drain the excess oil. Season with a generous sprinkle of salt as soon as the *cuculli* come out of the oil, and serve warm.

Clam, Scallop, and Oyster Crostini

Crostini di Mare alla Genovese

To me, this is a quintessential summer appetizer. Picture this: *aperitivo* by the beach at sundown sipping a glass of chilled white wine or—why not?—a refreshing cocktail. What could complement this better than a seafood crostino? You can replace the clams, scallops, and oysters with any shellfish you like: shrimp, calamari, or lobster tails work quite well. And if all you have is a bigger loaf of bread, such as a ciabatta, don't hesitate to make crostoni (large crostini).

SERVES 4

8 small oysters

12 large clams

1 medium-size baguette

3 tablespoons extra-virgin olive oil

2 large cloves garlic

8 sea scallops

¼ cup dry white wine

1 teaspoon salt

1 tablespoon unsalted butter

½ teaspoon cayenne pepper

1 teaspoon finely chopped parsley

Freshly ground black pepper

2 tablespoons lemon juice

Shuck the oysters and set them aside in the refrigerator, reserving 2 tablespoons of the liquid.

Barely cover the bottom of a large saucepan with water and bring it to a boil. Reduce to a slow simmer and add the clams. Cover and cook just until all the clam shells are wide open, discarding any unopened ones. Don't overcook the clams or they'll get gummy. Set aside.

Preheat the oven to 350°F. Cut the bread in eight 1-inch slices. With your fingers, carve out some of the soft center of the bread to form a small dimple. Don't throw away the carved-out bread, reserve it for later.

Place the crostini on a rimmed baking sheet, drizzle them evenly with 1 tablespoon of the olive oil, and toast them in the oven for about 10 minutes, or until crispy but not browned. Reserve.

Crush the garlic cloves with the flat blade of a chef's knife.

In a large skillet, heat 1 tablespoon of the olive oil over medium-high heat and add the garlic. After about 2 minutes (just enough time to infuse the oil with garlic flavor without burning the garlic), remove the garlic and add the scallops. Brown them on both sides over medium-high heat, 3 to 4 minutes per side. Transfer them to a clean cutting board. Add the oysters, white wine, and oyster liquid to the pan and cook over medium-high to high heat for another 3 to 4 minutes, or until the liquid has almost completely evaporated. Turn off the heat. Cut the scallops into quarters (or eighths if they're very big). Add the clams and scallops back to the pan with the oysters, sprinkle with the salt, and stir the contents of the pan well.

Meanwhile, melt the butter in an 8-inch skillet over medium heat. When it stops bubbling, add the reserved bread and cook it in the butter over medium-high heat for 2 to 4 minutes, until crispy and lightly golden. Let it cool and chop it coarsely.

Place the shellfish in a bowl and add cayenne pepper, parsley, and the toasted chopped bread. Adjust seasoning with salt and pepper. Arrange the seafood mixture on the concave side of the reserved crostini. Drizzle the remaining olive oil over each crostino and put the pan back in the oven for 2 minutes or less, just enough to heat the ingredients through. Drizzle with the lemon juice and serve immediately.

Crostini with Lemon-Scented Olive Paste

Crostini con la Pasta di Olive

My very first food memories associated with Liguria date back to before Bonassola. My paternal grandparents spent their retirement years on the *riviera di ponente* in a town called Pietra Ligure. Every time we visited, my grandmother had *pasta di olive* ready for us, spread on some crusty peasant bread. It was one of the best parts of my visit. She got the paste from an olive farmer near Imperia, where she also bought her olive oil. My parents stocked up on these small jars of olive paste and took them back to Torino, so we could enjoy them year-round. *Pasta di olive* is admittedly quite similar to Provençal tapenade, which is not surprising given that the two regions are adjacent and that the very eastern limb of Provence was once part of Italy. Over the centuries, there has been a great deal of cultural as well as political back and forth, and a number of similarities appear in the regions' cuisines.

SERVES 6 TO 8

FOR THE OLIVE PASTE

2 cups pitted black olives, preferably gaeta, kalamata, or niçoise

2 sprigs thyme, leaves only

1 small sprig rosemary, leaves only

1 large clove garlic

1 teaspoon finely grated lemon zest

Freshly ground black pepper

½ cup extra-virgin olive oil

TO ASSEMBLE

16 (½-inch) slices bread, cut on the bias (use a baguette or similar bread)

2 tablespoons extra-virgin olive oil

Preheat the oven to 425°F.

MAKE THE PASTE Place the olives, thyme, rosemary, garlic, lemon zest, and pepper in the bowl of a food processor and run the motor until you obtain a fairly smooth paste. With the processor still running, add the olive oil in a thin stream. And voilà, your zesty olive paste is ready. You shouldn't need to add any salt, as the olives are already quite briny. But taste and add salt if needed.

ASSEMBLE Arrange the slices of bread on a large rimmed baking sheet, drizzle them with the olive oil, and toast them in the oven for about 5 minutes, or until nice and crispy.

Let the bread cool just a little. Spread the olive paste onto each bread slice and serve.

Bruschetta with Cherry Tomatoes, Black Olives, and Basil

Bruschetta con Ciliegine, Olive Nere, e Basilico

No Italian meal, especially in summertime, should ever begin without a bruschetta. That's my take, anyway. Bruschetta is not necessarily a Ligurian specialty (in one form or another, it's eaten all over Italy), but we always make this one at our house in Bonassola. It's a great, undemanding way to use the *terreno*'s gorgeous produce. When I make it at home in the United States, I like using colorful heirloom cherry tomatoes. But if all you can find at the market are regular old red tomatoes, they'll work just as well—just make sure they're ripe and juicy. You can add a little ricotta or crumbled goat cheese on top, if you like.

SERVES 6 TO 8

2 cups ripe cherry tomatoes

1 medium-size baguette or ciabatta bread

½ cup extra-virgin olive oil, plus more for drizzling

½ cup coarsely chopped pitted black olives, preferably gaeta or niçoise

Salt

Freshly ground black pepper

2 large cloves garlic, cut in half lengthwise

8 large basil leaves, coarsely chopped

Preheat the oven to 425°F.

Do all your prep first. Quarter the cherry tomatoes (if they're bigger, cut them into ¼-inch dice).

Cut the bread into eight ½-inch slices if it's a ciabatta, into sixteen ½-inch slices on the bias if it's a baguette (as it's narrower). Place the slices on a large rimmed baking sheet, drizzle them evenly with 2 tablespoons of the oil, and toast them in the oven for about 5 minutes, until they're just starting to turn golden.

In a medium-size bowl, toss the chopped tomatoes and olives with the remaining olive oil and season with salt and pepper to taste.

As soon as you take the bread out of the oven, rub the garlic onto the warm bread, making sure the cut section of the clove is rubbing against the bread.

Top the bread with some of the chopped tomato mixture and sprinkle the top with the basil. Drizzle with a little more olive oil, if you like, and serve. Don't let the bruschetta sit out too long or it'll get soggy.

Crostini with Crescenza Cheese, Sautéed Pears, and Rosemary

Crostini con Crescenza, Pere al Salto, e Rosmarino

On a recent trip to San Francisco I paid a quick visit to my old neighborhood in the city, North Beach, and ate at one of my favorite restaurants on the Columbus strip, Rose Pistola. Although the restaurant has an American sensibility, it's heavily influenced by Italian cuisine—Ligurian cuisine, in fact, as it pays homage to the neighborhood's original Italian settlers from the Ligurian coast. The Crescenza crostini on the menu that day were so fabulous, I decided to try some of my own, inspired by Rose Pistola's and, of course, by the flavors of Liguria. (See Sources for where to find Crescenza.)

SERVES 6 TO 8

1 tablespoon unsalted butter

1 small Bosc pear,
cored and cut into ¼-inch slices

Salt

Freshly ground black pepper

16 (½-inch) slices bread,
cut on the bias
(use a baguette or similar bread)

1 tablespoon extra-virgin olive oil

½ cup (5 ounces) Crescenza cheese

1 tablespoon finely chopped rosemary

Preheat the oven to 425°F.

In a 12-inch skillet heat the butter over medium-high heat. Season the pear slices generously with salt and pepper. When the butter is hot and stops bubbling, add the pear slices and cook them for 3 to 4 minutes on each side, or until they acquire a nice brown color. Set them aside.

Arrange the bread slices on a large rimmed baking sheet and drizzle the olive oil evenly over them. Toast in the oven for 5 minutes, or until the bread is crispy.

Spread each bread slice with some of the Crescenza cheese (a generous tablespoon per slice), and top with a pear slice and with some of the chopped rosemary.

Sprinkle a little salt and pepper over each crostino and cook in the oven for 3 to 5 minutes, just until the cheese has melted a bit. Serve immediately.

Crostini with Crescenza Cheese, Caramelized Onions, and White Truffle Oil

Crostini con Crescenza, Cipolle Caramellizzate, e Olio al Tartufo Bianco

Another crostino inspired by Rose Pistola and Liguria. (See Sources for where to find Crescenza.)

SERVES 6 TO 8

4 tablespoons extra-virgin olive oil

1 large sweet onion, chopped (about 2 cups)

Salt

1 tablespoon finely chopped thyme

16 (½-inch) slices bread, cut on the bias (use baguette or similar bread)

½ cup (5 ounces) Crescenza cheese

Freshly ground black pepper

White truffle oil, for drizzling

Preheat the oven to 425°F.

Heat 3 tablespoons of the olive oil in a 10-inch skillet over medium-high heat. When the oil is hot, add the onions. Add a pinch of salt and cook, stirring frequently, for 10 to 15 minutes, adding warm water a few tablespoons at a time when the onions start browning and sticking to the pan a little. Allow the onions to acquire an amber, light brown color without burning. Turn the heat down to medium-low and cook the onions for about 20 more minutes, stirring occasionally, and adding a few tablespoons of water when they seem to be getting too dry. The onions should be a deep brown color and glistening. Stir in the chopped thyme and set aside.

Arrange the bread slices on a large rimmed baking sheet and drizzle the remaining olive oil evenly over them. Toast in the oven for 5 minutes, or until the bread is crispy.

Spread each bread slice with some of the Crescenza cheese (a generous tablespoon per slice) and top with the caramelized onion mixture.

Sprinkle a little salt and pepper over each crostino and cook in the oven for 3 to 5 minutes, just until the cheese has melted a bit. Drizzle a drop or two of the truffle oil over each crostino and serve immediately. (Be careful not to pour too much truffle oil; a little goes a long way.)

Ligurian Soft Chickpea Flatbread with Extra-Virgin Olive Oil

Farinata

If you say *farinata*, a particularly vivid image comes to mind: my uncle Franco clad in shorts, sandals, and nothing else but a large apron enveloping his not-so-willowy form. He is shoving a large round *teglia*, a baking sheet, coated with a yellowish chickpea (garbanzo bean) flour batter inside the al fresco wood-burning oven of his Bonassola house with one of those long shovels used for pizza. What comes out of the oven is a pancakelike flatbread that's wonderfully balanced: soft on the inside and crispy on the outside, oily enough to make you want to lick your fingers yet still not a complete mess—by far the best *farinata* I've ever tasted, even in the most acclaimed Ligurian joints.

SERVES 4 TO 6

NOTE
THE BATTER NEEDS TO REST
FOR AT LEAST 4 HOURS

2 cups (½ pound) chickpea flour

3 cups water

1 tablespoon plus ½ teaspoon salt

½ cup extra-virgin olive oil

Freshly ground black pepper

Place the chickpea flour in a large bowl and slowly add the water, whisking constantly and energetically to prevent clumps from forming. You'll end up with a fairly liquid batter.

Add the salt, stir, and let the batter rest, covered with plastic wrap, for at least four hours at room temperature.

Preheat the oven to 425°F. With a large slotted spoon, remove any foam that might have formed on the surface of the batter and stir it well.

Pour the olive oil in a 17 × 13-inch rimmed baking sheet (preferably nonstick) and pour in the batter. Spread it with the back of a wooden spoon to cover the pan and to incorporate the oil. The batter should form only a thin layer, about ¼ inch thick.

Bake for 35 to 40 minutes, or until the *farinata* turns a nice golden brown. Let it rest for a few minutes and sprinkle on some pepper (three or four generous grinds should do, but if you like it more peppery, add more). Use a pizza cutter to cut it in slices of any size you like, and serve warm.

Soft Chickpea Flatbread with Onions and Thyme

Farinata con Cipolle e Timo

This is a variation on the *farinata* theme. You can make your own delicious creations using your favorite toppings. But to stay true to the uncomplicated spirit of Italian cooking, limit yourself to just one or two fresh ingredients. You won't be disappointed.

SERVES 4 TO 6

NOTE

THE BATTER NEEDS TO REST
FOR AT LEAST 4 HOURS

2 cups (½ pound) chickpea flour

3 cups water

1 tablespoon plus ½ teaspoon salt,
plus more for seasoning the onions

½ cup plus 3 tablespoons
extra-virgin olive oil

2 small sweet onions, thinly sliced

2 tablespoons chopped thyme

Freshly ground black pepper

Place the chickpea flour in a large bowl and slowly add the water, whisking constantly and energetically to prevent clumps from forming. You'll end up with a fairly liquid batter.

Add the salt, stir, and let the batter rest, covered with plastic wrap, for at least four hours at room temperature.

In a 12-inch skillet, heat 3 tablespoons of the olive oil over medium-high heat. When the oil is hot, add the onions. Add a small pinch of salt and cook, stirring frequently, over medium-high heat for about 8 minutes, allowing the onions to brown a little without burning. Add 1 or 2 tablespoons of water if the onions start sticking to the pan or become too dark. Turn down the heat to medium and continue cooking the onions for another 15 minutes, stirring frequently and adding a few tablespoons of warm water as the onions begin to dry. At the end, the onions should be a light brown color and glossy. Set them aside.

Preheat the oven to 425°F.

With a large slotted spoon, remove any foam that might have formed on the surface of the batter, and stir the batter well. Pour the remaining olive oil in a 17 × 13-inch rimmed baking sheet (preferably nonstick) and pour in the batter. Spread it with the back of a wooden spoon to cover the pan and to incorporate the oil. The batter should form only a thin layer, about ¼ inch thick.

CONTINUED

Soft Chickpea Flatbread with Onions and Thyme

CONTINUED

Top the batter with the onions and the chopped thyme, distributing them evenly.

Bake for 35 to 40 minutes or until the *farinata* turns a nice golden brown. Let it rest for a few minutes and sprinkle on some pepper (three or four generous grinds should do, but if you like it more peppery, add more). Use a pizza cutter to cut it in slices of any size you like, and serve warm.

COOKING AND SERVING *farinata*

Farinata is best when cooked in a wood-burning oven. But I share the limitations faced by city dwellers worldwide and I know from experience that a regular oven works just fine. If you have a nonstick rimmed baking sheet, use it, as *farinata* tends to stick to the pan. But, *farinata* is a rustic affair, so it's okay if it sticks a little and you can't cut perfect slices. In Liguria, *farinata* is not usually served as part of a meal. It's more of a midmorning or midafternoon snack. But I think it makes a delicious appetizer, especially if you get creative and add a few fresh herbs and caramelized onions (see recipe page 37). Although it may not make for elegant entertaining, it's perfect for a casual cookout with friends. The best way to enjoy *farinata* is when it's still warm, just out of the oven.

Veal Polpettine with Goat Cheese and Fresh Herbs

Polpettine di Vitello alla Genovese con Caprino

I serve these mini-meatballs as appetizers or as fun finger food at cocktail parties. To make for a more dramatic presentation, I like to stick toothpicks into each *polpettina*—this also makes them easy to pick up. If I'm serving them as a main course (usually at lunch or for a casual meal), I accompany them with a salad or a side of roasted potatoes. Their texture is soft and moist with an intense, cheesy flavor—and I mean that in a *good* way.

SERVES 4 TO 6

2 ounces day-old white bread, crusts removed, cut into 1-inch dice (scant 2 cups)

¼ cup whole milk

1 tablespoon pine nuts

1 tablespoon finely chopped parsley

1 teaspoon finely chopped marjoram

1 small clove garlic, finely chopped almost to a paste

½ cup fresh goat cheese (about 4 ounces), softened

1 teaspoon salt

Freshly ground black pepper

A pinch of freshly grated nutmeg

1 large egg, beaten

1 pound ground veal

½ cup unbleached all-purpose flour

¼ cup extra-virgin olive oil

Soak the bread in the milk in a small bowl for about 10 minutes, or until the bread has almost completely absorbed the liquid.

Grind the pine nuts with a mortar and pestle or in a small food processor, until you obtain a coarse paste.

In a large bowl, combine the pine nuts, bread (and whatever milk is left in the bowl), parsley, marjoram, garlic, goat cheese, salt, pepper, and nutmeg. Mix well with a wooden spoon. Add the egg and ground veal, and mix well to incorporate the ingredients.

To make the *polpettine*, take a small quantity of the mixture the size of a walnut and form a small sphere, rolling the meat mixture between the palm of your hands until you have a fairly regular round shape. Repeat until you run out of mixture.

Place the flour in a shallow bowl and dredge each *polpettina* in flour.

Heat the olive oil in a 12-inch nonstick skillet over medium-high heat. When the oil is hot and shimmers, add the *polpettine*. Arrange enough *polpettine* in the pan to fit snugly without overcrowding it (you may need to do this in two batches). Cook the *polpettine* over medium-high heat for 4 to 5 minutes, turning them over at least once to make sure they're evenly browned. Drain them on paper towels and serve warm.

Zucchini Blossom Tempura

Fiori di Zucchini Fritti

In June and July, the *terreno* in Bonassola churns out more zucchini than anyone can handle. With them come their beautiful flowers, the color of sunshine. I think these fried zucchini blossoms make the perfect Italian-style "bar food" (though they're not served in Italian bars at all), and they're certainly great crowd pleasers at any party. The traditional batter used in Liguria is a little different from that in this recipe. It usually contains flour, water or milk, and eggs. But I'm using a beer-based tempura-style batter because I think it makes the blossoms lighter and more effectively brings out their flavor. You can find zucchini blossoms in the summertime at farmers' markets or in gourmet grocery stores. To clean them, cut off the green portions attached to the stems and remove the pistil inside.

SERVES 4

At least 6 cups extra-virgin or virgin olive oil or a blend of canola and olive oil, for frying

1 cup unbleached all-purpose flour

1¼ cups pale ale beer

20 zucchini blossoms

Salt

Pour the oil into a large saucepan and bring it to frying temperature, 365°F, over medium-high heat. If you don't have a thermometer to check the temperature of the oil, throw in a tiny bit of batter (see next step). If it starts fizzing, the oil is ready.

Put the flour in a large bowl and slowly pour in the beer, whisking vigorously to prevent lumps from forming.

Dip the zucchini blossoms in the batter one at a time, shaking off the excess batter, and fry them in the oil until they turn golden and crispy, about 5 minutes.

Drain them on paper towels, season generously with salt, and serve immediately.

Frittata with Baby Zucchini, Caramelized Onions, Goat Cheese, and Fresh Herbs

Frittata di Bonassola

This frittata came on the spur of the moment. It was past lunchtime and we had nothing ready to eat, which didn't happen very often in Bonassola. We needed to throw together something quick and delicious. So we turned to the garden and the pantry. The *terreno* gave us plenty of zucchini, onions, and fresh herbs, and we had eggs and cheese in the refrigerator. Frittata was the obvious choice. This is the one we came up with.

Frittata is easy to prepare and can be very tasty, provided you use fresh, high-quality ingredients. And it's fun because you can improvise. Once you've made this recipe a couple of times and have become acquainted with the basics, you can make your own with whatever's in season or available at home. This is a summer frittata, but who says you can't turn it into a winter one using delicata or acorn squash instead of zucchini? I like to serve it cut in little squares as an appetizer or as finger food. But it can also be a light meal. In the latter case, I cut it in triangular wedges, like I would a pie (as a light main course, it serves four). While frittata is good warm, I think it's even better lightly chilled.

SERVES 8

5 tablespoons extra-virgin olive oil

1 medium onion, thinly sliced

2 teaspoons salt, plus more for seasoning the onions and zucchini

8 baby or 3 medium zucchini, thinly sliced crosswise into rounds (about 1½ cups)

1 teaspoon finely chopped marjoram

½ teaspoon finely chopped thyme

1 tablespoon finely chopped parsley

1 tablespoon finely chopped chives

Preheat the oven to 350°F.

Heat 2 tablespoons of the olive oil in a 10-inch nonstick ovenproof skillet over medium-high heat. When the oil is hot, add the onions. Add a pinch of salt and cook, stirring frequently, for 10 to 15 minutes, adding warm water a few tablespoons at a time when the onions start browning and sticking to the pan. Allow the onions to acquire an amber, light brown color without burning. Turn down the heat to medium-low and cook the onions for about 20 more minutes, stirring occasionally, adding a few tablespoons of water when they seem to be getting too dry. The onions should be a deep brown color and glistening. Transfer them to a plate.

Add the remaining olive oil to the skillet and cook the zucchini with a pinch of salt over medium-high heat, stirring frequently to avoid burning and sticking, 8 to 10

CONTINUED

CONTINUED

Frittata with Baby Zucchini, Caramelized Onions, Goat Cheese, and Fresh Herbs

CONTINUED

8 large eggs

¼ cup heavy cream

½ cup finely grated Parmigiano-Reggiano

½ cup crumbled fresh goat cheese

Freshly ground black pepper

minutes. You want the zucchini to be slightly caramelized but not charred. Remove the pan from the heat, add the herbs, and let everything cool.

Meanwhile, beat the eggs in a large bowl and add the heavy cream, Parmigiano, and goat cheese. Add the cooled down onions and zucchini and mix well so that the ingredients are well distributed inside the egg mixture. Season with 2 teaspoons of salt, grind on some pepper, and transfer the egg mixture back to the skillet.

Cook, covered, over very low heat for about 15 minutes. Uncover and finish cooking in the oven for another 10 to 15 minutes, or until the eggs have completely set in the center.

Dandelion Greens and Crescenza Cheese Pie

Torta di Bietole e Stracchino

Liguria is the land of savory pies. If you poke your head in any Ligurian *gastronomia*, the ubiquitous Italian food emporiums packed with cured meats and cheeses of all kinds as well as a slew of delicious prepared foods, you'll surely find a huge selection of *torte salate*, savory pies. They range from things that look more or less like American pies to shell-less *torte* that look like frittatas. And they're all delicious. I like this one because it's simple and distinct. The dandelion greens give it a slight bitter zing that pairs very well with the delicate tanginess of the cheese. This pie can be served warm or at room temperature.

MAKES 1 PIE; SERVES 6 TO 8

FOR THE DOUGH
2½ cups unbleached all-purpose flour

1 teaspoon salt

¼ cup extra-virgin olive oil

½ to ⅔ cup cold water

FOR THE FILLING
2 tablespoons extra-virgin olive oil, plus more for oiling and brushing

1 small onion, finely chopped (about 1 cup)

¾ pound dandelion or beet greens, washed, tough stems removed, and coarsely chopped (about 7 cups tightly packed)

1¼ teaspoons salt

1 teaspoon chopped marjoram

1 full cup (½ pound) Crescenza cheese, at room temperature

2 large eggs, beaten

1½ cup grated Parmigiano-Reggiano

Freshly ground black pepper

MAKE THE DOUGH In the bowl of a stand mixer, combine the flour and salt. Begin mixing at medium speed with the dough attachment. Slowly add the olive oil, then ½ cup of the water, scraping the sides of the bowl. Continue mixing, increasing the speed to medium-high, until the dough forms. If the dough has a hard time coming together and is still very dry and crumbly, add the remaining water. Remove it from the food processor and knead it with your hands for a few minutes, until a smooth dough forms. Cover with plastic wrap and let it rest in refrigerator for 30 minutes.

MAKE THE FILLING In a 12-inch skillet, heat the olive oil over medium-high heat. When the oil is hot, add the onions and cook, stirring frequently, over medium-high for about 5 minutes, or until they start to soften. Add the greens and ¼ teaspoon of salt, and cook for 6 to 8 minutes over medium-high heat, until the greens are soft and the water is completely absorbed. (Note: when you wash the greens, don't shake off too much of the water. That will help keep the greens soft while cooking.) Add the marjoram, stir to combine, and turn off the heat. Let the vegetables cool.

In a bowl, stir together the Crescenza, eggs, Parmigiano, and the cooled greens. Add the remaining 1 teaspoon of salt and a few grinds of pepper, and mix well until the filling is smooth and creamy.

CONTINUED

Dandelion Greens and Crescenza Cheese Pie

CONTINUED

ASSEMBLE THE PIE Preheat the oven to 350°F.

Take the dough out of the refrigerator. Cut it in half, keeping one of the halves inside the plastic wrap.

With a rolling pin, roll out the other half until you obtain a thin circle (about 1/16 inch thick). Oil a 9-inch pie dish with a little extra-virgin olive oil and line it with the rolled-out dough, cutting the excess hanging from the edges.

Roll the remaining dough into a circle, trying to make it even thinner than the first, if you can.

Pour the filling into the lined pie dish, spreading it evenly with the back of a spoon or an offset spatula, and cover the pie with the thinner dough sheet, cutting the excess dough hanging from the edge. Carefully press the edges all around the pie with your fingers to make the two pieces of dough stick together. Cut a few deep slits on the top layer to let out the steam while baking, brush the top lightly with olive oil, and bake the pie for 55 minutes to 1 hour, or until the top is nice and golden. Serve warm or at room temperature.

CRESCENZA OR STRACCHINO?

Stracchino and Crescenza are two very similar types of cheeses often confused for one another in Italy. Both are soft-ripened, rindless cow's milk cheeses with a creamy texture and a slightly sour flavor. But Stracchino is a government-protected artisan cheese produced exclusively in the region of Lombardy; it's ripened a few days longer than Crescenza, developing a light exterior film, almost like a very thin rind. Crescenza is more commonly produced on a larger scale and tends to have a tangier, sharper taste and a slightly softer texture. Although Crescenza is by far the more popular of the two, most people in Italy mistakenly call it Stracchino (most likely because of the similarity between the two cheeses). So when you see an Italian recipe that calls for Stracchino, it's perfectly fine to use Crescenza—that's most likely what the authors were thinking of anyway.

Fresh Ricotta and Artichoke Millefoglie Pie with Marjoram

Torta Pasqualina

Torta pasqualina (*Pasqua* means Easter in Italian) is a specialty enjoyed by many Ligurians at Easter time. Traditionally, it's an extremely complicated savory pie with all of thirty-three layers of dough and a rich filling containing loads of Prescinseua cheese (see sidebar p. 47) and twelve whole hard-boiled eggs. The preparation is quite convoluted, too, involving straws blowing air between each paper-thin layer of dough so they stay separate and get a little crispy. The recipe that follows is my own interpretation—and simplification—of this classic. I reduced the number of layers to ten (let's face it, who's going to roll thirty-three nearly transparent sheets of dough?) and I eliminated the hard-boiled eggs altogether. This may not be the classic *torta pasqualina*, but at least it can be prepared in a single afternoon—and not two days of solid work in the kitchen!

MAKES 1 PIE; SERVES 6 TO 8

FOR THE DOUGH

2½ cups unbleached all-purpose flour

1 teaspoon salt

¼ cup extra-virgin olive oil

½ to ⅔ cup cold water

FOR THE FILLING

2 large or 8 baby artichokes

Juice of 1 lemon

3 tablespoons extra-virgin olive oil, plus more for oiling and brushing

1 medium onion, finely chopped (about ¾ cup)

1 tablespoon finely chopped parsley

1 tablespoon finely chopped marjoram

1 cup dry white wine

MAKE THE DOUGH In the bowl of a stand mixer, combine the flour and salt. Begin mixing at medium speed with the dough attachment. Slowly add the olive oil and then ½ cup of the water, scraping the sides of the bowl. Continue mixing, increasing the speed to medium-high, until the dough forms. If the dough has a hard time coming together and is still very dry and crumbly, add the remaining water. Remove it from the food processor and knead it with your hands for a few minutes, until a smooth dough forms. Cover with plastic wrap and let it rest in refrigerator for 30 minutes.

MAKE THE FILLING Clean the artichokes by cutting the tough stems and about ½ inch to 1 inch off the top and by removing the outer, tough leaves until you reach the tender, light green leaves near the center. Cut each artichoke in half lengthwise and remove the hairy white core inside of each. Immediately place the halves in a bowl of water with the lemon juice or else they'll turn very dark. Cut each half lengthwise into eight sections (cut them only in four if you're using baby artichokes). Leave the slices in the acidulated water until you're ready to cook them.

CONTINUED

CONTINUED

Fresh Ricotta and Artichoke Millefoglie Pie with Marjoram

CONTINUED

3 teaspoons salt

4 large eggs, beaten

½ cup heavy cream

1 cup (about ½ pound) fresh ricotta

2 cups finely grated Parmigiano-Reggiano

Heat 3 tablespoons of olive oil in a 10-inch skillet over medium-high heat. When the oil is hot and shimmering, add the onion and cook, stirring frequently, for 6 to 8 minutes, or until translucent and lightly golden.

Drain the artichokes and pat them dry with a paper towel. Add them to the onions and add the parsley, ½ tablespoon of marjoram, and the wine. Reduce the heat to low, add 1 teaspoon of salt, partially cover, and cook for about 30 minutes, or until the artichokes are tender (the cooking time will vary with the size of the artichokes). You may need to add a few tablespoons of water or vegetable stock if the content of the pan gets too dry. When finished cooking, remove the artichoke mixture from the heat and let it cool.

In a large bowl, mix the eggs and cream. Fold in the ricotta, Parmigiano, remaining marjoram, remaining salt, and the cooled-down artichokes. Mix well until all the ingredients are well blended. Keep the filling covered in the refrigerator while you work with the dough.

ASSEMBLE THE TORTA Preheat the oven to 350°F.

Take the dough out of the refrigerator. Cut it in half, keeping one of the halves inside the plastic wrap.

Cut the other half in five small pieces of equal size. While you work with each piece of dough, keep the others wrapped so they don't dry out. With a rolling pin, roll each piece of dough on a lightly floured surface until you obtain a paper-thin circle with a diameter of about 11 inches. You should be able to see through it somewhat.

CONTINUED

Oil a 9-inch pie dish with a little extra-virgin olive oil and line it with the five circles of rolled out dough, brushing the top of each with a thin layer of olive oil before adding the next. Cut the excess dough hanging from the edges.

Roll out the remaining dough into five paper-thin circles as you did before.

Pour the filling into the lined pie dish, spreading it evenly with the back of a spoon or an offset spatula, and cover the pie with the remaining five dough sheets, brushing the top of each evenly with a thin layer of olive oil before adding the next. Again, cut the excess dough hanging from the edge. Carefully press the edges all around the pie with your fingers so the top and bottom layers of dough stick together. Cut one deep slit on the top layer to let out the steam while the pie is baking, brush the top lightly with olive oil, and bake for about 1 hour and 15 minutes, or until the top is golden brown and crispy. Serve the pie warm or at room temperature.

IS *prescinseua* AN ITALIAN WORD?

Actually, it's not. It's a word in Ligurian dialect that refers to a soft, creamy dairy product more similar to yogurt than to cheese. It's obtained by curdling fresh milk with rennet (the first step in the production of any cheese) in a process that lasts no more than two days. The result is a tangy, slightly sour cream that can be spread and is often eaten with a dash of sugar as a dessert. Rennet is called *caglio* or *presame* in Italian and *presu* in Ligurian dialect, which is where the word *prescinseua* comes from. Prescinseua is used primarily in Genova and east of Genova (it's so local that when I asked a grocer near Imperia—on the opposite side of the region— if they had Prescinseua, they looked at me like I was speaking another language) and is a fundamental ingredient in many traditional Ligurian preparations, such as torta pasqualina and the filling for pansotti al preboggion. In this book, I've often replaced it with ricotta but, although ricotta is delicious, it's not exactly the same. If you want to get closer to the original, mix the ricotta with some good yogurt or sour cream to yield the amount required by the recipe.

Warm Squid and Baby Octopus Salad with Potatoes, Garlic, and Olive Oil

Insalata di Mare Tiepida del Pescatore

Nearly every coastal town in Italy serves some form or another of seafood salad with *calamari* (squid) or octopus, or both. Liguria is no exception. To me the perfect seafood salad is one in which the squid and octopus are so spectacularly tender they almost melt in your mouth. One of the best *insalata di mare* I've had in Liguria was at the restaurant of the Cenobio dei Dogi Hotel, in Camogli. This recipe was inspired by their wonderful dish. If you have a hard time finding baby octopus (often available only in the fall), use just squid and double the amount listed below.

SERVES 4

1 pound squid, cleaned

1 pound baby octopus, cleaned

1 teaspoon white wine vinegar

½ pound medium shrimp, shelled and deveined

1 small Yukon gold potato, peeled and cut into ½-inch dice (about ½ cup)

¼ cup extra-virgin olive oil, plus more as needed

2 teaspoons freshly squeezed lemon juice, more to taste

Salt

Freshly ground white pepper

A pinch of cayenne pepper

1 tablespoon coarsely chopped parsley

1 medium clove garlic, thinly sliced

8 pitted black olives, roughly chopped, preferably gaeta or niçoise

6 very thin slices pancetta, cut into ½-inch-thick strips (optional)

Rinse the squid and baby octopus under cold running water (even if they're already clean, I like to give them a little extra rinse).

Cut the body of the squid into ½-inch rings as if you were making calamari. Cut the tentacles in half if too big. As for the baby octopus, separate the "heads" from the tentacles. Cut the "heads" into ½-inch rings and cut the tentacles in half if too big.

Place the octopus in a large pot and add water to barely cover. Add the vinegar. Bring to a boil, reduce the heat to low, and simmer, covered, for about 40 minutes, or until tender. If you see you're running out of liquid, just add a little more warm water. When done, let the octopus cool down to room temperature in its own liquid.

Meanwhile, bring a medium-size saucepan of lightly salted water to a boil and add the squid. Reduce the heat the medium-low and simmer for 4 to 5 minutes. Remove with a slotted spoon and set aside. Add the shrimp and cook for 3 to 4 minutes, or until it turns pink and is cooked through. Drain, transfer to a plate, and set aside. Fill the saucepan with water, bring it to a boil, and add the potatoes. Cook until fork tender, 8 to 10 minutes. Drain and set aside.

In a small bowl, whisk together the olive oil and lemon juice to form a loose emulsion.

Drain the cooled octopus and transfer to a large bowl. Add the reserved shrimp and squid and pour in the olive oil emulsion. Season with salt to taste, sprinkle with pepper and a tiny pinch of cayenne, and add the parsley, garlic, and olives. (I like for the garlic to give out its flavor, but I remove it before serving.)

Let the "salad" rest in the refrigerator, covered with plastic wrap, for at least 1 hour before serving.

If you're using the pancetta, heat an 8-inch skillet over medium-high heat just before serving. Cook the pancetta until crispy, about 2 minutes, and set aside

When you're ready to serve, reheat the "salad" gently in a large skillet over very low heat. You don't want it to be hot but just barely warmed. You may need to add 1 tablespoon of olive oil or water if it appears to be too dry when you reheat it. If using, add the pancetta and the rendered fat from the pan, toss well, and serve. You can certainly forgo the reheating step and serve the seafood chilled, if you prefer.

Baby Octopus Drowned in White Wine and Tomato Sauce

Moscardini Affogati

Silvana makes these *moscardini* all the time and everyone in my family is a big fan. It's hard to find real *moscardini* in the United States, but regular baby octopus (which are a little larger and come into season in the fall) will work just fine.

SERVES 4

2 pounds baby octopus, cleaned

1 (14-ounce) can whole tomatoes

3 tablespoons extra-virgin olive oil

½ large onion, finely chopped (about 1 cup)

1 large clove garlic, finely chopped (about 1½ teaspoons)

2 tablespoons finely chopped parsley

Salt

1 cup dry white wine

½ cup fresh or frozen peas (optional)

Freshly ground black pepper

Rustic bread, for serving

Cut off the heads of the octopus and cut them in half. Cut the tentacles in bite-size pieces (keep in mind that they will shrink when cooking).

Drain the canned tomatoes and puree them in a food processor, pulsing for about 30 seconds.

Heat the olive oil in a 10-inch skillet over medium-high heat. When the oil is hot, add the onion, garlic, and parsley and cook for 2 to 3 minutes, just until the onions are soft and fragrant. Add the pureed tomatoes and a pinch of salt and cook, stirring occasionally, for another 5 minutes.

Add the octopus and the white wine, reduce the heat to medium-low, and cook, covered, for 25 minutes. Add the peas, if you're using them, and cook for another 25 to 35 minutes. Adjust the seasoning with salt and pepper and serve warm on chunks of rustic bread, if you like.

Deep-Fried Fresh Sardines with Mildly Hot Salsa Verde

Sardine Fritte con Salsa Verde Piccantina

In Liguria it's usually fresh anchovies that people fry (or even little bait fish called *bianchetti*), but because sardines are so much easier to find in the United States, I tried them instead—and they work quite well. My aunt Silvana's fried anchovies are a legend in Bonassola. People will try to snag an invitation just for the privilege of savoring these tiny fish lightly dusted with flour and fried in sizzling olive oil. My father is a die-hard fan and I, too, love their delicate crunch and subtle taste of the sea. Use the salsa verde as a dip or pour a dollop on top of the finished sardines.

SERVES 4

FOR THE SALSA VERDE

1½ cups packed parsley leaves

1 large clove garlic

6 tablespoons extra-virgin olive oil

1 teaspoon red wine vinegar

1 teaspoon freshly squeezed lemon juice

⅛ teaspoon cayenne pepper, more to taste

Salt

Freshly ground black pepper

FOR THE SARDINES

At least 6 cups extra-virgin or virgin olive oil or a blend of canola oil and olive oil, for frying

2 pounds fresh sardines, cleaned and filleted

1 cup unbleached all-purpose flour

MAKE THE SALSA VERDE Chop the parsley and garlic very finely or process in a small food processor (such as a Cuisinart MiniPrep).

Transfer to a bowl and add the remaining salsa verde ingredients, mixing well with a spoon to combine them. Cover with plastic and set aside in the refrigerator.

FRY THE SARDINES Pour the oil into a large saucepan and bring it to frying temperature, 365°F.

Dredge the sardine fillets uniformly in the flour and fry them in the hot oil until they turn golden brown, about 3 to 4 minutes. Do this in batches, as you don't want to overcrowd the pan and bring down the temperature of the oil.

With a slotted spoon, transfer the sardines to a plate lined with paper towels and sprinkle them generously with salt.

Serve immediately with the sauce on the side.

Focaccia with Extra-Virgin Olive Oil and Sea Salt

Focaccia

What more can I say about focaccia? To me, it's emblematic of what Ligurian food is all about: making something deliciously addictive with the simplest, freshest, tastiest ingredients available. All there is to focaccia is flour, salt, water, a little yeast, and abundant fruity extra-virgin olive oil. Yet, the result is sinfully good.

I'm giving you two slightly different methods: an easy and quick one that produces a mighty tasty focaccia, and one that's closer to how bakers make it Liguria, which involves a little more time. I like to cut a large batch in thin strips and serve them as an appetizer, with aperitivo, or as a simple, scrumptious snack. Try focaccia for brunch with coffee like Ligurians do, or make delicious sandwiches with prosciutto and fontina cheese or just a few slices of good mortadella. A word of advice: focaccia doesn't age well. Even a couple of hours after it's been out of the oven, it's not quite as good as when it's just baked. It's at its best when it's still warm and fresh.

SERVES 8 TO 10

EASY METHOD

FOR THE DOUGH

4 ¼ cups unbleached all-purpose flour

2 teaspoons salt

2 cups warm water

1 (¼ ounce) package active-dry yeast

¼ cup extra-virgin olive oil, plus more for oiling

FOR THE TOPPING

1/3 cup fruity extra-virgin olive oil

1 teaspoon coarse sea salt

EASY METHOD

In a large bowl, mix the flour with the salt.

Pour the water in the bowl of a stand mixer and sprinkle the yeast in it, stirring a few times until it's incorporated in the water. Let it rest for 5 minutes, then add ¼ cup of the olive oil.

Start mixing on low speed with a dough attachment and slowly add the flour mixture. Increase the speed to medium-high and keep mixing until you obtain a smooth, sticky dough. The dough should be rather wet and loose and will stick to your fingers a little. It's almost more like a thick batter than a dough.

CONTINUED

Oil a large clean bowl, scrape the dough from the mixer into the bowl, cover it tightly with oiled plastic wrap, and let the dough rise in a warm place until doubled in size, about 40 minutes.

Oil a 13 × 17-inch rimmed baking sheet and spread the dough with your hands to cover the surface of the pan completely.

Preheat the oven to 425°F.

Oil the fingers of one hand and dig a few random dimples on the surface of the stretched focaccia dough. Cover it with oiled plastic wrap and let the dough rest in the pan for another 30 minutes, until it has risen and doubled in size once again.

Before baking, top the dough with the 1/3 cup of olive oil, spreading it gently with your hands to cover the surface evenly. In particular, make sure it gets into the dimples. At this point, your dough will look very oily but don't worry, the oil will get absorbed while baking and it'll make the focaccia soft and delicious. Sprinkle the dough with the coarse salt and bake for 30 to 35 minutes, or until it turns a nice golden brown and it's cooked through. Cut and serve immediately.

TRADITIONAL METHOD

FOR THE SPONGE

⅔ cups warm water

1 (¼ ounce) package active-dry yeast

1 cup unbleached all-purpose flour

TRADITIONAL METHOD

MAKE THE SPONGE Pour the water in the bowl of a stand mixer and sprinkle the yeast in it, stirring a few times until it's incorporated in the water. Add the flour and mix on low speed with a dough attachment until well incorporated. Cover the bowl with plastic wrap, and let it rest for about 30 minutes, or until the content has doubled in size. It will look bubbly and kind of "spongy."

CONTINUED

CONTINUED

Focaccia with Extra-Virgin Olive Oil and Sea Salt

CONTINUED

FOR THE DOUGH

2⅔ cups unbleached all-purpose flour

2 teaspoons salt

½ cup water

½ cup dry white wine

⅓ cup extra-virgin olive oil

FOR THE TOPPING

⅓ cup extra-virgin olive oil

1 teaspoon coarse sea salt

MAKE THE DOUGH In a large bowl, mix the flour with the salt.

Add the water, white wine, and olive oil to the rested sponge in the bowl of the stand mixer.

Begin mixing on low speed and slowly add the flour mixture. Increase the speed to medium-high and keep mixing until you obtain a smooth, sticky dough. The dough should be quite moist and loose, and will stick to your fingers a little.

Oil a large clean bowl, scrape the dough from the mixer into the bowl, cover it tightly with oiled plastic wrap, and let the dough rise in a warm place until doubled in size, about 40 minutes.

Oil a 13 × 17-inch rimmed baking sheet and spread the dough with your hands to cover the surface of the pan completely.

Preheat the oven to 425°F. Place a small oven proof container filled with water in the oven and leave it throughout the cooking of the focaccia. It will help keep it moist.

Oil the fingers of one hand and dig a few random dimples on the surface of the stretched focaccia dough. Cover it with oiled plastic wrap and let the dough rest in the pan for another 30 minutes, until it has risen and doubled in size once again.

Before baking, top the dough with the ⅓ cup of olive oil, spreading it gently with your hands to cover the surface evenly. In particular, make sure it gets into the dimples. At this point, your dough will look very oily but don't worry, the oil will get absorbed while cooking. Sprinkle the dough with the coarse salt and bake for 30 to 35 minutes, or until it turns a nice golden brown and is cooked through. Cut and serve immediately.

Focaccia with Sweet Onions

Focaccia con le Cipolle

SERVES 8 TO 10

FOR THE DOUGH

See focaccia dough recipes on pages 52–54.

FOR THE TOPPING

2 tablespoons plus ⅓ cup fruity extra-virgin olive oil

1 large sweet onion, thinly sliced

½ teaspoon salt

1 teaspoon coarse sea salt

Follow either focaccia dough recipe on pages 52–54, but don't bake it.

Preheat the oven to 425°F.

Heat 2 tablespoons of the olive oil in a 10-inch skillet over medium-high heat. When the oil is hot, add the onion and salt and cook over medium heat for about 10 minutes, until the onions are soft and translucent and turn a warm golden color.

After the dough has risen the second time in the baking sheet, and before baking, top it with the remaining ⅓ cup of olive oil, spreading it gently with your hands to cover the surface evenly. Sprinkle the cooked onions evenly over the stretched focaccia dough, sprinkle with the coarse salt, and bake for 30 to 35 minutes, or until it turns a nice golden brown and is cooked through. Cut it and serve immediately.

Focaccia with Fresh Herbs

Focaccia alle Erbe

In this recipe I use rosemary and thyme, but you can use any herb you like. Sage works quite well, too.

SERVES 8 TO 10

FOR THE DOUGH

See focaccia dough recipes on pages 52–54.

FOR THE TOPPING

⅓ cup fruity extra-virgin olive oil

1 tablespoon chopped rosemary

1 tablespoon chopped thyme

1 teaspoon coarse sea salt

Follow either focaccia dough recipe on pages 52–54, but don't bake it.

Preheat the oven to 425°F.

Once the dough has risen the second time in the baking sheet, and before baking, top it with ⅓ cup of olive oil, spreading it gently with your hands to cover the surface evenly. Sprinkle the herbs and the coarse salt evenly over the dough and bake for 30 to 35 minutes, or until it turns a nice golden brown and is cooked through. Cut it and serve immediately.

Focaccia with Crescenza Cheese from Recco

Focaccia al Formaggio di Recco

Cheese focaccia from Recco is an altogether different thing from the focaccia we've all come to eat and love. This doesn't mean it isn't as delicious. *Focaccia al formaggio* is nothing more than two paper-thin layers of unleavened bread with a generous slathering of soft Crescenza cheese in between. When made well, it's lusciously cheesy with a slight tang from the Crescenza. My family used to get *focaccia al formaggio* from Bianchetto's in Bonassola, who made something very close to the real thing. But on a recent trip to Liguria, I went to visit the Panificio Moltedo in Recco, where they've been making this local specialty (which originated in Recco) for over two hundred years, one generation after another. Today, the Moltedos are the only people in Recco still baking *focaccia al formaggio* in the classic method. Titta Moltedo, the owner, shared his recipe for authentic *focaccia al formaggio* (see sidebar, page 58) with me. I tweaked it a little, eliminating one layer of dough, which I think makes things a lot easier for the home cook, but still maintains the flavor.

MAKES 2 *FOCACCE*; SERVES 8 TO 10

2 cups unbleached all-purpose flour

1½ teaspoons salt

2 teaspoons extra-virgin olive oil, plus more for oiling

⅔ to 1 cup water

2 full cups (1 pound) Crescenza cheese

Preheat the oven to 450°F.

Put the flour in the bowl of a stand mixer and add 1 teaspoon of salt. Start the mixer on low speed with the dough attachment and slowly add the olive oil. Increase the speed to medium and begin adding the water. Start with ⅔ cup and add the rest, if necessary. If the dough doesn't come together after adding 1 cup of water, stop the mixer and knead it by hand for a few minutes. The dough should be smooth and elastic and fairly wet, but not too sticky (definitely, less sticky than regular focaccia dough). Remove it from the mixer bowl and shape it into a ball. Cover it in plastic wrap and let it rest for 30 minutes.

Meanwhile, cut the Crescenza in small pieces the size of a walnut.

Cut the dough in half. Keep one piece wrapped in plastic and roll the other with a rolling pin over a lightly floured surface until you obtain a paper-thin circle (less than

CONTINUED

Focaccia with Crescenza Cheese from Recco

CONTINUED

$\frac{1}{16}$ inch thick). It should easily fit into a round pan with the diameter of about 15 inches. If you don't have a round baking pan that wide, roll out the dough in a rectangle that will fit a 13 × 17-inch rimmed baking sheet. Repeat with the other piece of dough (if you don't have two pans the same size, bake the first focaccia, and reuse the same pan).

Oil the pan(s) and line with the rolled-out dough.

Arrange the Crescenza pieces on top of the dough, distributing them evenly between the two pans, and sprinkle with the remaining salt. Trim any excess dough on the edges.

Cook in the oven for 10 to 15 minutes, or until the top is slightly browned, and serve immediately.

focaccia al formaggio
ACCORDING TO TITTA MOLTEDO

Titta Moltedo, the owner of Recco's historic Panificio Moltedo, is not what you'd expect an artisanal bread baker to be like. Skinny—emaciated almost—with a crowd of smoke-tinted teeth in his mouth and an infectious boyish energy, he's the enfant terrible of traditional *focaccia al formaggio*. His anecdotes of travels to New York City hint at years of debauchery and legend-making good times, but nothing has stopped Titta (short for Giovanni Battista) from spending the better part of his life making *focaccia al formaggio* in the same time-honored way his ancestors have made it for nine generations.

When I visited his bakery on a sunny afternoon in late June, he explained what distinguished his very traditional focaccia from most others in town and beyond. He cooks his wafer-thin flatbread directly on the surface of the oven, which is made with a material intended to reproduce slate, as in the old hearths used to bake *focaccia al formaggio*. He doesn't use a *tegame*, a baking sheet, as do most other bakers nowadays.

For the dough, Titta mixes one kilo of flour (half Canadian flour from Manitoba—which he swears was what his ancestors used—and half type "00," commonly found in Italy), salt, one large spoonful of extra-virgin olive oil, and water. After cutting the dough in two pieces, he rolls both in paper-thin circles, between 1 and 2 millimeters thick—something that takes years of practice (I, for one, can't get anywhere near that kind of thinness without breaking the dough). He transfers one circle onto a wooden board with a handle (similar to the one used to shove pizza in the oven, but much bigger), which he sprinkles with cornmeal. He tops the dough with a good kilo of small Crescenza pieces (that he calls Stracchino, as does everyone else in Liguria), and covers it with the other paper-thin sheet of dough, pressing around the cheese pieces to let the air out. To prevent the cheese from oozing from the sides while baking, Titta makes a little fold he calls *uegin*, dialect for the Italian *ripieghino*. A sprinkle of salt and a drizzle of olive oil and the bread is shoved in his blistering hot oven for less than ten minutes. The result: hands-down, the best *focaccia al formaggio* I've ever eaten.

Focaccia with Tomatoes, Onions, and Olives

Pizza all'Andrea

There's a bit of controversy over the origins of this pizza. The French claim it's their creation (in Nice they make a suspiciously similar *pissaladière*), the Italians say they conceived it to honor Andrea Doria, the illustrious admiral of Genova's glory days as a maritime republic. Given the fuzzy borders along the Riviera, I wouldn't be surprised if it were indeed the same bread that migrated. Although it's called "pizza," it's really more a focaccia with a thin layer of tomato sauce topping and a taste that's very similar to what you get in Italy when you order a pizza in a *panetteria* (a bread bakery).

SERVES 8 TO 10

FOR THE DOUGH

See focaccia dough recipes on pages 52–54.

FOR THE TOPPING

1 (14-ounce) can whole tomatoes

¼ cup plus 4 tablespoons extra-virgin olive oil

½ small onion, finely chopped (about ½ cup)

2 small cloves garlic, smashed with the blade of a chef's knife

½ teaspoon salt

½ teaspoon granulated sugar

½ cup pitted black olives

4 oil-packed anchovy fillets, drained

1 tablespoon salted capers, rinsed

3 large basil leaves

1 teaspoon dry oregano

Freshly ground black pepper

Follow either focaccia dough recipe on pages 52–54, but don't bake it.

Preheat oven to 425°F.

Place the tomatoes with their juices in the bowl of a food processor and pulse until pureed.

In a 10-inch skillet, heat 4 tablespoons of the olive oil over medium-high heat. When the oil is hot, add the onion and garlic and cook for about 5 minutes, stirring frequently and making sure not to burn the garlic. Add the tomatoes, salt, and sugar and cook for another 5 minutes, stirring frequently. Reduce the heat to medium-low, add the olives, anchovies, capers, basil, oregano, and pepper, and simmer for 20 minutes. Stir occasionally and add a few tablespoons of warm water if the sauce seems too dry. Remove the chunks of garlic.

Once the dough has risen the second time in the baking sheet, and before baking, top it with ¼ cup of olive oil, spreading it with your hands to cover the surface evenly. Smear a thin layer of the tomato sauce all over the surface of the focaccia (don't overdo the tomato sauce, it's supposed to be a very thin layer), including the borders.

Bake for 30 to 35 minutes. Cut it and serve immediately.

MAKING PASTA IN THE STORM

The first floor of the old rental house in Bonassola was an open, cavernous room spread across two levels. It had soaring ceilings and plain white walls and was sparingly decorated with a blend of phony Chippendale-style furniture and cut-rate modern pieces purchased, in all likelihood, circa 1950. They'd become vintage by then, but many stood still wrapped in the protective plastic they came with. Anyone who sat at the faux-formal dining table in shorts (not uncommon in summertime) experienced a painfully loud sucking noise as their skin unglued itself from the chairs' plastic when they tried to get up. No wonder nobody sat at that table. And as if that weren't enough, with both French windows crowded in the front, the dining area at the back of the room—with its austere furniture and an intricately carved mahogany cabinet crowned by a colossal dark-rimmed mirror—was consigned to permanent dimness and gloom. Who'd want to spend their time there when everything outside radiated cheerful sunlight?

The kitchen was on the lower level, close to the room's two big windows, a step down from the dining area. While certainly brighter, it suffered an awkward charm of its own. It was a large and unadorned room, stripped to its bare essentials: a tiny white refrigerator with no freezer; an ancient white ceramic sink mapped by scratches; a fifties-style pale green plastic countertop; and a gas stove from that same era. The stove wasn't connected to any kind of gas plumbing. Instead, it was fed by a tank the size of a small waste bin, called a *bombola del gas*. Many houses in Liguria, especially on the hills, have never been connected to a gas main. The ruggedness of the land, I guess, renders big excavations required to run gas pipes impractical. So many people's gas stoves operate thanks to these outdated metal barrels filled with propane, whose flow is regulated by a small valve latched onto the stove. When you run out of gas—literally—it's time to get a refill. You can spot locals hauling their empty *bombole* to the deposit near the train station, where they exchange them for full ones—the vacationers prefer to wait for the guy who runs the town's *bombole* delivery business to drive by each week on his overloaded *Ape*.

What redeemed the old kitchen were the two sizeable French windows on opposite sides of the room. They were always open, letting in wafts of briny sea air and plenty of light from the terrace—and us, flowing in and out of the kitchen with ease in our lithe summer clothes. This effortless access to the outdoors, the almost complete lack of boundaries, is something I've come to appreciate deeply. Few of us get to experience it—confined as we are in our office buildings, trapped in our apartment lives.

The only time I remember being forced to stay inside the big downstairs was when a huge storm hit the *riviera di levante*, heralded by ominous, charcoal clouds, blasting winds, deafening thunder, and waves taller and fiercer than anything I've seen on the Mediterranean before or since. It rained as though someone was tilting huge vats of water over the house. We were forced to shut the windows, and sitting out on the terrace was out of the question.

Instead, we made *pansotti*, triangular Ligurian ravioli with eggless pasta. Before that day, I'd eaten plenty of fresh pasta—my grandmother and grand-aunt made amazing Piedmontese *agnolotti*—but when it came to making these things, I'd always been a happy spectator. It had never seemed like much fun. This time, with nothing else to do, I had no choice but to help.

"Laura can make the dough. She'll have fun," said Silvana.

She was the creative one, expert at keeping kids busy with arts and crafts and hands-on activities. My mother was more cautious; she had, I knew, catastrophic visions of me covered in flour from head to toe, white puffs occasionally blowing in the air, settling on the dining room's dark mahogany table. But she held her tongue.

I looked skeptically at the mound of flour Silvana had shaped as a volcano crater on the kitchen table. How could this dry, dusty mess turn into pasta? But with Silvana's help, the miracle happened. Simply kneading the flour with salt, some white wine, and water, we transformed it into a soft, supple dough. It was that easy. And although food processors and stand mixers have since turned pasta making into a cinch, I make pasta by hand to this day. I like to whisk eggs or water in the well and feel the dough slowly take shape in my hands. I like the physicality of kneading the resilient lump with my palms until it becomes smooth and limber.

Silvana reached into a canvas bag in which she carried produce from the *mercato* (the local farmers' market) or the *terreno*, fishing out bunches of leafy greens I couldn't identify. They were neither spinach nor chard, at least not the big-leaf variety I grew up with.

"What are these?" I asked with fresh curiosity.

"They're wild herbs that grow around here. We call them *preboggion*," replied Silvana. "These are from the *terreno*. If you don't learn to recognize them, you'll step right on them, thinking they're weeds."

The old Ligurians knew better than to toss out herbs they could cook with, especially when there was never much else growing in the fields. If most of Italy cooks with a relatively standard assortment of fresh aromatics—parsley and basil, of course, with thyme, rosemary, and oregano in tow—Ligurians go wild when it comes to herbs, using many that grow only on their own sun-baked soil.

With my mother's help, Silvana blanched the leaves, then chopped and mixed them with ricotta, eggs, Parmigiano, and a pinch of salt and pepper, making a fragrant filling for our *pansotti*. I helped spoon tiny dollops of it onto long, floury ribbons of rolled-out pasta. It was a calm and soothing task. I got so immersed in the methodical, repetitive act of lining up miniature balls of filling on the sheets, cutting the dough into big squares and folding them over to make triangles, that I forgot all about the ghastly weather. Even the dreariness of the closed room vanished for a while, as I absorbed myself in the minutiae of creating flawless *pansotti*. To this day, the hypnotic power of hand-making fresh pasta is one of the few things that truly relaxes me at the end of a busy, stressful week.

With the pasta water at a rolling boil, Silvana dropped a large chunk of butter into a pan on the stove and let it melt slowly with a handful of sage. We laid a wrinkled cotton tablecloth over the dining table, sat on the plastic-covered chairs, and savored the delicate, wafer-thin stuffed triangles lightly doused with the sage-infused butter, bursting with the essence of Ligurian land and air. The rain, the thunder, the distant noise of the menacing waves, the dim sadness of the closed room with its sticky plastic—everything vanished before this plate of glorious food.

PASTA & SOUPS

pasta e minestre

Fresh Eggless Pasta Dough

Pasta Fresca senza Uova

Because this pasta dough has no eggs, it's very dry and I only use it to make *trofie*. Many Ligurians use eggless pasta to make *pansotti* (Ligurian ravioli) as well, but I find that the dough is easier to work with if you add an egg, as in the fresh pasta recipe that follows on page 67.

MAKES ABOUT 1 POUND

2¼ cups unbleached all-purpose flour

1½ teaspoons salt

½ to ¾ cup cold water

Pour the flour in a large bowl and add the salt. Slowly add the water as you mix with your hands until a compact dough forms. Alternatively, put the flour and salt in the bowl of a stand mixer. Begin mixing on medium speed with the dough attachment, slowly add the water, raise the speed to medium-high, and continue mixing until a compact dough forms. Knead it for about 5 minutes with the palms of your hands. Pat it into a round shape and let it rest, covered in plastic wrap, for about 20 minutes. You can freeze the dough for later use, if you like.

Fresh Pasta Dough for *Pansotti*

Pasta Fresca per Pansotti

Ligurians often use dry white wine to make doughs, from pasta to focaccia. With the exception of the egg—which I used to give a little more strength to the dough—this is a rather traditional Ligurian pasta recipe.

MAKES ABOUT 1½ POUNDS

3 cups unbleached all-purpose flour

1½ teaspoons salt

¼ cup dry white wine

⅓ to ½ cup cold water

1 large egg

BY HAND Place the flour in a mound on a flat surface. Make a well in the center and add the salt, wine, ⅓ cup of water, and the egg. With a fork, start incorporating the flour from the inside walls of the well with the liquid a little at a time until about two-thirds of the flour are mixed in. When the mixture gets too sticky and hard to beat with the fork, start working with the palms of your hands until a smooth dough forms. The dough will be slightly crumbly at the beginning. If it doesn't come together after a few minutes of kneading, add the rest of the water.

Note that, at this point, you'll have a main mass of dough and lots of smaller dough crumbs that won't incorporate into the bigger dough ball. Remove these crumbs from the work surface and throw them away, adding more flour to the surface if it's too sticky. Knead the dough with the palms of your hands for about 5 minutes. Pat it into a round shape, cover it with a dry towel or plastic wrap, and set it aside for about 30 minutes. You can freeze the dough for later use, if you like.

WITH A MIXER Don't be afraid to use a mixer or food processor to make the dough, if you prefer. I use it when I'm in a hurry, although I still like to take the dough out of the mixer bowl and knead it by hand for a few minutes before setting it aside. Place the flour and salt in the bowl of a stand mixer fitted with the dough attachment. Run it on slow speed and slowly add the white wine, ⅓ cup of water, and the egg, increasing the speed to medium-high and scraping the sides. Add the rest of the water if the dough doesn't come together. Knead it by hand for the last 5 minutes. Pat it into a round shape, cover it with a dry towel or plastic wrap, and set it aside for about 30 minutes.

Fresh Egg Pasta Dough

Pasta Fresca all'Uovo

This dough is closer to the egg-rich pasta doughs from Piedmont and Emilia Romagna. It doesn't have quite as many eggs as those do, but it's richer than most Ligurian fresh pastas. I use it for ravioli and lasagne in this book.

MAKES ABOUT 1½ POUNDS

3 cups unbleached all-purpose flour

4 large eggs

1 teaspoon extra-virgin olive oil

1½ teaspoon salt

¼ cup cold water

BY HAND Pour the flour in a mound on a wide, flat surface—wood and plastic are preferable to marble because the coldness of marble counteracts the elasticity of the dough. Create a well in the middle of the flour mound, break the eggs into the well, then add the olive oil, salt, and 2 tablespoons of the water. With the help of a fork, whisk the eggs inside the well, working in the flour from the rims a little at a time until about two-thirds of the flour are mixed in with the eggs. When the mixture gets too sticky and hard to beat with the fork, start working with the palms of your hands. If the dough doesn't come together, add the rest of the water or more, if needed.

Note that, at this point, you'll have a main mass of dough and lots of smaller dough crumbs that won't incorporate into the bigger dough ball. Remove these crumbs from the work surface and throw them away, adding more flour to the surface if it's too sticky. Knead the dough for a good 5 minutes with the palms of your hand, until it becomes smooth and malleable. Pat it into a round shape, cover it with a towel or plastic wrap, and set it aside for about 30 minutes. You can freeze the dough for later use, if you like.

WITH A MIXER Don't be afraid to use a mixer or food processor to make the dough, if you prefer. I use it when I'm in a hurry, although I still like to take the dough out of the mixer bowl and knead it by hand for a few minutes before setting it aside. Place the flour in the bowl of a stand mixer fitted with the dough attachment. Run it on slow speed, adding the eggs one at a time. Add the olive oil, salt, and 2 tablespoons of the water and increase the speed to medium-high. Add the rest of the water if the dough doesn't come together. Knead it by hand for the last 5 minutes. Pat it into a round shape, cover it with a dry towel or plastic wrap, and set it aside for about 30 minutes.

Trofie with Pesto, Green Beans, and Potatoes

Trofie con Pesto alla Genovese

My aunt Silvana makes the best pesto I've ever tasted. She learned it from her husband Franco's mother, an authentic Ligurian who told her always to use Genovese basil from Prà, on the hills to the west of Genova. And that is the true secret behind classic authentic pesto, which is lighter in color and sweeter and milder in flavor, without the minty hints of other pestos. Yes, I know what you're thinking: how on earth am I going to get my hands on some of that Prà basil? Don't fret. You can come close to Genovese pesto by selecting the smallest leaves from a bunch of store-bought basil. Leave the larger, darker leaves for flavoring a tomato sauce or ratatouille. Or you can grow your own Genovese basil from seeds available in most seed catalogs (see Sources).

Traditionally, pesto is made by grinding the basil and pine nuts with a little salt in a mortar and pestle, before adding the other ingredients. Today, however, almost everyone in Liguria makes pesto in a blender or a food processor. If you have a mortar and pestle, I encourage you to try it. The flavors are often more vivid and intense. But you can still make a delicious pesto without it. Use pecorino toscano or sardo, but don't use the "Romano" cheese you commonly find in grocery stores. It's often too salty and doesn't have the right flavor profile.

SERVES 4

FOR THE PASTA DOUGH
1 Fresh Eggless Pasta Dough recipe, page 66

Toothpicks

FOR THE PESTO
3 cups tightly packed basil leaves

1 medium clove garlic

2 tablespoons pine nuts

Salt

½ cup extra-virgin olive oil

2 tablespoons finely grated pecorino, preferably toscano or sardo

3 tablespoons finely grated Parmigiano-Reggiano, plus more for garnishing

2 ounces green beans, washed, trimmed, cut into 1-inch pieces

1 small Yukon gold potato (about 6 ounces), peeled and cut into ½-inch dice (about ¾ cup)

PREPARE THE PASTA Follow the instructions for Fresh Eggless Pasta Dough, page 66.

To shape the *trofie*, pull from the dough a very small amount, the size of a pea. On a flat surface, gently roll the piece of dough around a toothpick. To do this, place the toothpick flat against the center of the tiny ball of dough and, applying gentle pressure, roll the dough evenly around the toothpick with your fingers, forming a small, twisted cylinder. Then slide the dough off the toothpick. The little dumpling should be slender and no more than 1 inch long. Repeat until you finish all the dough, making sure to keep it covered while you roll the *trofie* to prevent it from drying up. Set the *trofie* in a single layer on a flat, lightly floured surface and let them dry for at least 1 hour. If you're not planning to cook them right away, put them in a plastic bag once they're dry, and store them in the refrigerator. They can also be frozen for up to 3 months.

CONTINUED

STORE-BOUGHT *trofie*

Trofie, originally from Recco but popular all over Liguria, can be a bit laborious and time-consuming to make. You can certainly opt for store-bought *trofie*, which you can find in Italian specialty markets or online (see Sources), or use another type of pasta. Ligurians also enjoy pesto with a kind of pasta called *trenette*, similar to linguine but less flat, with an elliptical cross section. If you're using store-bought pasta, you'll need about one pound for four people.

IT'S ALL IN THE BASIL

The mild sweetness and creamy quality of true Genovese pesto is due in most part to the type of basil used. The basil that will get you those results is the Basilico Genovese (Genovese basil) grown across a few acres on the hills to the west of Genova, in an area called Prà. The Genovese basil that grows there (in large greenhouses in the winter) is quite small, with oval light green leaves that bow slightly downward. And it isn't very happy at temperatures hovering around 30°F, thus the greenhouses; it wants at least 60°F, but really a temperature between 70° and 78°F is ideal for its germination. The basil plants are harvested by hand when the leaves are still young, which contributes to its mildness and light color. Prà basil is sold in markets in Genova and surrounding towns, but you can buy Genovese basil seeds and grow it elsewhere—although different soils and climactic conditions will invariably produce different results. In fact, Genovese basil has recently become a government protected variety and can only be sold as authentic Basilico Genovese if grown in Liguria. (But it's a known fact among Ligurians that the one grown in Prà is the best.)

Trofie with Pesto, Green Beans, and Potatoes

CONTINUED

PREPARE THE PESTO AND ASSEMBLE THE PASTA

Put the basil, garlic, pine nuts, a pinch of salt, and 1 or 2 tablespoons of the olive oil in the bowl of a food processor. Start mixing, adding a little more olive oil if the ingredients don't easily combine into a paste. Stop the food processor, add the pecorino and Parmigiano, and continue processing until you obtain a smooth, creamy paste. Transfer to a bowl and mix in the remaining olive oil, reserving 1 tablespoon. Adjust seasoning with salt to taste. Pour the tablespoon of olive oil on top of the pesto to form a thin layer, which prevents it from discoloring. Cover the bowl with plastic wrap and set it aside (refrigerate it if you don't plan on using it right away).

Bring a large pot of generously salted water to a boil. Add the green beans and the potatoes, together with the prepared *trofie*, and cook for 8 to 10 minutes, or until the pasta is soft and the vegetables are tender but not mushy.

Drain the pasta along with the vegetables, making sure to reserve about ½ cup of the cooking water. Toss the pasta and vegetables with the reserved pesto and a few tablespoons of the cooking water. Add more water if the pasta is dry, but be careful not to make your sauce too watery. Serve the pasta topped with a little more grated Parmigiano, if you like.

Ligurian Herb Ravioli with Walnut Cream Sauce
Pansotti al Preboggion con Salsa di Noci

Given that *preboggion* (a medley of wild herbs that grow spontaneously in Liguria) is virtually impossible to find in Italian markets—let alone American ones—traditional *pansotti al preboggion* can be a bit elusive. However, if you can find unusual little greens such as baby Swiss chard, dandelion and beet greens, watercress, and chervil, you're in good shape. And if all fails, you can always use spinach—you'll still make some mighty tasty *pansotti*. (The word, by the way, derives from the Italian *panciuti*, which means "plump, with a belly," because they're packed with filling.)

A word of advice: You'll make your life a lot easier if you purchase a hand-cranked—or motorized—pasta machine. The two main available brands, Atlas and Imperia, are sold in many kitchen appliance stores for about forty dollars. Both get the job done just fine and will save you a lot of time and effort—unless you enjoy rolling out pasta dough by hand, that is. Even with the help of a pasta machine, however, *pansotti*—and other filled pastas in this book—are not an easy ride. Making them will likely take you back to bygone times when people had the luxury of spending an entire day in the kitchen. So be prepared to give up at least an afternoon, possibly more. I prefer to prepare the filling first, so the pasta doesn't dry out too much while it's waiting to be filled.

SERVES 4 TO 6

FOR THE FILLING

½ pound *preboggion* (a variety of mixed herbs including dandelion greens, beet greens, baby Swiss chard, watercress, and chervil)

¾ cup finely grated Parmigiano-Reggiano

1 large clove garlic, finely chopped almost to a paste

¾ cup fresh ricotta

1 teaspoon salt, plus more to taste

Freshly ground black pepper

PREPARE THE FILLING Bring a large pot of water to a boil and blanch the *preboggion* greens (leave out the chervil) for 3 minutes. Drain them, shock them in ice water or under cold running water, and squeeze out the excess water either by wringing them in a kitchen towel or using a potato ricer.

Finely chop the blanched greens and the raw chervil, if using, in a food processor or with a sharp knife. Transfer them to a bowl and add the remaining filling ingredients, leaving the egg for last so you can taste the filling for seasoning. Mix well to incorporate all the ingredients. You should have a smooth filling that you'll set aside in the refrigerator covered with plastic wrap as you prepare the dough.

CONTINUED

CONTINUED

Ligurian Herb Ravioli with Walnut Cream Sauce

CONTINUED

¼ teaspoon freshly grated nutmeg

1 large egg

FOR THE PASTA DOUGH

1 Fresh Pasta Dough for
Pansotti recipe, page 67

FOR THE SAUCE

¾ cup shelled walnuts

¼ cup pine nuts

1 medium clove garlic

¼ cup finely grated
Parmigiano-Reggiano

⅓ cup extra-virgin olive oil

½ cup fresh ricotta

Salt

Freshly ground black pepper

¼ cup heavy cream

PREPARE THE *PANSOTTI* Follow the instructions for Fresh Pasta Dough for *Pansotti*, page 67.

Cut the dough into four pieces and cover three of them with plastic wrap. Run the remaining piece through the widest setting of a hand-cranked pasta machine. You should obtain a thick, flat slice of dough. Fold it in three parts (like a letter), then put it back through the machine from its shortest side at the same setting. Repeat this process at least three times. Then start running the dough through at progressively narrower settings until you reach the very last one, always flouring both sides of the dough and inserting the shortest side first. Set the resulting long sheet of dough aside on a lightly floured surface, and cover it with a kitchen towel to keep it moist. Repeat with the other three pieces of dough. This dough is very delicate and can be a bit sticky. Make sure you dust all surfaces generously with flour when working with it.

With a dough cutter or knife, cut all the dough sheets in half lengthwise. Then, from each sheet, cut out squares about 3 inches across. Spoon about 1 teaspoon of the filling at the center of each square and fold it in half to form a triangle, sealing two of the sides with a quick brush of water. Don't worry, this is not an exact science. If the edges don't match perfectly, just trim them with a dough cutter or a knife. Continue filling and folding until you run out of dough and filling. Arrange the *pansotti* in a single layer on a lightly floured surface and cover them with a kitchen towel. You can freeze them at this point, if you're not planning to use them right away.

PREPARE THE SAUCE AND ASSEMBLE THE DISH Preheat the oven to 350°F.

Scatter the walnuts on a baking sheet and lightly toast them in the oven for about 5 minutes. Take them out and let them cool. Place the cooled walnuts, pine nuts, garlic, and Parmigiano in the bowl of a food processor and puree until creamy, about 2 minutes. With the processor still running, add the olive oil in a thin stream and continue to process until a smooth, creamy sauce forms. Transfer to a bowl and add the ricotta, mixing with a wooden spoon to incorporate it in the sauce. The mixture should be smooth but fairly dense. Add salt and pepper to taste. (Add a little more salt than you think you need, as the flavors get diluted a bit with the addition of cream at the end.)

Bring a large pot of generously salted water to a boil. Cook the *pansotti* for 4 to 5 minutes, or until they're soft and pliable (taste one; if it's too hard and chewy, it needs a little more time).

Meanwhile, transfer the sauce to a 12-inch skillet, add the heavy cream, and stir to incorporate over medium-low heat, 2 to 3 minutes.

Drain the *pansotti*, reserving ½ cup of the cooking water, and toss them with the sauce. If the sauce seems too dry, add the cooking water 1 or 2 tablespoons at a time (this may not be necessary). Serve immediately.

Fish Raviolini with Red Mullet Sauce

Raviolini di Pesce con Salsa di Triglie

The recipe for this sauce is adapted from a recipe by chefs Vittorio Baracchini and Emilio Pagani of the Cenobio dei Dogi restaurant in Camogli. It's delicious with other types of pasta, too. Try it with fresh angel hair or dried rigatoni. While I recommend you use red mullet, I know it can be tricky to find in American markets. So I tried replacing it with other types of fish and I found that trout works quite well as a substitution.

SERVES 4 TO 6

FOR THE FILLING

1½ pounds whole red mullet or 1 pound red mullet or trout fillets, cleaned

1 tablespoon unsalted butter

¾ pound medium shrimp, peeled and deveined

¾ cup fresh ricotta

1 teaspoon chopped marjoram

2 large egg whites

2½ teaspoons salt

Freshly ground black pepper

¼ cup heavy cream

FOR THE PASTA DOUGH

1 Fresh Egg Pasta Dough recipe, page 68

MAKE THE FILLING If your fish is whole, skin and fillet the red mullet as best you can. It's a small fish with lots of little bones that make it very hard to fillet. Since you need to chop it later, it's not very important to have whole fillets. Remove all the pesky bones with a pair of tweezers (I use clean eyebrow tweezers). Cut the fillets in 2- to 3-inch chunks.

Heat the butter in a 12-inch skillet over medium-high heat. When the butter stops bubbling, add the fish chunks. Sauté for 3 to 4 minutes over medium heat turning once, remove from the pan, and let cool. Remove any remaining skin and bones, and finely chop.

In the bowl of a food processor, combine the shrimp, ricotta, marjoram, and egg whites. Process for about 1 minute. Add the cooled-down red mullet, salt and pepper, and turn the motor on again. Pour in the cream slowly in a thin stream and process for 1 or 2 more minutes, until you obtain a smooth mixture. Store the filling in the refrigerator covered with plastic wrap as you prepare the dough.

MAKE THE PASTA DOUGH Follow the instructions for Fresh Egg Pasta Dough, page 68.

Cut the dough in four pieces and cover three of them with plastic wrap. Run the remaining piece through the widest setting of a hand-cranked pasta machine. You

1½ pound red mullet or trout fillets, cleaned

3 medium cloves garlic

⅓ cups plus 1 tablespoon extra-virgin olive oil

3 pounds fresh or canned tomatoes (scant 2 28-ounce cans), peeled, seeded, and chopped

Salt

Hot water as needed

½ medium onion, finely chopped (about ¾ cups)

1 tablespoon finely chopped parsley

½ medium celery stalk, finely chopped (about ⅓ cup)

½ pound squid, finely chopped

½ pound medium shrimp, peeled, deveined, and finely chopped

Freshly ground white pepper

⅓ cup dry white wine

1 tablespoon coarsely chopped parsley

should obtain a thick, flat slice of dough. Fold it in three parts (like a letter), then put it back through the machine from its shortest side at the same setting. Repeat this process at least three times. Then start running the dough through at progressively narrower settings until you reach the very last one, always flouring both sides of the dough and inserting the shortest side first. Set the resulting long sheet of dough aside on a lightly floured surface, and cover it with a kitchen towel to keep it moist. Repeat with the other three pieces of dough.

ASSEMBLE THE RAVIOLINI Take one pasta sheet and drop small bean-size dollops of filling (about ½ teaspoon) at an equal distance of about 1 inch, creating three rows on the sheet. Brush the outer edges of the pasta sheet with water and cover it with a second sheet so that the borders match. With your hands, press firmly all around the filling to remove any air and to seal the two sheets together. Roll a pastry or ravioli cutter around the filling to form even little squares, tracing around the areas you had already pressed with your hands. The raviolini should be fairly small (the word means "small ravioli").

Repeat the same procedure with the remaining pasta sheets. Arrange the raviolini in one layer on a lightly floured surface and cover with a kitchen towel. If you don't have enough space to spread them out in one layer, you can stack them in several layers each separated by a lightly floured kitchen towel.

MAKE THE SAUCE AND ASSEMBLE THE DISH Chop the red mullet fillets coarsely and set aside.

Smash one of the garlic cloves with the blade of a chef's knife and chop the remaining two cloves. Set aside.

CONTINUED

Fish Raviolini with Red Mullet Sauce

CONTINUED

Heat 1 tablespoon of the olive oil in a 10-inch skillet over medium-high heat. When well heated, add the smashed garlic clove, the chopped tomatoes, and ½ teaspoon of salt and cook for 3 to 4 minutes, or until it starts simmering vigorously. Lower the heat to medium and cook, stirring frequently, for 25 to 30 minutes, adding hot water 1 tablespoon at a time when the tomato sauce starts getting dry. Remove the garlic and set aside.

In a separate 12-inch skillet, heat the remaining olive oil over medium-high heat. When the oil is hot and shimmering, add the chopped garlic, onion, parsley, and celery, and cook for 4 to 5 minutes over medium-high heat, stirring occasionally.

Add the squid and sauté for 1 minute, stirring frequently, then add the shrimp and sauté for another 1 or 2 minutes. Add the red mullet, a generous pinch of salt, a couple of grinds of pepper, the white wine, and the reserved tomato sauce and cook, stirring frequently, for 4 or 5 more minutes. Season with salt and pepper to taste and remove from the heat.

Bring a large pot of generously salted water to a boil. Cook the raviolini for 8 to 10 minutes, or until they are soft and pliable (taste one; if it's too hard and chewy, it needs a little more time). Drain them, reserving ½ cup of the cooking water. Toss the raviolini with the sauce adding 1 or 2 tablespoons of the cooking water if the sauce is too dry (you may not need to add water at all or you may need a little more). Serve immediately garnished with the parsley.

Pennette with Langoustines in a Light Tomato Sauce

Pennette con gli Scampi di Vernazza

This is my attempt to recreate that perfect plate of *pennette* I had at Vernazza's Gambero Rosso restaurant some time in the mid-eighties. I didn't bother going back to the restaurant to ask for the recipe as the Gambero Rosso is not quite the eatery it used to be. Besides, they don't have this pasta on the menu anymore. A word on scampi: many people erroneously think they're the same as shrimp or prawns. That's not the case. Scampi, also known in America by their French name of langoustines, are like tiny lobsters with little claws, which shrimp most definitely don't have. They are fished only in the Mediterranean or in certain parts of the Atlantic close to the European shore. Hence, they're quite hard, if not impossible, to find in American markets. Unless you happen upon some nice scampi at the market or you're on the Mediterranean, opt for shrimp or prawns instead.

SERVES 4

1 pound scampi (or medium shrimp)

½ small carrot, coarsely chopped (about ¼ cup)

½ medium onion, quartered

½ medium celery stalk, coarsely chopped

2 sprigs parsley

½ cup dry white wine

⅔ cup extra-virgin olive oil

3 small cloves garlic, finely chopped (about 1½ teaspoons)

2 tablespoons chopped parsley, plus more for garnish

⅔ cup tomato puree

Salt

Peel the scampi (if using shrimp, also devein before using) and cut them into ¼-inch pieces, reserving the shells and heads. Set aside.

Make a quick broth: Pour 4 cups of water in a medium-size saucepan and add the carrot, onion, celery, parsley sprigs, scampi or shrimp shells and heads, and the wine. Bring to a boil and reduce to a simmer. Cook, uncovered, for about 30 minutes. Strain and reserve the broth.

Heat 4 tablespoons of the olive oil in a 10-inch skillet over medium heat, add the garlic and parsley, and cook for about 3 minutes, stirring frequently. (Lower the heat if the garlic starts burning.) Add the tomato puree and a pinch of salt and continue cooking for about 20 minutes over medium heat, stirring occasionally, adding the broth in ¼-cup increments to make sure the sauce doesn't dry out. It's hard to say how much broth you'll end up using, as the quantity of liquid you need will vary depending on the pan and the temperature.

CONTINUED

CONTINUED

Pennette with Langoustines in a Light Tomato Sauce

CONTINUED

Freshly ground black pepper

1 pound dried pennette (small penne pasta)

In the last 3 to 4 minutes of cooking, add the reserved scampi, season with salt and pepper to taste, and add the remaining olive oil, as you give the pan a few stirs.

Bring a large pot of generously salted water to a boil. Cook the pasta in boiling water according to package instructions until al dente.

Drain the pasta and toss it with the sauce. Garnish with extra chopped parsley, if you like, grind on some more pepper, and serve immediately.

Seafood Risotto with Clams, Mussels, and Shrimp

Risotto ai Frutti di Mare

Risotto is often believed to be labor-intensive and hard to make. I actually think it's quite simple. Once you nail the basic technique, you can make it over and over again with your own flavor preferences. You sweat the onion in butter or olive oil (I use butter for heartier risottos), you toast the rice so it's coated by the fat, you add some white wine and let it evaporate, then ladle in broth in small increments while stirring constantly. When it's almost done, you finish with a dollop of butter and some grated cheese. But be warned: no cheese on seafood! This is a strict Italian rule, very seldom broken. And certainly no cheese goes on this seafood risotto. Its flavor is so delicate and, well, "sealike" that cheese would spoil it. When cooking with clams or mussels, always discard shellfish whose shells are open and won't close after a gentle tapping. Once cooked, discard any shellfish that refuse to open.

SERVES 4

12 large clams

12 mussels

¼ cup water

3 tablespoons extra-virgin olive oil

1 tablespoon finely chopped garlic (about 3 medium cloves)

2 sprigs parsley

5 cups homemade shrimp broth (see recipe page 209)

3 tablespoons unsalted butter

½ large onion, finely chopped (about 1 cup)

Salt

2 cups arborio or carnaroli rice

1 cup dry white wine

CONTINUED

Scrub the clam and mussel shells well under cold running water. Discard any open shells.

Pour the water and 1 tablespoon of olive oil in a 12-inch pan (the liquid should just barely cover the bottom). Bring to a boil and reduce to a very slow simmer. Add half the garlic and parsley sprigs, followed by the clams and mussels. Cover and simmer until all the shells have opened, discarding the ones that didn't open. (Mussels will tend to open sooner than clams, so you may want to add the mussels a few minutes after adding the clams.) Strain the liquid through a fine-mesh strainer and reserve.

You can opt to leave the clams and mussels in their shells, shell them all, or shell some and leave the others in their shells. I like a few shells for decoration, but mostly I remove the shells.

Heat the shrimp broth in a saucepan over medium heat. When it starts simmering, reduce the heat to low and cover so it doesn't evaporate.

CONTINUED

Seafood Risotto with Clams, Mussels, and Shrimp

CONTINUED

1 large tomato, peeled, seeded, and coarsely chopped

16 medium shrimp, peeled and deveined

Freshly ground black pepper

½ teaspoon red pepper flakes

1 tablespoon coarsely chopped parsley

In a 10-inch sauté pan with straight sides, heat 1 tablespoon of olive oil and 1 tablespoon of butter over medium-high heat. Add the onions, the remaining garlic, and a pinch of salt and cook for 8 to 10 minutes over medium heat, stirring frequently and making sure not to burn the garlic.

Add the rice and stir well to coat it with the oil and butter, cooking it for 2 to 3 minutes over medium-high heat. Add the white wine and cook for another 2 to 3 minutes, always stirring, until it has almost completely evaporated.

Add the tomato, the reserved seafood cooking liquid, and another pinch of salt and begin ladling in the broth in ½-cup increments, stirring constantly, for 12 to 14 minutes. Make sure the liquid is almost completely absorbed before you add the next ladle. Maintain the heat at medium-high; the liquid should be bubbling.

At this point, you should have added about 4 cups of broth. Add the shrimp and the remaining broth, and cook about 4 minutes (the broth should be almost completely absorbed so that the texture of the risotto is soft and loose but not too soupy). Finish with the remaining 1 tablespoon of the olive oil and 2 tablespoons of the butter. Turn off the heat, stir in the shelled clams and mussels, season with the red pepper flakes and salt and pepper to taste, and sprinkle over the chopped parsley. Serve immediately garnished with the shellfish still in the shell, if using.

Hearty Baked Risotto with Sausage, Artichokes, and Mushrooms

Riso del Campagnolo di Ponente

When doing research for this book, I stumbled upon a recipe that means something like "rice of the western countryman." I was intrigued, so I decided to try it. It turned out to be quite a hearty and delicious dish, perfect for a cold winter Sunday. (It's not true risotto, in that the rice is first boiled, then baked.)

SERVES 4 TO 6

1 ounce dried porcini mushrooms (about 1 cup)

4 baby or 2 regular artichokes

Juice of 1 lemon

2 large links sweet Italian sausage (about ½ pound)

2 tablespoons extra-virgin olive oil

½ medium onion, chopped (about ¾ cup)

2 ounces fresh shiitake mushrooms, thinly sliced (about 1 cup)

4 ounces fresh cremini mushrooms, thinly sliced (about 2 cups)

¼ cup fresh or frozen peas

Salt

Freshly ground black pepper

2½ cups homemade (see recipe page 210) or low-sodium canned chicken broth

2½ cups vialone nano or arborio rice

2 cups finely grated Parmigiano-Reggiano

3 tablespoons unsalted butter

Soak the dried porcini in 1 cup of warm water for 30 minutes. Drain them and pat them dry, reserving the liquid (strain it before using).

Preheat the oven to 350°F.

Clean the artichokes by cutting the tough stems and about ½ inch to 1 inch off the top and by removing the outer, tough leaves until you reach the tender, light green leaves near the center. Cut each artichoke in half lengthwise and remove the hairy core. Then cut it into very thin slices (¼ to ⅛ inch thick) and drop them in a bowl of water with the lemon juice. When you're ready to cook them, drain and pat them dry with a paper towel.

Take the sausage out of its casing. Heat the olive oil in a 12-inch skillet over medium-high heat and add the sausage to the pan. Cook for about 3 minutes, or until it's lightly browned, breaking it up with a wooden spoon. Add the onion and cook for another 3 to 4 minutes, until the onion is soft. Add the dried and fresh mushrooms, 4 tablespoons of the mushroom soaking liquid, the peas, and artichokes, and season to taste with salt and pepper. Cook for another 1 to 2 minutes, stirring frequently, then add 1 cup of broth and cook until the liquid is almost completely evaporated, 8 to 10 minutes.

CONTINUED

Hearty Baked Risotto with Sausage, Artichokes, and Mushrooms

CONTINUED

Meanwhile, bring a large pot of generously salted water to a boil. Add the rice and parboil it for about 10 minutes (the rice should still be quite firm and very al dente, about two-thirds cooked through). Drain it in a colander or strainer over the sink.

Pour the drained rice in a 9 × 13-inch baking dish and add the sausage mixture. Add the Parmigiano, butter, and remaining broth. Mix the ingredients well so they're evenly distributed, and taste for seasoning. Level the surface with the back of a wooden spoon and bake for about 20 minutes. Serve immediately.

Butternut Squash Ligurian Ravioli with Browned Butter and Sage

Pansotti di Zucca

Even in Liguria people get tired of the same old stuff, so they experiment a little with new flavors and combinations. While not traditional, I've seen winter squash pansotti on the menu of more than one restaurant in the region. I like to make these *pansotti* slightly larger than the more traditional herb *pansotti* so that five or six are enough for one serving. This makes them perfect for a fancier occasion.

SERVES 4 TO 6

FOR THE FILLING

1½ **pound butternut squash**

¼ **cup extra-virgin olive oil**

Salt

Freshly ground black pepper

2 **large eggs**

½ **cup fresh ricotta**

1 **cup finely grated Parmigiano-Reggiano**

1 **medium clove garlic, chopped to a paste**

¼ **teaspoon chopped marjoram**

¼ **teaspoon finely grated lemon zest**

¼ **cup homemade bread crumbs (see recipe, page 211)**

PREPARE THE FILLING Preheat the oven to 450°F.

Cut the butternut squash in half, drizzle both open sides with the olive oil, and sprinkle liberally with salt and pepper. Cook in the oven for 50 to 60 minutes, or until soft when pierced with a fork.

Meanwhile, in a large bowl combine the eggs, ricotta, Parmigiano, garlic, marjoram, lemon zest, and bread crumbs. Add 1½ teaspoons of salt, grind on some pepper, and mix well to incorporate all the ingredients.

When the squash is ready, scoop out the seeds with a large spoon. Spoon the squash pulp out of its skin, let it cool, and mix it in with the filling. Cover the bowl with plastic wrap and refrigerate.

PREPARE THE *PANSOTTI* Follow the instructions for Fresh Pasta for *Pansotti*, page 67.

Cut the dough in four pieces and cover three of them with plastic wrap. Run the remaining piece through the widest setting of a hand-cranked pasta machine. You should obtain a thick, flat slice of dough. Fold it in three parts (like a letter), then put it back through the machine from its shortest side at the same setting. Repeat this

CONTINUED

CONTINUED

Butternut Squash Ligurian Ravioli with Browned Butter and Sage

CONTINUED

FOR PASTA DOUGH
**1 Fresh Pasta Dough for *Pansotti*
recipe, page 67**

FOR THE SAUCE
5 tablespoons unsalted butter

14 sage leaves

¼ teaspoon salt

Freshly ground black pepper

process at least three times. Then start running the dough through at progressively narrower settings until you reach the very last one, always flouring both sides of the dough and inserting the shortest side first. Set the resulting long sheet of dough aside on a lightly floured surface, and cover it with a kitchen towel to keep it moist. Repeat with the other three pieces of dough. This dough is very delicate and can be a bit sticky. Make sure you dust all surfaces generously with flour when working with it.

Cut out of each pasta sheet into squares of about 5 inches across. Spoon about 1 tablespoon of the filling at the center of each square and fold it in half to form a tri-angle, sealing two of the sides with a quick brush of water. Don't worry, this is not an exact science. If the edges don't match perfectly, just trim them with a pastry cutter or a knife. Continue filling and folding until you run out of dough and filling. Arrange the *pansotti* in a single layer on a lightly floured surface and cover them with a kitchen towel. You can freeze them at this point if you're not planning to use them right away.

PREPARE THE SAUCE AND ASSEMBLE THE DISH In a 12-inch skillet, melt the butter over medium heat and cook until it barely starts turning brown, 3 to 4 minutes. Imme-diately, remove the pan from the heat, add the sage, and steep it for 10 minutes.

Bring a large pot of generously salted water to a boil. Cook the *pansotti* for 4 to 5 minutes, or until they are soft and pliable (taste one; if it's too hard and chewy, it needs a little more time).

Drain the *pansotti* and add them to the pan with the butter and sage. Turn on the heat to medium-low, add the salt and a few grinds of pepper, and toss them so they're completely coated in butter. Serve immediately. You can grate on some extra Parmigiano at the table, if you like.

Fresh *Trenette* with Leeks, Zucchini, and Pecorino

Trenette con Porri e Zucchine

Trenette and pesto go hand in hand in Liguria—they're a classic regional dish. But I almost prefer this pasta (which resembles linguine, but is plumper with an elliptical cross section) when it's accompanied by leeks, zucchini, and pecorino. If you don't want to go through the trouble of making the pasta, you can use dried *trenette* or linguine, or even penne or rigatoni instead.

SERVES 4

FOR THE PASTA DOUGH

½ **Fresh Egg Pasta Dough recipe, page 68**

FOR THE SAUCE

½ **cup extra-virgin olive oil**

1 **small onion, finely chopped (about 1 cup)**

4 **medium leeks (white and light green parts only), sliced (about 4 cups)**

1 **medium zucchini, finely sliced crosswise (about 1 cup)**

Salt

Freshly ground black pepper

1 **tablespoon chopped parsley**

1 **cup finely grated pecorino, preferably toscano or sardo**

MAKE THE PASTA DOUGH Make half Fresh Egg Pasta Dough recipe, page 68.

Cut the dough in four pieces and cover three of them with plastic wrap. Run the remaining piece through the widest setting of a hand-cranked pasta machine. You should obtain a thick, flat slice of dough. Fold it in three parts (like a letter), then put it back through the machine from its shortest side at the same setting. Repeat this process at least three times. Then start running the dough through at progressively narrower settings until you reach the very last one, always flouring both sides of the dough and inserting the shortest side first. Set the resulting long pasta sheet aside on a lightly floured surface, and cover with a kitchen towel to keep it moist. Repeat with the other three pieces of dough.

Cut each pasta sheet into smaller, 10-inch-long sheets and run each through the *trenette* (or linguine) cutter of your hand-cranked pasta machine (while linguine cutters come with most machines, you have to buy *trenette* cutters separately). Arrange the *trenette* in a single layer on a lightly floured surface, sprinkle with more flour, and cover with a kitchen towel.

MAKE THE SAUCE AND ASSEMBLE THE DISH In a 12-inch skillet, heat ¼ cup of the olive oil over medium-high heat. Add the onions and cook for 4 to 6 minutes, stirring frequently, until very soft and translucent with a few browned bits. Add the leeks

CONTINUED

Fresh Trenette with Leeks, Zucchini, and Pecorino

CONTINUED

and zucchini, season with a pinch of salt and pepper and cook, stirring occasionally, for another 10 minutes, or until all the vegetables are very soft and tender. You may need to add 1 or 2 tablespoons of water if the vegetables start drying out too much. Add the remaining oil and parsley, toss, and remove from the heat.

Bring a large pot of generously salted water to a boil. Add the *trenette* and cook for 4 to 6 minutes, or until they're soft and pliable (taste one; if it's too hard and chewy, it needs a little more time). Drain, reserving about ½ cup of the cooking water, and toss them with the sauce and the pecorino. Add some of the water if they appear too dry. Serve immediately.

Riviera-Style Spaghetti with Anchovies and Capers in a Light Tomato Sauce

Spaghetti alla Rivierasca

This pasta is quick and easy—perfect for a weeknight. And you can pretty much make it with ingredients from the pantry, provided your pantry is filled with some of the staples of Ligurian cooking—extra-virgin olive oil, of course, but also salted anchovies and capers, parsley, tomatoes, and garlic.

SERVES 4

⅔ cup extra-virgin olive oil, plus more for drizzling

4 salted anchovy fillets, rinsed and chopped

2 tablespoons salted capers, rinsed and chopped

2 medium cloves garlic, finely chopped (about 2 teaspoons)

1 tablespoon chopped parsley

4 small plum tomatoes or 4 whole canned tomatoes, peeled, seeded, and chopped

1 pound dried thick spaghetti or bucatini

Salt

Freshly ground black pepper

Heat the olive oil in a 10-inch skillet over medium heat. Add the anchovies, capers, garlic, and half of the parsley, and cook for 3 to 4 minutes. If the garlic starts burning, turn down the heat. Add the tomato and cook for another 6 to 8 minutes, stirring occasionally, until the tomatoes are soft and have broken down into a sauce. Turn off the heat.

Meanwhile, bring a large pot of generously salted water to a boil. Drop in the pasta and cook it according to package instructions.

Add the remaining parsley to the pan with the sauce and adjust seasoning with salt and pepper (you probably won't need much salt because the anchovies and capers are already quite salty).

Drain the cooked pasta and toss it with the sauce. Add a drizzle of olive oil, if you like, and serve immediately.

Fresh *Corzetti* Pasta with Pine Nut and Marjoram Pesto

Corzetti con Salsa di Pinoli

I didn't even know *corzetti* existed before a recent trip to Bonassola, when I found a pack of round, coin-shaped pasta in Silvana's pantry, imprinted with what looked like a seal. Curious, I asked her about this "new" type of pasta. It turns out they were anything but new. *Corzetti* are a time-honored pasta in the *levante*, especially between the towns of Recco and Chiavari, imprinted with artisanal wooden stamps (see sidebar). You can find dry, packaged *corzetti* in Italy, but they're virtually impossible to find in the United States. To make them at home, you need to get a hold of one or more *corzetti* stamps, which can be tricky to come across (the only place I found in the United States that sells them is A. G. Ferrari Foods; see Sources). If you're willing to forgo the seal, you can make do with a shot glass that has a diameter of about one and a half to two inches.

SERVES 4 TO 6

FOR THE PASTA DOUGH

2 cups unbleached all-purpose flour

2 large eggs

1 teaspoon extra-virgin olive oil

½ teaspoon salt

2 teaspoons finely chopped marjoram

¼ cup cold water

FOR THE PESTO

¾ cup pine nuts

⅓ cup tightly packed marjoram leaves

1 small clove garlic

1½ cups extra-virgin olive oil

⅓ cup heavy cream

Salt

Freshly ground black pepper

½ cup finely grated
Parmigiano-Reggiano

MAKE THE PASTA DOUGH Pour the flour into a mound on a wide, flat surface—wood and plastic are preferable to marble because the coldness of marble counteracts the elasticity of the dough. Create a well in the middle of the flour mound, break the eggs into the well, then add olive oil, salt, marjoram, and 2 tablespoons of water. With the help of a fork, whisk the eggs inside the well, working in the flour from the rims of the well a little at a time until about two-thirds of the flour is mixed in with the eggs. When the mixture gets too sticky and hard to beat with the fork, start working with the palms of your hands. If the dough doesn't come together, add the rest of the water. At his point you'll have a main mass of dough and lots of smaller dough crumbs that won't incorporate into the bigger dough ball. Remove these crumbs from the work surface and throw them away, adding more flour to the surface if it's too sticky. (You can use a mixer or food processor to make the dough. Place the flour and salt in the bowl of a stand mixer fitted with the dough attachment. Run it on slow speed, adding the oil, marjoram, and eggs one at a time. Add 2 tablespoons of the water and increase the speed to medium-high. Add more of the water if the dough isn't coming together. I like to knead it by hand for the last 5 minutes.)

Knead the dough for a good 5 minutes with the palms of your hands, until it becomes smooth and malleable. Pat it into a round shape, cover it with a towel or plastic wrap, and set it aside for about 30 minutes. You can freeze it, if not using right away.

Cut the dough in four pieces and cover three of them with plastic wrap. Run the remaining piece through the widest setting of a hand-cranked pasta machine. You should obtain a thick, flat slice of dough. Fold it in three parts (like a letter), then put it back through the machine from its shortest side at the same setting. Repeat this process at least three times. Then start running the dough through at progressively narrower settings until you reach the very last one, always flouring both sides of the dough and inserting the shortest side first. Set the resulting long pasta sheet aside on a lightly floured surface, and cover with a kitchen towel to keep it moist. Repeat with the other three pieces of dough.

Press a *corzetti* stamp on each sheet of dough at an equal distance so that you obtain little disks of pasta imprinted with the image on the stamp. Lay the disks in a single layer on a lightly floured work surface and let them dry for at least 2 hours.

MAKE THE PESTO Place the pine nuts, marjoram, garlic, and olive oil in the bowl of a food processor and process until you obtain a smooth paste. Stop the motor, add the heavy cream, and process for another minute to incorporate. The sauce should be smooth and creamy. Add a generous pinch of salt and grind on some pepper. Taste for seasoning and add more salt and pepper, if necessary.

ASSEMBLE THE DISH Bring a large pot of generously salted water to a boil. Cook the *corzetti* for about 5 minutes, or until they're soft and pliable (taste one; if it's too hard and chewy, it needs a little more time). Drain them, reserving 1 or 2 tablespoons of the cooking water, and toss them with the sauce. Add the reserved water if the sauce looks too dry. Sprinkle the Parmigiano over the pasta and serve immediately.

WHAT ARE *corzetti* STAMPS?

They're hand-carved, round-shape wooden stamps with a diameter of one and a half to two inches. Because *corzetti* are a local specialty confined to the area around Recco and Chiavari, the stamps used to make them are not mass produced. They're still carved by hand by local artisans. Traditionally, *corzetti* stamps represented designs related to the glorious maritime republic of Genova or to the Doria family, which is to Liguria what the Medici were to Tuscany. Rich noble families would imprint *corzetti* with their own seals and arms symbols. The word itself means "little crosses," which leads to speculation that the original designs might have had something to do with Genovese Crusaders of the thirteenth century. Nowadays, you'll also find more modern, abstract representations, including fish, sailboats, and flowers. My own two *corzetti* stamps represent an old-style sailboat and a large fish happily jumping out of the sea.

Fresh *Maltagliati* with Spicy Purple Pesto

Maltagliati con Pesto Piccantino

Apricale Da Delio is a gourmet restaurant worthy of any urban area—except it's nowhere close to the hustle and bustle of a city. It's at the foot of a spectacular medieval village called Apricale in the *entroterra* behind Ventimiglia, right on the border with France. This is the area where Liguria's most famous wines are produced, including Rossese di Dolceacqua, where *stoccafisso* (stockfish) is on every menu, and where pesto is deconstructed. Da Delio was where I first had pesto that wasn't blended. "*Maltagliati con Pesto Piccantino*" ("badly cut pasta" with mildly spicy pesto), said the menu. Nothing betrayed the fact that this wasn't your standard pesto. Yet Delio Viale's *maltagliati* with large pieces of basil leaves, whole toasted pine nuts, pecorino shavings, and a generous dose of olive oil were fabulous. I've tried to recapture their essence in this recipe. The use of purple basil is mine, however, inspired by a Saturday morning visit to the Union Square farmers' market in New York City. You can certainly use regular basil if you can't find the purple variety.

SERVES 4

FOR THE PASTA DOUGH
½ **Fresh Egg Pasta Dough recipe, page 68**

FOR THE PESTO
⅓ **cup extra-virgin olive oil**

2 **large cloves garlic, smashed with the blade of a chef's knife**

2 **cups purple basil leaves, cut into ½-inch-wide strips**

2 **cups finely grated Parmigiano-Reggiano**

½ **small serrano pepper, finely chopped**

½ **cup pine nuts, lightly toasted**

Salt

Freshly ground black pepper

MAKE THE PASTA DOUGH AND *MALTAGLIATI* Make half Fresh Egg Pasta Dough recipe, page 68.

Cut the dough in four pieces and cover three of them with plastic wrap. Run the remaining piece through the widest setting of a hand-cranked pasta machine. You should obtain a thick, flat slice of dough. Fold it in three parts (like a letter), then put it back through the machine from its shortest side at the same setting. Repeat this process at least three times. Then start running the dough through at progressively narrower settings until you reach the very last one, always flouring each side of the dough and inserting the shortest side first. Set the resulting long pasta sheet aside on a lightly floured surface, and cover with a kitchen towel to keep it moist. Repeat with the other three pieces of dough.

With a sharp paring knife, cut each dough sheet in strips about 1 inch wide. Then cut each strip on the bias every 3 inches. Repeat until all the dough sheets are cut up. Arrange the *maltagliati* in a single layer on a lightly floured surface, sprinkle them with more flour, and cover with a large kitchen towel.

ASSEMBLE THE DISH Bring a large pot of generously salted water to a boil. Cook the pasta for about 5 minutes, or until it's soft and pliable (taste one; if it's too hard and chewy, it needs a little more time).

Meanwhile, heat the olive oil in a large skillet over medium heat and add the garlic. Cook for about 5 minutes, being careful not to burn it. Remove the garlic from the skillet and add the basil, Parmigiano, serrano pepper, and pine nuts. Adjust seasoning with salt and pepper. Drain the pasta, reserving about ½ cup of the cooking water, and toss in the hot pan for 1 minute to incorporate the flavors. Add some of the water if the pasta appears too dry. Serve immediately.

TIP

To toast pine nuts, place them in a skillet over medium-high heat and cook them, shaking the pan occasionally, for about 5 minutes, or until they've turned golden brown. Transfer them to a cold plate so they don't continue to toast and burn. Toasting extracts the nuts' oils and brings out more flavor.

Fresh *Picagge* Pasta with Asparagus in a Light Cream Sauce

Picagge con gli Asparagi

Picagge is Ligurian for tagliatelle or fettuccine. It's also the word for a cook's apron strings. But in Liguria, *picagge* are seldom plain. They're green, made with borage leaves or spinach, or even *matte* (crazy), made with chestnut and whole wheat flours. While *picagge* are commonly enjoyed with pesto (and are delicious that way), I experimented with a different sauce, one inspired more by Berkeley's Chez Panisse, where I once had a terrific asparagus pasta, than by traditional Ligurian fare. You can choose to make your own fresh *picagge* or buy packaged fresh fettuccine to speed up the prep time.

SERVES 4

FOR THE PICAGGE

½ Fresh Egg Pasta Dough recipe, page 68

FOR THE SAUCE

1 pound asparagus, tough stem ends removed

2 tablespoons extra-virgin olive oil

1½ tablespoons chopped shallots

Salt

½ cup heavy cream

Freshly ground black pepper

MAKE THE *PICAGGE* Make half Fresh Egg Pasta Dough recipe, page 68.

Cut the dough in four pieces and cover three of them with plastic wrap. Run the remaining piece through the widest setting of a hand-cranked pasta machine. You should obtain a thick, flat slice of dough. Fold it in three parts (like a letter), then put it back through the machine from its shortest side at the same setting. Repeat this process at least three times. Then start running the dough through at progressively narrower settings until you reach the very last one, always flouring both sides of the dough and inserting the shortest side first. Set the resulting long pasta sheet aside on a lightly floured surface, and cover with a kitchen towel to keep it moist. Repeat with the reserved three pieces of dough.

Cut each pasta sheet into smaller, 10-inch-long sheets, add the appropriate attachment to the pasta machine, and run each sheet through the medium-width pasta cutter (don't use the smallest one or else you'll get linguine). Turn the crank slowly and make sure you capture the *picagge* as they roll out so they don't stick to one another. Lay them in a single layer on a floured surface, sprinkle them with more flour, and let them dry for 20 minutes or so. If it's very humid, they may need to rest longer.

MAKE THE SAUCE Bring a large pot of water to a boil and blanch the asparagus in it for 2 to 3 minutes. Drain and shock them under cold running water or in a bowl of iced water. When cool, drain again, blot dry with a kitchen or paper towel, and cut on the bias into very thin slivers, $\frac{1}{8}$- to $\frac{1}{16}$ inch thick.

Heat the olive oil in a 10-inch skillet over medium-high heat. Add the shallots and cook for 5 minutes, stirring occasionally. Be careful not to burn them, although it's fine if they get slightly browned on the edges—that'll lend the dish a pleasant caramelized flavor.

Add the asparagus to the pan with a pinch of salt, and cook for another 5 minutes, lowering the heat if the asparagus start to burn. Reduce the heat to medium, add the cream, and cook for 3 to 4 more minutes, stirring frequently to amalgamate the cream with the remaining ingredients. Season with more salt and grind on a generous amount of pepper. Don't be shy here: for four people, a good five or six strong twists of the pepper grinder won't hurt. And if you're a pepper aficionado, add more.

Bring a large pot of generously water to a boil. Cook the pasta for about 5 minutes, or until it's soft and pliable (taste one; if it's too hard and chewy, it needs a little more time).

Drain the pasta, reserving $\frac{1}{2}$ cup of the cooking water, and toss it with the sauce. It shouldn't need the addition of any cooking water, but use it in case the sauce appears to be too dry.

Serve immediately, grinding a little more fresh pepper on each plate, if you like.

Rigatoni with Swordfish, Olives, Rosemary, and Sage

Rigatoni col Pesce Spada

This may just be the perfect pasta for a busy weeknight. It's quick, easy, and delicious. It's a variation on a recipe my mother passed along to me. We make it a lot in Bonassola, as well as in Torino when we need something light, tasty, and simple for lunch or dinner. You can substitute tuna or halibut for the swordfish, if you like.

SERVES 4

2 medium celery stalks

½ large carrot

½ large onion

1 medium clove garlic

1 small sprig rosemary, leaves only

5 medium sage leaves

5 tablespoons extra-virgin olive oil

½ teaspoon salt

⅓ cup pitted black and green olives, coarsely chopped

1 pound dried rigatoni pasta

1½ pounds swordfish, cut in ½-inch dice

Freshly ground black pepper

Place the celery, carrot, onion, garlic, rosemary, and sage in the bowl of a food processor and process for about 1 minute. You want to chop the vegetables finely but not make a watery puree.

In a 12-inch skillet, heat the olive oil over medium-high heat. When the oil is hot, add the chopped vegetables and the salt. Cook for about 7 minutes, stirring frequently, until the vegetables are soft and fragrant. Add the olives and cook for another 7 to 8 minutes.

Meanwhile, bring a large pot of generously salted water to a boil. Add the rigatoni and cook according to package instructions.

Add the swordfish to the skillet and cook, stirring often, for 3 to 4 minutes, just enough time to cook the fish through without making it tough. Adjust the seasoning with salt and pepper to taste and turn off the heat.

Drain the pasta, reserving a few tablespoons of the cooking water, and toss it with the sauce. Add the reserved cooking water only if the pasta appears to be too dry. Serve immediately.

Vegetarian Pesto Lasagne with Fresh Ricotta and Toasted Pine Nuts

Lasagne col Pesto

Lasagne with pesto are quite common all over Liguria. Everyone has their own trusted recipe and they're all slightly different. This one's my twist on a classic. To avoid making your lasagne too oily, you may want to consider using about two-thirds of the oil required in the pesto recipe on page 69. (I, for one, don't mind it as long as the oil is good.) Also, if you plan on refrigerating the lasagne to serve later, the oil will dry up a bit.

SERVES 6 TO 8

FOR THE PASTA DOUGH
1⅔ cups unbleached all-purpose flour

2 large eggs

1 teaspoon extra-virgin olive oil

½ teaspoon salt

2 to 3 tablespoons cold water

FOR THE BÉCHAMEL
¼ cup unsalted butter

¼ cup unbleached all-purpose flour

2 cups hot whole milk

Salt

Freshly ground pepper

Freshly grated nutmeg

FOR THE FILLING
1 tablespoon extra-virgin olive oil

1½ cups pesto
(double the recipe on page 69, without the green beans and potatoes)

MAKE THE PASTA DOUGH AND LASAGNE SHEETS Pour the flour in a mound on a wide, flat surface—wood and plastic are preferable to marble because the coldness of marble counteracts the elasticity of the dough. Create a well (it'll look somewhat like a crater) in the middle of the flour mound, break the eggs into the well, then add the olive oil, salt, and 2 tablespoons of water. With the help of a fork, whisk the eggs inside the well, working in the flour from the rims of the well a little at a time until about two-thirds of the flour is mixed in with the eggs. When the mixture gets too sticky and hard to beat with the fork, start working with the palms of your hands. If the dough doesn't come together, add a little more water. At his point you'll have a main mass of dough and lots of smaller dough crumbs that won't incorporate into the bigger dough ball. Remove these crumbs from the work surface and throw them away, adding more flour to the surface if it's too sticky. (You can use a mixer or food processor to make the dough. Place the flour and salt in the bowl of a stand mixer fitted with the dough attachment. Run it on slow speed, adding the oil and eggs one at a time. Add 2 tablespoons of water and increase the speed to medium-high. Add more of the water if the dough isn't coming together. I like to knead it by hand for the last 5 minutes.)

Knead the dough for a good 5 minutes with the palms of your hands, until it becomes smooth and malleable. Pat it into a round shape, cover it with a towel or plastic wrap, and set it aside for about 30 minutes.

CONTINUED

CONTINUED

Vegetarian Pesto Lasagne with Fresh Ricotta and Toasted Pine Nuts

CONTINUED

1½ pounds fresh ricotta
(about 3 cups)

2 cups finely grated
Parmigiano-Reggiano

Freshly ground black pepper

Salt

1 tablespoon pine nuts, lightly toasted

Cut the dough in two pieces and cover one with plastic wrap. Run the remaining piece through the widest setting of a hand-cranked pasta machine. You should obtain a thick, flat slice of dough. Fold it in three parts (like a letter), then put it back through the machine from its shortest side at the same setting. Repeat this process at least three times. Then start running the dough through at progressively narrower settings until you reach the very last one, always flouring both sides of the dough and inserting the shortest side in the machine first. Set the resulting long pasta sheet aside on a lightly floured surface, and cover with a kitchen towel to keep it moist. Repeat with the other piece of dough.

Cut the pasta sheets in even rectangles so each fits an 8 × 10-inch baking dish. Keep in mind that pasta dough expands when cooking, so cut the rectangles a little smaller than the size of your pan. You should end up with six or seven rectangles. (While one rectangle is usually enough for each lasagna layer, you may need a little more to patch each layer.) Set them aside in a single layer on a lightly floured surface and cover with a large kitchen towel. If you have any leftovers, you can freeze them and use them for your next lasagne. Just put parchment or sprinkle semolina flour between sheets to prevent them from sticking.

MAKE THE BÉCHAMEL Melt the butter in a medium-size saucepan over medium-low heat and slowly add the flour, whisking constantly. Cook the mixture for 2 to 3 minutes, always whisking, then slowly pour in the hot milk. Cook, whisking constantly, for another 8 to 10 minutes, or until the béchamel thickens. Add the salt, pepper, and nutmeg to taste. Keep warm and stir occasionally to remove the "skin" that will form on the surface. Add a little more hot milk and stir vigorously if the béchamel thickens too much while it sits.

ASSEMBLE THE LASAGNE Preheat the oven to 400°F.

Bring a large pot of generously salted water to a boil. Add the lasagna rectangles. Cook for about 5 minutes, or until the rectangles turn a pale, creamy color and feel very soft and tender. Shower them with cold water in a colander and drain them very carefully (I prefer to take them out of the pot one by one with a large slotted spoon). When they're cool enough to handle with your hands, lay them flat on a cooling rack (you can overlap them a bit as long as you pour a little olive oil between pasta rectangles so they won't stick).

Oil the bottom of your baking dish with 1 tablespoon of olive oil. Place the first lasagna rectangle on the bottom, trimming the sides or adding a patch if it doesn't fit perfectly. Spread a thin layer of pesto over it, then a thin layer of ricotta, a generous sprinkle of Parmigiano, and some of the béchamel. Grind on a little pepper and sprinkle with a pinch of salt, but be careful not to oversalt, as both the pesto and noodles are already salted. Make sure to portion out the ingredients so you have enough for five layers of filling. Follow the same procedure for the remaining four layers, finishing with the pesto, ricotta, béchamel, and Parmigiano.

Bake the lasagne for 35 to 40 minutes and serve immediately, topped with the toasted pine nuts.

"Coral" Lasagne with Shrimp and Clams

Lasagne al Corallo

These lasagne are called "coral" in Italian because the tomato and seafood sauce, mixed with the béchamel, turns a delightful coral color. To make them, as well as those on page 95, you can buy ready-made dried lasagna noodles; but I find they're often too thick. When making lasagne, I always run the pasta dough through the next to last setting of the hand-cranked pasta machine in order to get a super-thin noodle. This, in turn, makes the lasagne light and delicate. If the noodles are too thick, lasagne can be coarse and tough.

SERVES 6 TO 8

FOR THE PASTA DOUGH
See Lasagne recipe, page 95.

FOR THE FILLING
2 pounds medium shrimp

2 sprigs parsley

½ medium onion, quartered

5 tablespoons extra-virgin olive oil

1 cup chopped onions

2 medium cloves garlic, chopped (about 2 teaspoons)

1 tablespoon chopped parsley

20 plum tomatoes, peeled, seeded, and coarsely chopped, or 2½ (28-ounce) cans whole tomatoes, coarsely chopped

1 teaspoon salt, more as needed

40 large clams
(a scant ½ pound when shelled)

Freshly ground black pepper

2 tablespoons unsalted butter

MAKE THE PASTA DOUGH AND LASAGNE SHEETS Follow the instructions on pages 95-96.

MAKE THE FILLING Peel and devein the shrimp. With the shells, make a quick shrimp broth: Pour 6 cups of water into a large pot and add the parsley sprigs, quartered onion, and shrimp shells. Bring to a boil and reduce to a simmer. Simmer for 30 minutes, then drain and reserve the broth.

In a 12-inch skillet, heat 4 tablespoons of the olive oil over medium heat. When the oil is hot, add the onions, garlic, and chopped parsley, and cook for 5 minutes over medium heat, until the onions are soft and translucent. Add the tomatoes and the salt, raise the heat to medium-high, and cook the sauce for 30 to 35 minutes, stirring frequently. Ladle in some of the shrimp broth when the sauce starts getting dry. There's really no fixed amount of broth you should add. It all depends on the heat of your stovetop, how much water was originally in the tomatoes, and the thickness of the pan. Focus on the result: You don't want a watery sauce, but neither a sauce that's too thick and dry. The balance between the two is the optimal result.

While the sauce is cooking, coarsely chop three-quarters of the shrimp and reserve the rest. Heat 1 cup of water in a large skillet and cook the clams, covered, over

FOR THE BÉCHAMEL

¼ cup unsalted butter

¼ cup unbleached all-purpose flour

2 cups hot whole milk

Salt

Freshly ground pepper

Freshly grated nutmeg

medium-low heat, until the shells open. Discard any clams whose shells don't open. Remove the clams from the opened shells and coarsely chop them.

Add the chopped shrimp to the tomato sauce and cook over medium-high heat, stirring frequently, for 4 to 5 minutes, or until the shrimp are cooked. Add the chopped clams, remove from the heat, and set aside. Add more salt, if necessary, and a little pepper.

Melt the butter in a 10-inch skillet over medium-high heat. When the butter stops foaming, add the reserved unchopped shrimp and cook for 4 to 5 minutes, until slightly browned on the edges. Transfer them to the bowl of a food processor and pulse until finely minced. Set them aside.

MAKE THE BÉCHAMEL Melt the butter in a medium-size saucepan over medium-low heat and slowly add the flour, whisking constantly. Cook the mixture for 2 to 3 minutes, always whisking, then slowly pour in the hot milk. Cook, whisking constantly, for another 8 to 10 minutes, or until the béchamel thickens. Add the salt, pepper, and nutmeg to taste. Keep warm and stir occasionally to remove the "skin" that will form on the surface. Add a little more hot milk and stir vigorously if it thickens too much while it sits.

ASSEMBLE THE LASAGNE Preheat the oven to 400°F.

Pour the béchamel in a large bowl and add the prepared tomato sauce and pureed shrimp. Mix well with a large spoon to incorporate the ingredients. Taste and adjust seasoning with salt and pepper as needed.

CONTINUED

"Coral" Lasagne with Shrimp and Clams

CONTINUED

Cook the lasagne noodles following the instructions on p.97.

Oil the bottom of a 8 × 10-inch baking dish with 1 tablespoon of olive oil. Place the first lasagna rectangle on the bottom, trimming the sides if it doesn't fit perfectly. Spread a layer of the filling and grind on a little pepper. Make sure to portion the filling out so you have enough for five layers of filling. Follow the same procedure for the remaining four layers, finishing with the filling.

Bake the lasagne for 35 to 40 minutes and serve immediately.

Ligurian Seafood Bisque with Paprika Crostoni

Ciuppin con Crostoni di Paprika

I called this a bisque because it reminds me of the creamy French pureed and strained soup, but it's really not a bisque in a traditional sense. In Liguria it's called *ciuppin*, and it may well be the ancestor of the famed—and much heartier—San Francisco cioppino. In some parts of Liguria, *ciuppin* is a chunky seafood soup, not dissimilar to *buridda*. In others, it's pureed into a liquid cream, as in this recipe. You have two options: you can stop after pureeing the fish in the blender, for a more rustic soup; or proceed to strain the puréed soup for something a bit more refined. If you strain it, it'll serve about two; if you don't strain it, it can serve up to four.

SERVES 2 TO 4

2 pounds white fish fillets, such as grouper, nile perch, cod, tilapia, or red mullet, skinned

¼ cup plus 3 tablespoons extra-virgin olive oil

1 small onion, finely chopped (about 1 cup)

1 small celery stalk, finely chopped (about ⅓ cup)

1 small carrot, finely chopped (about ½ cup)

3 small cloves garlic, finely chopped (about 1½ teaspoons)

1 tablespoon chopped parsley, plus more for garnish

½ teaspoon finely chopped marjoram

Salt

1 cup dry white wine

4 medium tomatoes, peeled, seeded, and coarsely chopped

Clean the fish, removing all the bones (which can be pretty pesky in certain fish, such as red mullet), and cut the fillets into 2-inch chunks.

In a small Dutch oven or in a straight-sided, lidded 10-inch pan, heat ¼ cup of the olive oil over medium-high heat. When the oil is hot and shimmering, add the onion, celery, carrot, garlic, parsley, marjoram, and a pinch of salt, and cook, stirring frequently, for 5 to 7 minutes, until the vegetables are fragrant and begin to soften.

Add the white wine and simmer vigorously until the wine is reduced by half, 2 to 3 minutes.

Add the tomatoes and just a little more salt. Continue cooking for about 5 minutes, or until the liquid is mostly reduced (it may take longer if the tomatoes are very watery).

Add all the fish and the fish broth. Reduce the heat to medium-low and simmer for 40 to 45 minutes, with the pan partially covered.

Preheat the oven to 450°F.

CONTINUED   CONTINUED

Ligurian Seafood Bisque with Paprika Crostoni

CONTINUED

2 cups homemade fish broth (see recipe page 208)

1 teaspoon Hungarian paprika

2–4 (½-inch) slices ciabatta bread or any other type of large bread (cut 4–8 slices if using a baguette)

Freshly ground black pepper

Working in two or three batches, transfer the fish and the liquid to a blender and puree until very smooth, 2 to 3 minutes each time.

OPTION 1 You can stop here, transfer the pureed soup (which is now basically a *passata*) to a clean saucepan and reheat it for 5 minutes over low heat. This way, the soup will be more rustic.

OPTION 2 One more step will give you a slightly more refined soup, closer to a real bisque. Pass the pureed soup through a fine mesh strainer into a bowl, pressing the soup down with the back of a ladle or large spoon to squeeze out as much liquid as possible. Because there will be a lot of solids left in the strainer, this is more likely to serve two instead of four. Transfer the soup to a clean saucepan and reheat it for 5 minutes over low heat. (You can use the solids as a filling for ravioli.)

While the soup is warming up, heat the remaining 3 tablespoons of olive oil in an 8-inch skillet over medium-high heat, add the paprika, and cook for about 1 minute, stirring frequently. Dip the bread slices into the paprika oil and place them on a rimmed baking sheet. Transfer them to the oven and toast for about 5 minutes, or until the crostoni are crisp and slightly browned.

Serve the heated soup (rustic or not) with the crostoni, a grind of pepper, and a sprinkle of parsley.

Hearty Vegetable Minestrone with Pesto

Minestrone alla Genovese

This minestrone is hearty and outright delicious. It can be served nice and hot, at room temperature, or even slightly chilled in the summer. It's satisfying either way. The texture is soft and creamy—almost pureed—because the vegetables are cooked (some might say overcooked) until they break down into the soup. If you prefer your vegetables firmer, reduce the cooking time by 1 hour or more. Traditional *minestrone alla genovese* has spaghettini or vermicelli pasta in it, but I prefer to leave the pasta out and let the vegetables shine. One of the secrets to making a great minestrone is to simmer it with a rind of Parmigiano; so next time you're left with a hard crust after grating every single bit, think twice before you throw it away. I usually scrape the outer side with a grater to remove any residual wax before adding it to the bubbling soup. And, since I was a kid, it was always a treat to eat the supple, slow-cooked crust right before enjoying the minestrone.

SERVES 4 TO 6

FOR THE PESTO

See Pesto recipe page 69, without green beans and potatoes.

FOR THE MINESTRONE

10 cups (2½ quarts) cold water

2 teaspoons salt, plus more for seasoning

1 small carrot, peeled and cut in ½-inch dice

1 small Italian eggplant, cut ½-inch dice

½ large onion, chopped

1 small Savoy cabbage, cut in ¼-inch strips

1 Yukon gold potato, cut in ½-inch dice

MAKE THE PESTO See Pesto recipe page 69.

MAKE THE MINESTRONE Bring the water to a boil in large pot, add 2 teaspoons of salt, and reduce to a slow simmer.

Add the carrot and eggplant, and simmer for about 5 minutes.

Add the onion, cabbage, potato, green beans, and the Parmigiano rind and simmer for another 10 minutes.

Add the zucchini, leek, tomatoes, beans (only if the beans were dried and pre-soaked; hold them if they were canned), and a pinch of salt and continue simmering, uncovered, for 1½ to 2 hours.

Add the spinach and beans (if canned) and simmer for another 5 minutes. At this point the vegetables should be very soft and the liquid should have reduced a bit.

CONTINUED

CONTINUED

Hearty Vegetable Minestrone with Pesto

CONTINUED

**4 ounces green beans,
trimmed and cut in ½-inch pieces**

1 small Parmigiano-Reggiano rind

2 zucchini, cut in ½-inch dice

1 medium leek, cut in ½-inch dice

**3 plum tomatoes,
peeled, seeded and coarsely chopped**

**1 cup dried cannellini or borlotti beans,
presoaked (or use canned beans)**

1 cup coarsely chopped spinach leaves

3 tablespoons fruity extra-virgin olive oil

Freshly ground black pepper

Remove the rind, stir in the olive oil, adjust the seasoning with salt and pepper and let the minestrone cool off the heat. Serve the minestrone warm, at room temperature, or cold, topped with a generous dollop of pesto. (Use any leftover pesto to make pasta or for another batch of minestrone).

Silvana's Chunky Seafood Soup

Buridda come la fa Silvana

The word *buridda* sounds awfully similar to a fish soup made in the south of France called *bourride*. In all likelihood, *buridda* is a variation of the same dish. As I've mentioned, there are a number of similarities between the cuisines of Liguria and Provence due to the proximity of the two regions, their shared history, and the constant flow of ideas and ingredients back and forth. This is Silvana's famed version of traditional *buridda*, a dish that is perfect for both cold and warm months. The seafood makes it light and summery, but its "stewy" nature makes it also cozy and ideal for a cold winter day. And it's quick, too—especially if your fishmonger cleans and bones the fish for you. Traditionally, *gallette del marinaio*—round, dry bread buns—were soaked in the soup instead of bread.

SERVES 4

8 mussels

8 large clams

4 whole walnuts, shelled,
or 2 tablespoons pine nuts

3 tablespoons extra-virgin olive oil

1 large clove garlic, finely chopped
(about 1½ teaspoons)

1 small onion, finely chopped
(about 1 cup)

1 tablespoon finely chopped parsley,
more for garnish

1 teaspoon finely chopped
fresh oregano

2 small tomatoes, peeled, seeded,
and coarsely chopped

1 teaspoon salt,
plus extra for seasoning the fish

½ cup dry white wine

½ cup homemade fish broth
(see recipe page 208)

1½ pound flaky white fish,
such as nile perch, cod, or tilapia,
cleaned and cut in bite-size pieces

Freshly ground black pepper

4 (½-inch) slices bread, toasted

Wash the mussels and clams carefully under cold water to eliminate any residue of sand—you don't want that in your stew.

Crush the walnuts with a mortar and pestle or in a food processor until you obtain a smooth paste, and set aside.

In a medium-size Dutch oven or a 12-inch straight-sided, lidded sauté pan, heat the olive oil over medium heat. Add the garlic, onion, parsley, and oregano, and cook for about 5 minutes, stirring occasionally, until the vegetables are soft and fragrant.

Add the tomatoes, 1 teaspoon of salt, and half of the wine and cook for 5 minutes, or until the wine has almost completely evaporated.

Add the clams, the rest of the wine, the nuts, and broth. Lower the temperature to medium-low and cook, partially covered, for about 5 minutes. Meanwhile, season the fish with salt and pepper and add it to the stew along with the mussels. Cook for 4 to 5 minutes, or until the fish is done and all the shellfish have opened (discard unopened shellfish). Adjust seasoning with salt and pepper, sprinkle with chopped parsley, and serve immediately with slices of toasted bread.

Butter Lettuce Rolls in Warm Veal Broth

Lattughe in Brodo

The first time I had lettuce rolls in broth was at La Brinca, a Ligurian restaurant in the middle of no-where—really. And it wasn't a dingy place, either. My husband and I drove for what seemed like an eternity into the deep *entroterra*, winding our way up high hills. By the end, the road was so tight there was barely room for one car. There was no village in sight, no houses, no lights—only a desolate church. We were sure we'd lost our way. But we kept going, and finally, in the distance, we spotted a few bright lights, then rows of cars parked in a small driveway. There it was: the restaurant. To our surprise, La Brinca was an elegant spot, with waiters in black jackets, a pretty hostess, a sommelier, and pristine white tablecloths. We could've easily been in Genova—or Manhattan, for that matter.

These small, bright green lettuce rolls were swimming in a clear, pale yellow broth inside a simple square bowl reminiscent of an Asian dish. Each roll was a perfect bite: mildly grassy at first, then bursting with flavor, savory and delicate at the same time. You can substitute chicken broth for veal broth, but it's very important that the broth is homemade. Canned broths often have intense or off flavors that may work fine when added to a stew, but can hardly stand on their own.

SERVES 4

4 tablespoons extra-virgin olive oil

½ small onion, chopped
(about ½ cup)

1 large clove garlic, chopped
(about 1½ teaspoon)

1 small celery stalk, chopped
(about ⅓ cups)

1 tablespoon plus 1 teaspoon
chopped parsley

½ pound ground veal

4 ½ cups homemade veal broth
(see recipe page 210)

In a 10-inch skillet, heat the olive oil over medium heat. When the oil is hot and shimmering, add the onion, garlic, celery, and 1 tablespoon of parsley, and cook, stirring frequently, for about 5 minutes, or until the vegetables are soft. Add the ground veal and ¼ cup of the veal broth, 1 teaspoon of salt, and freshly ground pepper, and cook for about 3 minutes, just until the veal is no longer pink (it shouldn't be completely cooked through) and the liquid is absorbed. Transfer the meat mixture to the bowl of a food processor and let it cool to room temperature.

Soak the bread whites in a small bowl in ¼ cup of the broth for about 10 minutes.

Add the mortadella, marjoram leaves, bread whites, nutmeg, Parmigiano, 1 teaspoon salt, and more pepper to the food processor bowl containing the veal, and pulse for 1 or 2 minutes until you obtain a finely ground mixture. Taste it and adjust

**2 teaspoons salt,
plus more for seasoning**

Freshly ground black pepper

**1 ounce day-old white bread,
crust removed, cut into 1-inch dice
(a scant 1 cup)**

**2 ounces mortadella
(about 2 thin slices),
cut into large strips**

2 sprigs marjoram, leaves only

½ teaspoon freshly grated nutmeg

**1½ cups finely grated
Parmigiano-Reggiano**

2 large eggs

**24 medium-small Boston or butter
lettuce leaves (2 or 3 large heads)**

1 teaspoon chopped marjoram

seasoning, if necessary. Add the eggs and mix until you obtain a smooth pastelike filling. Set it aside, covered, in the refrigerator.

Wash and dry the lettuce. Choose leaves that are medium size and whole (usually the outer leaves are too big and tattered, and the inside ones too small).

Bring a large pot of water to a boil and blanch the lettuce leaves for 3 to 5 seconds each. Remove them immediately with a slotted spoon and place them in a bowl of ice water. Be very careful as the leaves are extremely delicate and tear easily. Drain and pat them dry with paper towels.

Cut about 1 inch of the tough white ends of the lettuce leaves and fill each with about 1 tablespoon of the prepared filling. Fold the top part first (where the removed white part was), then fold the two sides one on top of the other and seal by folding the bottom. You should obtain about twenty-four bite-size lettuce rolls. It's very important that they are sealed on all sides, otherwise the filling will leak while cooking. Arrange them on a baking sheet folded side down and refrigerate for at least 30 minutes.

Bring the remaining 4 cups of broth to a boil in a medium-size saucepan, salt to taste, and reduce to a slow simmer to keep it warm.

Bring a large pot of water to a boil (you can use the water used to blanch the lettuce). Reduce to a slow simmer and, using a skimmer or slotted spoon, dip two or three rolls in the simmering water for 1 or 2 minutes, enough for the egg in the filling to cook. Scoop the rolls out in batches and arrange them in serving bowls (six rolls per person). Pour about 1 cup of the hot broth into each bowl and serve immediately, garnished with the remaining chopped parsley and the marjoram.

Chickpea Soup with Swiss Chard and Mushrooms

Zimino di Ceci

I love to use chard with yellow, red, and white stems to brighten this soup. I've found that the soup improves if you let it sit away from the heat for a couple of hours after it's done simmering, so the flavors have time to meld. You can serve it at room temperature or reheat it and serve it warm. Add a little more liquid, whether it's broth or just water, if it has dried out while sitting.

SERVES 4

2 (15-ounce) cans chickpeas (about 3 ½ cups)

½ ounce mixed dried mushrooms

5 tablespoons extra-virgin olive oil

½ medium onion, finely chopped (about ¾ cup)

1 large clove garlic, finely chopped (about 1½ teaspoons)

1 medium celery stalk, finely chopped (about ½ cup)

3 plum tomatoes, peeled, seeded, and coarsely chopped

4 cups chopped Swiss chard

Salt

2 cups homemade or low-sodium canned chicken or vegetable broth (see recipes pages 209-210)

1 tablespoon freshly squeezed lemon juice

Freshly ground black pepper

Drain the chickpeas and rinse them under cold running water.

Soak the mushrooms in warm water for 30 minutes. Drain, pat them dry, and coarsely chop them.

Heat 3 tablespoons of olive oil in a 4- or 5-quart saucepan over medium heat. When the oil is hot, add the onion, garlic, and celery, and sweat for 6 to 8 minutes, stirring frequently, without browning. Add the tomatoes, chard, mushrooms, and a pinch of salt. Raise the heat to medium-high and cook for another 5 to 7 minutes, or until all the vegetables are soft. Add the chickpeas and continue cooking for another 3 minutes. Add the broth, another pinch of salt, and simmer over medium-low heat for about 30 minutes.

With a ladle, transfer about 1 cup of the soup to a blender and puree it until smooth. Pour the pureed soup back into the pan (this will help give a thicker, richer consistency to the soup), and stir. Adjust seasoning with salt; add the lemon juice and a generous grind of pepper. Serve warm or at room temperature with a drizzle of the remaining 2 tablespoons of olive oil.

BABY SOUP AT THE GRAND HOTEL

For the first twenty years of their marriage, Silvana and Franco were the fun couple of the family—the cool, childless, jet-setting pair who rode motorbikes across Corsica, sailed their own boat to Sicily, and took extravagant vacations in far-off places like Egypt or Tanzania, lodging in fancy hotels and eating at expensive restaurants. Growing up, I loved spending time with them. Precisely because they were not my parents, they'd allow me to do things my parents would never dream of. With them I could have ice cream at eleven in the morning; I could go swimming right after lunch skipping the two-hour wait all Italian parents inflict on their kids to ensure their frail digestions aren't severely blocked by the mere touch of the icy Mediterranean waters. (Italians' inexplicably weak digestive systems—as well as their panicky fear of *colpi d'aria*, "air strikes," is a subject onto itself, one worthy of an exclusive chapter in a social science book. When I lived there, I assumed everyone's digestive system required constant vigilance—that anyone faced life-threatening danger if they stood in an air current with a light sweat. I accepted that, as humans, we had to take necessary precautions to survive in a world of dangerous air wafts and digestive perils. When I first moved abroad, I wondered how the Brits and Americans could be so cavalier about breezes without winding up in the hospital. That's when it dawned on me that mine is a country of people obsessed with *colpi d'aria* and imaginary digestive problems, among other things.)

When I was only five, on a family camping trip to Sardegna, Franco took me on his fastest motorbike. We whizzed through the winding roads of this beautifully barren Mediterranean island. A few years later, during a road trip through the western states of North America, I spent hours in the back of a rented motor home with Silvana, sketching the colors of the Grand Canyon and the Monument Valley.

But all this was bound to change. At thirty-eight, ready to give up her dreams of motherhood, Silvana found she was pregnant.

They said that this wasn't going to change their lifestyle, that a child would never turn them into dull Methuselahs, but I knew things wouldn't stay the same. For one thing, I wouldn't be the only kid in the family anymore. It wasn't jealousy, exactly. Rather, I was hit by a sudden sense of loss, a precocious nostalgia for moments I knew would no longer be. No more off-hour ice creams or wind-swept motorbike rides, no more afternoons drawing landscapes of overseas deserts. Silvana and Franco would now have their own child to do these things with, and as they raised him, they too would begin to enforce the no-swimming-for-two-hours-after-lunch rule, along with the rest of the inventory of Italian child-friendly precautions.

Marco was born in December 1981. He was a gorgeous, seven-pound baby, with a pearl skin and a bald, pear-shaped head. It'll lose its edge in a few months, the doctors said. And it did. We all loved him. He was a good baby, quiet but smiling, smart, and simpatico from his earliest months.

The summer after his birth, Franco and Silvana stuck to their promise, refusing to be bogged down by an eight-month-old babe-in-arms. Defiantly, they booked a lavish vacation at a five-star hotel on the northern coast of Sardegna. (For the record, this is where the rich and famous spend their Italian seaside vacations—when they're not in Portofino. As you might guess, the place ranks poorly as a family destination.)

The vacation was a nightmare—for them and, I suspect, for their hotel room neighbors. Baby Marco proved himself allergic to fancy hotels and their sea view dining rooms. When the family walked in the first night for dinner, decked out in evening garb with infant in tow, heads turned and eyes glowered at the bizarre couple carrying—what, a baby? Must be from Germany. As soon as they'd sat down and the waiter had passed them the wine list, Marco burst into a wretched crying fit. Nothing, absolutely nothing but returning to the room and lulling him to sleep, would bring it to an end. The remaining days of that doomed vacation were spent ordering room service and making *minestrine*, "baby soups" at the grand hotel. Franco and Silvana succumbed. Next year they would rent a place in a quiet beach town, begin taking sensible, child-proof vacations. But where?

It was Silvana who suggested they go back to a place she had visited years before, back when she worked at a high school and had her summers off. From Genova, she often took the train with a friend to explore Ligurian beach towns. It was on one of these coastal expeditions that she ended up in Bonassola, a charmingly quiet village with a pristine beach and clear blue waters. Perfect for a couple with a small boy.

Looking for an apartment to rent in Bonassola was no walk in the park. Who would have guessed that by April such an out-of-the-way spot would be sold out for the summer? It wasn't Portofino, after all. They searched far and wide, inquiring in local stores and knocking on doors where *affitasi* ("for rent" signs) were still hanging, most of them just forgotten. They found nothing. Finally, as they were ready to give up and head back home, a small man in his seventies from the local *sale e tabacchi* (a store that sells cigarettes and other mismatched items, including, once upon a time, salt) came running after them.

"Go see Angiolina," the man shouted. "She may still have a place in via Roma!"

"Where can we find Angiolina?" asked Franco.

"In the *pollaio*," the man replied.

The hen house?

They looked at each other puzzled, but also amused, and certainly curious to meet Angiolina in the hen house. They asked the man for directions and drove there straight away. But Angiolina was nowhere to be found. They got out of the car and picked their way across the narrow and steep *terreno*, climbing up and down the terraces, until they finally spotted an old barefoot woman plucking weeds. She wore a faded blue knee-length dress topped by a worn white apron with red and yellow flowers, a maroon handkerchief wrapping her head. She didn't seem surprised to see them.

"Looking for something?" she asked.

"Someone in town said you have a place for rent. We'd like to see it," said Franco.

"Ah, yes, the old house. Let me get the keys and I'll show you." She picked up a strange boomerang-shaped knife and seemed to reconsider. "Actually, I'm having some work done there," she said. "But I can show you another just like it. "

And so Silvana and Franco found the old house. Without actually seeing it, they committed to a two-month lease, July and August. By the end of that fateful summer of 1982, their abiding love affair with Bonassola had begun—and the seeds had been planted for my own. They liked the place so much they decided to buy some land and build their own house. What they didn't know was that it would take them almost ten years. And during this time, they would continue to rent Angiolina's old house.

UNDER THE STARS

At dusk, in that surreal moment when the sun has vanished behind the sea line and the sky is a hushed silver blue, streaked with loud bursts of red and purple-pink, my favorite thing to do in Bonassola is take a stroll to the Madonnina, a small sanctuary to the Virgin Mary erected at the very tip of the *Punta della Madonnina* just outside town. Aside from a few other passersby enjoying the tranquility of the early evening, the road is quiet at this hour, and walking on the *strada* along the coast—a meandering extension of via Roma—you catch sight of a cemetery perched on a hill to the right, protected by a grove of tall, dark green cypresses. Tiny patchwork vineyards recline placidly on either side and a few sumptuous houses keep watch over well-groomed lawns, sheltered by shrubs and trees that remind me of giant umbrellas. The water is darker here, deepening as you move further from the bay to the open sea, and the scents that ooze from the plants and the salty waves are intoxicating.

At the end of the final stretch of road you can spot the pale pink sanctuary. It's like a miniature Spanish mission, with big airy arches on three sides and a tiny mission-style *campanile*. The only side of this peculiar square structure not open to the sea and wind contains a huge alcove inhabited by an imposing statue of the Virgin, who was believed to watch over seafaring fishermen. The position is dramatic. On one side, through the arches, you can see the entire town and hear the lively voices of kids on the distant beach. On the other, massive rocks plunge straight into the sea. Waves prowl over against them, making a sweet, lulling sound that grows roaring and thunderous on stormy days. Sitting under an arch with your eyes closed, nothing but sea and wind around you, life fills up with possibilities.

On one such clear early evenings, I leaned against the railing of the vine-covered terrace overlooking the bay, waiting for the first guests to arrive for the biggest dinner party of the summer. I had no time to walk to the Madonnina. Soon I'd have to go back to the kitchen to give Silvana and my mother a hand. Still, for a few minutes I lingered. Through the olive trees growing on the brief plateau beneath the house, I could see the water's intense blue, the village houses with their soft shades of ochres and reds and pinks and their windows framed in white, perched only feet behind the beach minia-turized by distance—the fancy ones strutting ornamental trompe l'oeils that mimicked elaborate moldings and window decorations. I gazed at the imposing hill behind them, overgrown with *macchia mediterranea*, its many shades of green disrupted only by small clusters of colorful dwellings in three of Bonassola's tiny *frazioni*: San Giorgio, Costella, and Serra. I could easily stay there for hours, I thought, taking in the breeze charged with the vigorous smells of cone-shaped pine trees and the million little plants that make this part of the world unique—a place of absolute quiet and beauty, of seren-ity and contemplation.

The dinner was set for the evening of August 14th, the day before *ferragosto*—the high point of Italy's vacation month, when cities like Milano and Torino wither into gigantic ghost towns, and beach and mountain resorts brim with vacationers. In Bonas-sola, *ferragosto* is also the day of the *festa degli incappucciati*, an odd and vaguely halloweenish local holiday in which Bonassola's male residents dress in long tunics and cover their faces with big, pointy hoods. On the night of the fifteenth, they march around town in an eerie procession reciting solemn lines in dialect over the slow beat of large drums. The lines, it turns out, are less grave than they sound. They poke fun at fellow residents (and sometimes at longtime vacationers, too), expose their misde-meanors, ridicule this one's stubbornness and that one's stinginess, and pass on good old-fashioned village gossip. Like when fisherman Elia fell asleep on his *peschereccio* after a drunken evening ashore and returned empty-handed—except for the great big excuse he handed his wife.

Silvana and my mother had planned the dinner menu for days. They wanted simple dishes they could prepare in advance, or that wouldn't take hours to put together. They'd serve *acciughe fritte*, fried fresh anchovies, as an appetizer—something they knew would please all crowds. The party of twenty-something invitees was bound to grow as word spread that Silvana was spending the afternoon at the stove, aided by her next of kin from Piemonte; they could only hope the fishmonger would have enough fresh anchovies to feed them all. For her part, my mother was going to make gargantuan quantities of her legendary *melanzane alla parmigiana*, thin slices of fried eggplant layered in homemade tomato sauce and melting mozzarella and Parmigiano cheese. The pièce de résistance would be Silvana's chunky seafood soup, followed by lettuce and tomatoes picked from the garden and tossed with olive oil from the *terreno*. And the grand finale: a big, tasty fruit salad with gelato from Bonassola's favorite, the Gelateria delle Rose.

In the morning Silvana called the fishmonger at the *mercato del pesce*, the fish market in Levanto, asking him to set aside all the seafood she needed. Later, she and I set out to pick it up and run a few other errands. I'd never been to the Levanto fish market before. My experience of Ligurian seafood shopping was limited to the meager fish stand at Bonassola's weekly market, which hardly had anything left after nine in the morning. Arriving in Levanto, I could scarcely hide my disappointment. Where were the colorful boats with their tangled nets crowding the little port? Where were the tan, crusty fishermen in their dirty damp shirts yelling *"pesci, donne!"*? The fish market was located in a far-off wing of an anonymous, boxy edifice that housed fruit and vegetable stands and all sorts of street bazaar junk. It was nothing more than four or five refrigerated booths that didn't look much different from the fish section at a supermarket. But I was reassured to meet Ennio, the fishmonger, who was every bit as tan and crusty and rugged as I'd imagined, with harsh manners to match. Silvana and Franco had known him since their first year in Bonassola. Ennio was a true seaman. He loved the sea, he knew all the currents and every sea floor from Porto Venere all the way to Genova. He knew which zones were good for *muscoli* and which bore generous yields of *pesce azzurro*. And he loved talking to Franco, who, in his own way, was a sea enthusiast, too. Franco wasn't a fisherman, of course, but he grew up in Genova and spent his whole life within sight of the Mediterranean. He even went so far to claim that the mountains made him sick—that he just couldn't survive too long away from the sea.

He runs a thriving ship repair business right in the port of Genova, guaranteeing he'd never be too far away.

Something else redeemed Levanto's lackluster fish market: the fish. Ennio's stock was truly beautiful. It had been delivered straight from the fishing boats that very morning, and everything—graceful *branzini* and *orate*, gaudy *gallinelle di mare*, ugly *scorfani*, and glistening silver anchovies—gleamed with freshness and smelled like the sea. At night, from anywhere on the coast, you can see these fishing boats far out at sea, their telltale lights bright like stars on the horizon. *Lampare*—the Italian name for these lights—is one of my favorite words; there's something both magical and sad in its mellifluous sound.

Ennio wrapped four kilos (eight pounds!) of anchovies for us and Silvana started pointing at various other fish she needed for the soup. *Un chilo di gallinelle e mezzo chilo di pesce cappone.* And then *pescatrice, occhiata,* scorpion fish, squid, scampi, shrimp, clams, and mussels. Ennio needed time to clean all those fish, so we decided to run the rest of our errands and come back.

"There's a very important ingredient for the soup we can't forget," exclaimed Silvana. "*Le gallette del marinaio.* We must get them!"

Gallette del marinaio are firm, round breads, once carried by fishermen and sailors on their long journeys at sea. The mariners soaked them in sea water, or vinegar when they were lucky, and ate them onboard. To me, *gallette* seemed nothing more than cute bread buns gone horribly stale. But, I would soon discover that, rubbed with garlic and soaked in good vinegar or the broth of a spicy fish soup, *gallette* became tasty enough to outclass any ordinary bread. We headed to Levanto's *carrugi.* Located in the historical center of every respectable Ligurian town, these dark and narrow little roads meander up and down in dazzling mazes of stone and dampness. Here Silvana crossed the threshold of a tiny store I'd barely noticed. It was a dim little bakery. The baker behind the counter was a snowy-haired old man with a slight hunch and a honeyed voice.

"You'll never catch me without them," the baker winked when Silvana asked him if, by chance, he had any *gallette*. He was the only baker in town still making them, he pointed out. *Why are all these people so old?* I was suddenly overcome by a fear that when the baker, the fishmonger, and all the other older folks who ran these ancient stores, making their goods and conducting their businessees in the traditional ways—when they died, I thought, no one would care about good food anymore and all these time-honored delicacies would be lost forever.

Heading back to the fish market to retrieve our gastronomic loot, we couldn't resist the call of an espresso machine, shrieking and clattering in a *bar* we walked by. We stopped for a glorious morning *cappuccino e cornetto*, a bastion of Italy's culinary wisdom and, among the country's many epicurean rituals, perhaps the one I miss the most when I'm away. On our way home we made a final stop in Bonassola to pick up something to snack on for lunch, as we wouldn't have a big meal until the evening. Bianchetto, as it often happened, had run out of focaccia, and the next batch was still in the oven, not destined to be ready before a good fifteen minutes. So we headed to La Ladrona, who gave herself a license to embezzle whenever occasion presented itself—particularly in the form of gullible foreign tourists who, unfortunately for her, were not very numerous in Bonassola. That day we had the honor of witnessing a quintessential instance. Two middle-aged German ladies in front of us purchased nothing more than a couple of slices of focaccia, a wedge of *torta di patate*, a small jar of tuna packed in olive oil, and a few olives. "Fifty thousand lire," La Ladrona advised them in the most courteous tone she could muster. Silvana and I could barely hold back our gasps. Surely, we thought, the two women knew they could buy a whole *prosciutto di Parma* with that kind of money. Yet, baffled by the absurd number of zeroes in the price of any Italian good in those days, the ladies counted their money out without protesting. It was time to intervene.

"There must be some mistake," Silvana said with a firm tone. La Ladrona shot her a nasty look. Before my aunt could explain the fraud to the bewildered tourists, La

Ladrona quickly cried out: "Oh, so sorry, *signore*, I must be losing my mind. It's *fifteen* thousand lire, *not* fifty." Silvana rolled her eyes. The tourists escaped and we bought our focaccia and some slices of savory pie, all free of mathematical blunders—and left the shop barely suppressing a chuckle at the thought of La Ladrona's insolence.

Back at the house, we lunched on tasty slices of soft, oily focaccia, *torta di patate* and *torta di riso*. We washed it all down with a little Cinque Terre wine and enjoyed a brief siesta under the vine trellis before getting to work. As Mom sliced eggplant for the *parmigiana*, I helped Silvana tackle the fish that still needed to be cut and skinned before she could start the soup. For what seemed like an eternity, I scrubbed a pile of mussels with an old toothbrush, butterflied a huge bag of anchovies, and chopped the heads off of so many fish I started feeling like a Jacobin executioner. Silvana used the heads to make a *brodetto di pesce*, a fish stock that became the foundation for the soup. She threw them in a pot of water with onions, celery, a chopped carrot, a little white wine, and a bunch of fresh herbs, and let it simmer on the stove, filling the kitchen with fragrant aromas of land and sea.

I watched Silvana make *soffritto* for the soup, finely chopping heaps of garlic, onions, and parsley and adding them to sizzling olive oil with a pinch of peperoncino. After a while, she poured in a glass of white wine, let it evaporate, and added fresh chopped tomatoes. Her secret, she told me, was rounding the flavors with a dash of pine nuts she'd crushed in a mortar. Then she added the fish, one kind after another according to their cooking times, reserving shrimp and scampi for the very end.

The sun was already setting and, as I helped Silvana and my mother take care of last-minute preparations, I heard Franco cheerfully welcome the first guests. A good portion of Genova's vacationing community was slated to be there that night. Some people I knew well, others I'd scarcely seen at the beach or on strolls through town. For the occasion, Franco had retrieved a few bottles of his favorite *prosecchino*, a light sparkling wine produced by a friend of his in the Veneto. He uncorked bottle after bottle, pouring generous glasses for the arriving guests. Everyone was tan, elegantly dressed in light summery colors, displaying that distinctive style that makes Italians stand out everywhere in the world. Most of all, everyone seemed happy to be there. The largest faction lingered on the terrace, entertained by Franco's lively banter. But some peeked into the kitchen to pay homage to the cooks, and to get a preview of their dinner in the making. While the soup fragrantly simmered, we began to fry the anchovies. We floured the ones I'd painstakingly butterflied just hours before and dipped them into a huge pan of blistering olive oil. Soon was time to gather everyone around the big table on the wider portion of the terrace, which had become pleasantly breezy following the *solleone*'s (the lion sun of midday) disappearance behind the hills. Glasses raised, the feast got underway.

When Franco finally broke out a treasured bottle of *sciacchetrà* he reserves only for the most special occasions (it's so expensive I'm surprised he shares it at all), our guests were in high spirits. Enrico Carniglia, known as "the Architect" and a mainstay of Bonassola's summer beach scene—summer in Bonassola just isn't summer until you spot Carniglia's smooth, bald head roaming the umbrellas at the Bagni Sabbia d'Oro making small talk with "the Doctor" or with Gianni, the owner—went to fetch his guitar and, when he got back with a tattered acoustic specimen, we all sang heartrending songs by Genovese songwriter Fabrizio De André, mixed with Beatles tunes no one remembered the words to.

Dinner was spectacular—and unforgettable. I was only a teenager, but I can still recall that evening in vivid detail. I look back at that night, as well as many others that followed in Bonassola, to remind me of the things I need most to be happy: delicious food and good company. It was well past two in the morning when the last guests left. Silvana, my mother, and I turned out all the lights, unfolded the lounge chairs on the terrace next to the long table still cluttered with dirty plates, and lay down for many long minutes to watch the patchwork of twinkling stars against the pure black cloudless sky. We each saw a falling star that night.

FROM THE SEA

dal mare

Roasted Orata with Black Olives and Baby Potatoes

Orata al Forno con Olive Nere e Patatine Arrosto

If there is one quintessentially Ligurian way to cook fish, this would probably be it. Silvana makes this all the time when she finds good orata at the fish market. It's similar to the way the kitchen prepares roasted orata at La Rosa restaurant in Camogli. It captures the essence of Ligurian cooking, its simplicity and expert use of prime ingredients. That's why, in order for this dish to be truly memorable, you have to start with the best olive oil and the freshest fish you can possibly find. If you cut corners there, your results are bound to be disappointing. If you don't find orata, you can easily replace it with another delicate white-fleshed fish, such as striped or black sea bass or red snapper.

SERVES 4

1 pound baby potatoes, cut in 1-inch dice (about 1½ cups)

2½ teaspoons salt

Freshly ground black pepper

1 cup plus 3 tablespoons extra-virgin olive oil

2 large whole orata (about 2 pounds each), cleaned, skin on

8 sprigs parsley

10 sprigs thyme

2 small cloves garlic, finely chopped (about 2 teaspoons)

½ lemon, thinly sliced

½ cup pitted black olives, preferably gaeta or niçoise

Preheat the oven to 425°F.

Bring a large pot of water to a boil and add the potatoes. Boil them for 8 to 10 minutes, or until almost fork tender but not quite done. Drain and toss them in a bowl with 1 teaspoon of the salt, pepper to taste, and 3 tablespoons of the olive oil.

Place the fish in a large baking pan (or two smaller pans; there shouldn't be much overlap, otherwise the fish won't cook properly). Season generously with the remaining salt and pepper (inside the cavity of the fish as well as outside), and arrange the parsley, thyme, garlic, lemon slices, and olives randomly inside the cavity and outside the fish.

Add the potatoes to the baking pan, drizzle the remaining olive oil over the fish and in the cavity and cook in the oven for 20 to 25 minutes, depending on the size. To serve, remove the skin (which should come off with only the help of a spoon if the fish is properly cooked), and carve four fillets following the bone line. Chances are, the fillets will fall apart when you try to extricate them from the bones. Don't worry, you haven't failed, it happens all the time. The flavor of the fish will make everyone forget the broken fillets. Serve on individual plates with the potatoes and drizzled with the roasting juices, making sure that each plate has a few olives as well.

Fennel Seed-Crusted Fresh Sardines

Sarde Fresche al Finocchio

In Liguria, I would make this dish with fresh anchovies but, because anchovies are so hard to find in American markets, I tried it with sardines. It worked! I serve the sardines either as a light second course, if the first course was big and hearty, or as an appetizer.

SERVES 4

12 fresh sardines, cleaned

2 tablespoons fennel seeds

Salt

Freshly ground black pepper

3 tablespoons extra-virgin olive oil

2 large cloves garlic, smashed with the blade of a chef's knife

2 teaspoons freshly squeezed lemon juice

Fillet the sardines or ask your fishmonger to do it. If you're doing it yourself, chop off the heads and tails and place each fish on a clean surface, belly down, and start to "massage" the back gently, but firmly. You'll feel that the backbone gives a little and begins to detach itself from the flesh. Turn over the fish and extricate the backbone, separating the two fillets. Wash the fillets carefully and pat them dry with a paper towel.

Grind the fennel seeds in a spice or coffee grinder until very fine.

Season the sardine fillets generously with salt and pepper, and coat the tops evenly with the ground fennel seeds.

Heat the olive oil in a large nonstick skillet (big enough to hold all the fish, or use two smaller skillets) over medium heat. When the oil is hot, add the garlic, sauté for 2 to 3 minutes (be careful not to burn it), and remove it. Raise the heat to medium-high and add the sardines to the pan, crusted side down. Cook for 2 to 3 minutes, then turn them over and cook for 1 more minute. Serve them warm or chilled with a drizzle of the lemon juice.

Salt Cod Stew with Olives, Tomatoes, and Pine Nuts

Stoccafisso Accomodato

In Liguria, cooks use stockfish, not cod, to make this dish. Stockfish is cod that's been dehydrated rather than preserved in salt. And it's nearly impossible to find in the United States except through mail order (see Sources). Salt cod works well as a substitution, as long as you don't forgo the somewhat laborious process of soaking it in multiple changes of water for at least two days. Without this step, your dish will be so salty no one will be able to eat it. Although stockfish is mostly popular in western Liguria in the area around Imperia and Dolceacqua, it's cooked all over the region.

SERVES 4

NOTE SALT COD NEEDS TO SOAK
FOR AT LEAST TWO DAYS

2 pounds salt cod or stockfish

¼ cup extra-virgin olive oil

**1 large clove garlic, finely chopped
(about 1½ teaspoons)**

2 tablespoons finely chopped parsley

**2 oil-packed anchovies,
drained and finely chopped**

1 tablespoon salted capers, rinsed

2 tablespoons finely chopped pine nuts

5 tablespoons tomato puree

⅔ cup dry white wine

⅓ cup black olives, pitted and chopped

**3 baby potatoes or 1 medium
Yukon gold, cut in ½-inch dices
(about ¾ cup)**

1 tablespoon whole pine nuts

**1 to 1½ cups homemade fish broth
(see recipe page 208)**

Freshly ground black pepper

Cut the salt cod into 4-inch slices crosswise and soak it in a large bowl for two days in at least eight changes of water or more. **This is a very important step.** If you skip or neglect it, your dish will be too salty. You can forego this step if you're using stockfish. Blot the cod dry with a kitchen towel or paper towels and cut it into bite-size chunks (1 to 1½ inches).

Heat the oil in a 12-inch skillet over medium-high heat. When the oil is hot and shimmering, add the garlic, parsley, anchovies, capers, and chopped pine nuts, lower the heat to medium, and cook, stirring occasionally, for 4 to 5 minutes. Add the tomato puree, stir to incorporate, and cook for another 2 to 3 minutes. Add the cod chunks, the wine, and olives and cook over medium-high heat for about 5 minutes, stirring frequently. The liquids should be bubbling pretty vigorously. Lower the heat to medium-low and simmer gently for about 25 minutes.

Add the potatoes and whole pine nuts, and continue to simmer for another 30 to 35 minutes, or until the potatoes are soft and the cod is tender, adding the fish broth in small increments as the contents of the pan starts getting dry. Remember that this is a stew, so you should end up with a fairly loose texture. You don't want it to dry out too much. The dish shouldn't need any salt as many of the ingredients used are inherently salty. But taste it and adjust seasoning if necessary (you may need salt if you're using stockfish). I do like to add a few generous grinds of pepper. Serve warm with a slice or two of fresh rustic bread.

Grilled Branzino with Fennel Seeds and Roasted Fennel and Potatoes

Branzino al Finocchio

I found a recipe similar to this one flipping through the pages of Alessandro Molinari Pradelli's book *La Cucina Ligure*. One summer in Bonassola I decided to try my own version and everyone loved it. Now it's become part of our family repertoire. You can replace *branzino*—a Mediterranean sea bass—with any delicate, white-flesh fish such as red snapper or striped bass. And you can certainly skip the roasted fennel and potatoes, and serve the fish with a salad on the side instead. Either way, it's a perfect summer dish. If you don't have a charcoal or gas grill, use a cast-iron stovetop griddle and finish the fish in the oven.

SERVES 2

1½ large fennel bulbs

2 small Yukon gold potatoes, cut into 1-inch dice

Salt

Freshly ground black pepper

½ cup plus 3 tablespoons extra-virgin olive oil, plus more for brushing

1 medium branzino (about 2 pounds)

1 tablespoon finely chopped parsley

1 small clove garlic, thinly sliced

½ tablespoon fennel seeds

Heat the grill to medium-hot and preheat the oven to 425°F.

Cut 1 fennel bulb in half, core it, then cut it lengthwise into ¼-inch wedges.

In a medium-size bowl, toss the cut fennel and the potatoes with a generous amount of salt and pepper and 3 tablespoons of the olive oil. Transfer to a 9 × 13-inch baking dish and bake for 35 to 40 minutes, or until the fennel is soft and begins to caramelize. Give the fennel and potatoes a little stir half way through the cooking.

Meanwhile, cut the remaining fennel in half, core the halves, and slice each as thinly as you can lengthwise. Arrange the thin slices in the cavity of the fish together with the parsley and garlic slices. Season generously with salt and pepper inside and outside the cavity and drizzle with 2 tablespoons of the olive oil.

IF USING A CHARCOAL OR GAS GRILL Brush the fish with more oil and cook it on the hot grill until the skin is marked and slightly charred, about 15 minutes on each side. Meanwhile, heat a small 8-inch skillet and toast the fennel seeds in it for 5 to 7 minutes, or until fragrant and lightly browned. Transfer to a cold plate. To serve, remove the skin (which should come off with the only help of a spoon if the fish is

CONTINUED

Grilled Branzino with Fennel Seeds and Roasted Fennel and Potatoes

CONTINUED

properly cooked), and carve two fillets following the bone line. Chances are, the fillets will fall apart when you try to extricate them from the bones. Serve the fish on individual plates with the roasted fennel and potatoes. Drizzle with the remaining olive oil and sprinkle with the toasted fennel seeds.

IF USING A STOVETOP GRIDDLE Brush the griddle with a little olive oil and cook the fish on it 6 to 8 minutes per side, just enough to create some grill marks and a little charring. Transfer the fish to a 9 × 13-inch baking pan, pour the remaining olive oil over it, sprinkle with the fennel seeds, and finish cooking in the oven for 12 to 15 minutes. To serve, remove the skin (which should come off with only the help of a spoon if the fish is properly cooked), and carve two fillets following the bone line. Chances are the fillets will fall apart when you try to extricate them from the bones. Serve on individual plates with the roasted fennel and potatoes, drizzled with the roasting juices.

Pan-Seared Tilapia in a Shrimp and Saffron Brodetto with Parsley-Tarragon Pesto

Pesce in Padella in Brodetto di Gamberi e Zafferano con Pesto al Prezzemolo e Dragoncello

This is one of those dishes that are really more inspired by Ligurian cuisine than authentically Ligurian—I don't think you can actually find tilapia in Liguria, and the pesto is nut-less and cheeseless. But the flavors could belong to any Ligurian kitchen. You can serve the pesto on the side or on top of the fish. I like to serve it with roasted vegetables or simple roasted potatoes (see recipe page 170). Creamy herb polenta would be nice in the winter months, too. You can add a few shrimp to the sauté pan and add those to the dish as well. If you feel that making the *brodetto* is too fussy, or you don't have the time, omit it altogether. The dish is still good without it. A note: the recipe for shrimp broth on page 209 is for eight cups, while you only need one for this dish. You can either make the entire broth recipe, reserve one cup, and freeze the rest. Or you can make a quarter of the recipe and freeze the leftover broth for the next time you make tilapia.

SERVES 4

FOR THE PESTO

1 medium clove garlic

2 cups tightly packed parsley leaves

¼ cup packed tarragon leaves

2 teaspoons freshly squeezed lemon juice

½ teaspoon finely grated lemon zest

½ cup extra-virgin olive oil

½ teaspoon salt, more to taste

FOR THE BRODETTO

1 cup homemade shrimp broth (see recipe page 209)

¼ cup dry white wine

PREPARE THE PESTO Place the garlic, parsley, tarragon leaves, lemon juice, and lemon zest in the bowl of a food processor or blender. Start the motor and add the oil in a thin stream until all the ingredients are completely blended. Season with the salt (adding more to taste), and set aside in the refrigerator.

PREPARE THE *BRODETTO* Pour the shrimp broth and wine in a medium-size saucepan. Bring to a boil and reduce to a simmer.

Add the saffron threads and simmer for 10 minutes. Strain the saffron and season to taste with salt. Keep warm and stir before serving.

ASSEMBLE THE DISH Salt the tilapia fillets generously with salt and pepper.

In two 10-inch ovenproof nonstick skillets (or in the same skillet in two batches), heat the olive oil over medium-high heat. When the oil is hot, add the fish and sauté

CONTINUED

CONTINUED

¼ teaspoon saffron threads

Salt

TO ASSEMBLE

4 large tilapia fillets

Salt

Freshly ground black pepper

2 tablespoons extra-virgin olive oil

1 tablespoon coarsely chopped parsley (optional)

it over medium-high to high heat for 4 to 5 minutes, or until lightly browned. Turn over to the other side and cook for another 2 minutes. What you're looking for is fish that has lost its translucency and has become somewhat opaque, but hasn't overcooked.

Divide the *brodetto* equally among four shallow bowls. Add the tilapia and top with a generous dollop of pesto. Sprinkle with the chopped parsley, if using. If you're using roasted vegetables, add some to the plate before you add the fish and scatter the rest around the fish. If you're using polenta, put a generous dollop of it on the plate before adding the fish. Serve immediately.

Trofie with Pesto,
Green Beans,
and Potatoes
(*Trofie con Pesto
alla Genovese,*
page 69)

The Ligurian Coast

Roasted Orata with
Black Olives and Baby
Potatoes (*page 122*)

Farinata (page 36)

Ligurian Ratatouille
with Black Olives and Toasted Pine Nuts
(*page 173*)

A meal on the terrace in Bonassola

Cured Olives and Vermentino

Corniglia, in the Cinque Terre

Butter Lettuce Rolls in Warm Veal Broth
(*page 106*)

Deep-Fried Sardines
with Mildly Hot Salsa Verde (*page 51*)

Octopus at the fish market

Red Snapper Fillet
in Parchment with
Baby Vegetables and
Pigato Wine
(*page 133*)

Braised Guinea Hen
with Grapes and Grappa
(*page 154*)

Vanilla Ice Cream Drowned in
Rossese Wine-Poached Cherries
(*page 202*)

Sweet Bread with Fennel Seeds, Dried Cherries, Pistachios, and Pine Nuts (*Pandolce Genovese,* *page 188*)

Fishermen's boats in Vernazza

Roasted Cod with Curried Parsley Pesto and Pine Nuts

Pesce ai Pinoli

I can't claim the addition of curry powder to this simple but tasty dish as my own twist. It's actually something Silvana does often. But to be sure, I checked in a few Ligurian cookbooks and found curry used in similar contexts. This isn't entirely surprising, given that the Ligurians, along with the Venetians, were well-known spice traders in the Mediterranean. In fact, I'm surprised Ligurian cuisine doesn't make wider use of spices. I like to serve this cod with some basmati white rice for an Indian twist, or with more conventional—but no less delicious—roasted potatoes (see recipe p. 170).

SERVES 4

3 cups tightly packed parsley leaves (about 1 large bunch)

2 teaspoons freshly squeezed lemon juice

1 medium clove garlic

2 teaspoons mild curry powder

Salt

Freshly ground black pepper

½ cup dry white wine

½ cup extra-virgin olive oil

1 medium yellow onion, thinly sliced

4 small tomatoes, peeled, seeded, and coarsely chopped

2 pounds fresh cod, hake, or halibut, cut into 1 to 1½-inch chunks

2 tablespoons pine nuts

Preheat oven at 400°F.

Place the parsley, lemon juice, garlic, curry powder, a pinch of salt, a generous grind of pepper, and white wine in the bowl of a food processor or blender, and process for 1 to 2 minutes (you may need to pulse at the beginning). You should end up with a fairly runny, homogeneous sauce.

In a 10-inch skillet, heat ¼ cup of the olive oil over medium-high heat. When the oil is hot and shimmering, add the onions and cook over medium-high heat, stirring frequently, for 5 minutes, until soft and slightly browned on the edges. Add the tomato, a pinch of salt, and cook for another 10 to 15 minutes, stirring frequently and adding a few tablespoons of warm water if the sauce begins to dry a little. You want to end up with a simple, "oniony" tomato sauce.

Season the cod chunks generously with salt and pepper and arrange them in one layer on the bottom of a 9 × 13-inch baking dish. Drizzle the remaining olive oil over the cod chunks and top them with the tomato sauce. Cook in the oven for 10 minutes. Drizzle about half the curried parsley pesto evenly over the fish and roast for another 10 minutes. Drizzle with the remaining pesto, sprinkle the pine nuts evenly over the fish, and roast for 5 to 10 minutes more, depending on the thickness of fish. Give the contents of the pan a little stir and serve immediately.

Seared Tuna Steaks
with Quick Porcini Mushroom Ragù

Tonno alla Genovese

Land and sea come together in perfect harmony in this dish, which is a great autumnal treat when you're not in the mood for meat braises or roasts. You may wonder how fresh tuna, which typically doesn't swim in the waters near Liguria, ended up at the Ligurian table nonetheless. Apparently, the old maritime Republic of Genova had fishing rights in an area between Sicily and Tunisia, where tuna is abundant. As a result, several fresh tuna dishes became part of the region's culinary repertoire.

SERVES 4

1 ounce dried porcini mushrooms
(about 1 cup)

4 fresh (1-inch-thick) tuna steaks
(6 to 8 ounces each)

Salt

Freshly ground black pepper

4 tablespoons extra-virgin olive oil

2 salted anchovies,
rinsed and coarsely chopped

1 large clove garlic, chopped
(about 1½ teaspoons)

3 tablespoons finely chopped parsley

2 teaspoons unbleached
all-purpose flour

1 cup dry white wine

1 tablespoon unsalted butter (optional)

1 teaspoon freshly squeezed
lemon juice

Soak the dried porcini mushrooms in warm water for at least 20 minutes. Drain and chop them.

Season the tuna steaks generously with salt and pepper. In a 12-inch skillet, heat 2 tablespoons of the olive oil over medium-high heat and add the steaks, making sure they don't overlap. (If you only have a smaller skillet, you will need to do this in two batches.) Sear the tuna for 3 to 4 minutes on each side over fairly high heat. You want to cook the steaks almost all the way through without overcooking them. Transfer to a plate near the burner.

In the same skillet, add the remaining olive oil, the anchovies, mushrooms, garlic, and parsley, and season with a pinch of salt and pepper. Cook for 4 to 5 minutes over medium heat. Add the flour, stir it around the pan with a spoon for 1 minute, then add the wine. Cook, scraping any residual bits from the bottom of the pan, for about 2 minutes more, or until the liquid has reduced by about half and the sauce has thickened a little. Add the butter, if using, and the lemon juice, stirring to incorporate the ingredients. Remove from the heat. If the sauce is too thick, add 1 or 2 tablespoons of warm water to loosen it up. Adjust the seasoning with salt and pepper.

Pour the ragù over the warm tuna and serve immediately.

Roasted Fresh Sardines with a Beet Greens, Garlic, and Parmigiano Topping

Sarde Ripiene

There is an unspoken rule throughout Italy that cheese and fish should go separate ways at the table. Anyone asking for a dash of grated Parmigiano on a seafood risotto or a plate of spaghetti with clams is looked at with mild contempt and is thought of as either an eccentric or a foreign tourist. But, like all rules, this one has exceptions. The no-Parm-with-fish rule is broken in this recipe. And it works.

SERVES 4

8 large sardines, cleaned

2 ounces day-old white bread, crust removed and cut into 1-inch dice (about 2 cups)

½ cup whole milk

8 ounces dandelion greens or spinach, washed, tough stems removed, and coarsely chopped (about 5 cups tightly packed)

2 tablespoons finely chopped parsley

2 small cloves garlic, chopped (about 1 teaspoon)

1 cup finely grated Parmigiano-Reggiano

2 large eggs

2 teaspoons salt

4 tablespoons extra-virgin olive oil

Preheat oven to 450°F.

Remove the backbone from the sardines, leaving them hinged at the back (or ask your fishmonger to do it for you). To do this, place each sardine on a clean surface, belly down, and start to "massage" the back gently but firmly. You'll feel that the backbone gives a little and begins to detach itself from the flesh. Flip the fish and extricate the backbone, leaving the two fillets hinged at the back.

Soak the bread in the milk for at least 5 minutes, squeeze out the excess milk, and chop finely. Set aside.

Rinse the greens (don't pat them dry) and cook them in a 12-inch skillet over medium-high heat for about 5 minutes, using only the rinsing water for moisture. Let them cool and chop finely.

In a large bowl, mix the greens with the reserved bread, the parsley, garlic, Parmigiano, and eggs. Season with 1 teaspoon of the salt and mix to combine well. Brush 2 tablespoons of the olive oil onto a baking dish big enough to hold all the sardines in one layer. Place the sardines in the baking dish skin side down, season them with the remaining salt and spoon a dollop of the filling over each open sardine. Drizzle the remaining olive oil over the stuffed sardines and roast in the oven for about 15 minutes. Serve warm or at room temperature.

Seafood Fritto Misto

Fritto Misto di Mare

Some form or other of *fritto misto*, whether with seafood or meats, can be found in almost every regional Italian cuisine. This Ligurian version is a surprisingly light *fritto* that Silvana makes all the time, just barely dredging the fish in flour, with no eggs or heavy breading. You can serve the *fritto misto* with the salsa verde on page 51, or with any dip that you like.

SERVES 4

1 pound squid, cleaned

16 mussels

At least 3 cups extra-virgin olive oil

At least 3 cups canola oil

1 pound large shrimp, peeled and deveined

1 pound cod fillet, cut into bite-size chunks

½ pound fresh sardine fillets

2 cups unbleached all-purpose flour

Salt

Freshly ground black pepper

4 fresh lemon wedges

Cut the tentacles from the squid and reserve them. Cut the "bodies" into rings about ¼ inch wide.

Barely cover the bottom of a large skillet with water. Arrange the mussels in the skillet and cook them, covered, until the shells are all open. Discard any unopened shells and take the mussels out of their shells.

Pour the olive and canola oils into a large pot and bring them up to frying temperature, 365°F. You'll know the oil is up to temperature when it starts shimmering and it fizzes if you dip in a tiny piece of fish. Coat each fish piece (including the squid, shrimp, and mussels) with flour and dip it into the sizzling oil for 3 to 5 minutes, depending on the size of the fish, or until it turns golden. Remove the fish from the oil with a slotted spoon and place it on a plate lined with paper towels to absorb the excess oil. Season generously with salt and pepper as soon as the pieces come out of the oil. Serve immediately with lemon wedges and, if you like, a dip of your choice.

Red Snapper Fillets in Parchment with Baby Vegetables and Pigato Wine

Filetti di Orata in Cartoccio

I love to cook fish *in cartoccio*, wrapped in parchment paper. The flesh inside gets lightly steamed, permeated by the juicy flavors "trapped" in the parchment. Fish cooked this way is easy and tasty, and once you get comfortable with the method, you can be creative with flavors. I prepared some nice *orata* fillets this way in Liguria one year and got rave reviews from some pretty fussy critics—namely, my uncle Franco and my aunt Silvana. So I decided to share that recipe in this book, using red snapper instead of *orata*, because it's much easier to find.

SERVES 4

4 tablespoons extra-virgin olive oil

½ large onion, sliced

Salt

4 large red snapper fillets, skins on

Freshly ground black pepper

4 very small carrots, cut in thin strips (about ⅛ × ⅛ × 2 inches)

3 baby zucchini and/or squash, cut into matchsticks (about ⅛ × ⅛ × 2 inches)

1 tablespoon coarsely chopped parsley

1 teaspoon finely chopped marjoram

½ cup dry white wine, preferably Pigato

4 large sheets of parchment paper (about 20 × 15 inches each)

In a 10-inch skillet, heat 2 tablespoons of the olive oil over medium-high heat. Add the onion. Sprinkle with a small pinch of salt and cook, stirring frequently, over medium-high heat for about 10 minutes, allowing the onions to brown a little without burning. Add a few tablespoons of water if the onions start sticking to the pan or become too dark. Turn down the heat to medium and cook the onions for another 15 to 20 minutes, stirring frequently and adding a few tablespoons of warm water when the onions start to dry. The onions should be a deep brown color and glossy. Set them aside.

Preheat the oven to 400°F.

Fold each sheet of parchment paper in half widthwise (to become about 10 × 15 inches). Using a pencil and starting from the folded side, draw a half-heart shape that takes up as much of the parchment surface as possible. Cut around the edges of the heart shape and open the parchment paper. You should have a full heart shape, the *cartoccio*.

Season the fillets generously with salt and pepper on both sides. Assemble each *cartoccio* package by placing each fillet skin down on one side of the unfolded "heart," preferably toward the top where the surface is bigger. Top the fish with the

CONTINUED

Red Snapper Fillets in Parchment with Baby Vegetables and Pigato Wine

CONTINUED

carrot and zucchini strips and the reserved onions, dividing them equally among the four open packages. Sprinkle with the herbs and drizzle the remaining olive oil and the wine evenly over the four packages. Fold the other half of the "heart" over the fish and crumple the edges tightly so no juices can escape (you can staple the edges for a tighter seal).

Arrange the packages on a large baking pan and bake for 15 to 20 minutes, depending on the size of the fish. To check doneness, open one packet slightly. If the fish has turned opaque and lost some of its sheen, it's ready. To serve, transfer the packages to individual serving plates and open them slightly.

Pan-Seared Grouper with Lemon Basil Pesto

Pesce con Pesto al Limone

There were two sources of inspiration for this dish: the freshness of Ligurian flavors and a midsummer visit to the Union Square farmers' market in New York City, where I came a cross a bunch of incredibly fragrant lemon basil and decided on the spot I had to do something with it. Lemon basil is a variety of basil that has a pronounced lemony flavor and scent. If you can't find lemon basil, use regular basil and 2 tablespoons of lemon juice instead. I like to serve this grouper with a fresh salad or with some roasted vegetables and potatoes on the side.

SERVES 4

FOR THE PESTO

2 cups tightly packed lemon basil (about 1 large bunch)

1 small clove garlic

1 teaspoon lemon juice

½ cup extra-virgin olive oil

Salt

Freshly ground black pepper

TO ASSEMBLE

4 large grouper fillets or other white fish, such as sole (about 2 pounds total)

Salt

Freshly ground black pepper

2 tablespoons extra-virgin olive oil

1 tablespoon unsalted butter

MAKE THE PESTO Put the basil leaves in the blender with the garlic and lemon juice. Start the blender on high and add the olive oil in a thin stream. If the leaves don't puree immediately, press them down with a metal spoon or small ladle while the blender is running (be careful not to touch the blades). Season with salt and pepper to taste and set aside.

ASSEMBLE THE DISH Rinse the grouper fillets and pat them dry with a paper towel. Season them generously with salt and pepper on both sides. In a 12- to 14-inch nonstick skillet (or two 10-inch skillets), heat the olive oil and the butter over medium-high heat. (If you use two pans, divide the olive oil and butter between the two pans.) Add the seasoned fillets to the pan when the butter stops bubbling. Put the "presentation" side of the fish (i.e., the side you intend to show face up on the plate) face down into the pan.

Cook the fish on each side for about 4 minutes over medium-high heat, until both sides are slightly browned. Use a fish spatula when turning the fish to avoid breaking it.

Carefully transfer the fillets to a serving platter or individual plates and spoon a generous dollop of the pesto on top. It's as simple as that! If you're working in two batches, keep the fish in the first batch warm by placing in on an ovenproof dish close to the burner where you're cooking the next batch.

Pan-Steamed Swordfish with Capers, Olives, and Toasted Pine Nuts

Pesce Spada con Capperi, Olive, e Pinoli

This dish is similar to *Pesce Spada alla Stimpirata*, which is really a traditional Sicilian dish. But I added a few Ligurian "touches" for this book. I love it: it's a quick and satisfying dish that you, too, will want to have in your repertoire. I make it often, in Liguria as well as in New York.

SERVES 4

¼ cup pine nuts

4 swordfish steaks
(about ½ pound each)

Salt

Freshly ground black pepper

4 tablespoons extra-virgin olive oil

½ large onion or 1 small onion,
thinly sliced

1 cup coarsely chopped olives
(black and green)

1 tablespoon salted capers, rinsed

½ cup Vermentino white wine

¼ cup homemade fish broth
(see recipe page 208) or water

Toast the pine nuts in an 8-inch skillet over medium-high heat until they turn slightly tan, about 4 to 5 minutes. Remove them from the heat and transfer them to a cold plate. This will stop the cooking.

Season the swordfish generously with salt and pepper.

Heat 3 tablespoons of the olive oil in a 12- to 14-inch nonstick skillet (or two 10-inch skillets) over medium-high heat. When the oil is hot, add the fish and sear it over medium-high heat for 3 to 5 minutes on each side. Transfer to a plate near the stove.

Add the remaining oil and the onions to the pan and cook over medium-high heat, stirring frequently, for about 7 to 8 minutes, until the onions are soft and start turning brown on the edges. Add the olives and capers, and cook for another 2 to 3 minutes. Add half of the wine and scrape the bottom of the pan with a wooden spoon. Let the wine completely evaporate. Add the fish back to the pan and pour in the rest of the wine and the broth (or water). Turn down the heat to medium and cook, partially covered, for 5 to 8 minutes, or until the fish is cooked through but not overdone. Remove from the heat, adjust seasoning with salt and pepper, and sprinkle the pine nuts over the fish. Serve immediately, making sure to spoon some onions, olives, and capers with each serving.

Roasted Skate with Mint, Basil, Lemon Zest, and Extra-Virgin Olive Oil

Razza ai Profumi

This is a wonderful summer dish, not only because the fish ends up being very light and fresh-tasting, but also because it's a breeze to make, requiring very little time at the stove. You can easily replace the skate with any other delicate white fish you like, such as sole or halibut, but you may have to adjust the cooking time.

SERVES 4

4 skate fillets (about 2 pounds total)

Salt

Freshly ground black pepper

6 tablespoons extra-virgin olive oil

¼ cup dry white wine

2 tablespoons roughly chopped parsley

2 tablespoons roughly chopped basil

1 tablespoons roughly chopped mint

1 teaspoon finely chopped thyme

1 teaspoon finely grated lemon zest

Preheat the oven to 450°F.

Season the skate generously with salt and pepper. Heat 2 tablespoons of the olive oil in a 12- or 14-inch nonstick skillet (or two 10-inch nonstick skillets) over high heat. When the oil is hot, add the skate and sauté for 2 minutes per side, trying to get a nice, even browning. Use a fish spatula to turn the fillets over.

Turn off the heat and, using a fish spatula, transfer the skate to a 9 × 13-inch baking dish. Drizzle the remaining olive oil and the wine over it and sprinkle two-thirds of the herbs and lemon zest.

Bake for about 10 minutes (or less, if your skate is very thin). Sprinkle the remaining herbs evenly over the cooked fish and serve, spooning some of the oil and juices gathered at the bottom of the pan.

Shrimp-Stuffed Cuttlefish in Vermentino Wine Sauce

Seppie Ripiene

The squid world seems to be a tad more complicated in Italy than it is over here—at least at the store. In the United States we have squid and, occasionally, cuttlefish; in Italy we have *seppie* (cuttlefish), *calamari* (squid), and *totani* (a different kind of squid for which I haven't found an American equivalent). To complicate things further, what Americans call "calamari" are squid (or cuttlefish) rings that have been breaded and deep-fried. Given that the chances of finding cuttlefish at your local market are slim, you can use squid to make this Ligurian classic.

SERVES 4

FOR THE FILLING

12 medium cuttlefish or squid, cleaned

3 tablespoons extra-virgin olive oil

4 ounces oil-packed tuna, drained

2 oil-packed anchovies, drained

6 ounces medium shrimp, peeled and deveined

½ cup pitted black olives

1 tablespoon salted capers, rinsed

3 sprigs parsley, leaves only (about ¼ cup)

8 large basil leaves

2 large egg whites

1½ teaspoons salt

Freshly ground black pepper

½ cup heavy cream

TO ASSEMBLE THE DISH

2 tablespoons extra-virgin olive oil

⅔ cup dry white wine, preferably Vermentino

PREPARE THE FILLING Chop the cuttlefish tentacles finely, reserving the main "body." In a 10-inch skillet, heat 1 tablespoon of the olive oil over medium-high heat and cook the tentacles for 2 to 3 minutes, just enough to cook them through and brown them slightly. Let them cool.

Place the tuna, anchovies, shrimp, olives, capers, parsley, basil, the remaining olive oil, egg whites, salt, and pepper in the bowl of a food processor and add the cooled cuttlefish heads. Start the processor and add the cream in a thin stream. Continue processing until smooth, about 1 minute.

ASSEMBLE THE DISH Stuff the cuttlefish "bodies" with the filling and secure the opening with a toothpick. Make sure you don't overstuff them. The filling will expand while cooking and force itself out of the cuttlefish.

Heat 2 tablespoons of olive oil in a 12- or 14-inch nonstick skillet over medium-high heat and brown the cuttlefish evenly on all sides, about 4 to 5 minutes per side. Pour in the wine, scraping the browned bits at the bottom of the pan. When the wine starts boiling vigorously, reduce the heat to medium-low and simmer, partially covered, for about 5 minutes, until the wine is reduced by about half. Serve immediately, spooning the wine sauce over the cuttlefish.

Whole Striped Bass Baked in a Coarse Sea Salt Crust

Pesce al Sale

Baking a whole fish in a salt crust is quite common all over Italy. It's easy and the results are delicious. You'd think the flesh would be very salty, but it's not. Instead it's just seasoned enough to eat without further enhancement—just a drizzle of high-quality extra-virgin olive oil. Choose delicate white-flesh fish and use some good coarse sea salt for best results.

SERVES 4

5 to 6 pounds coarse sea salt

2 whole striped bass, black bass, or red snapper (about 1½ pounds each), cleaned, scales on

½ cup fruity extra-virgin olive oil

Preheat the oven to 450°F.

Spread one-third of the salt on the bottom of two 9 × 13-inch baking dishes, making sure to cover the dish completely. Arrange each fish on top and cover thoroughly with the remaining salt.

Bake for 30 to 35 minutes. When done, break the salt with the tip of a knife. Remove the salt crust completely. Remove any skin from the fish that has not come off with the salt. Carve four fillets following the bone line (it's very hard even for a pro to get whole fillets out of this operation, so don't worry if they break apart). Arrange them in individual plates and drizzle the olive oil evenly over the top.

Grilled Jumbo Shrimp with Arugula, Shaved Fennel, Orange, and Chickpeas

Gamberoni alla Griglia con Insalatina di Rucola, Finocchio, Arancio, e Ceci

In Liguria, grilled jumbo shrimp—*gamberoni alla griglia*—are always served with their heads on. It's nice to get messy and eat them with your hands, as with lobster. My uncle Franco taught me that the best part comes when you finish the meaty bodies and start sucking out the heads. I know this may sound strange to any American not from Lousiana, but trust me, it's delicious. That being said, it can be difficult to find shrimp sold with their heads on in the United States, so this recipe uses the headless jumbo shrimp more commonly found in American markets. You can replace the orange segments with grapefruit or even watermelon pieces, if you like.

SERVES 4

FOR THE MARINADE

1 large clove garlic, finely chopped (about 1½ teaspoons)

¼ cup extra-virgin olive oil

1 tablespoon finely chopped parsley

1 teaspoon finely chopped mint

A pinch of cayenne powder

1 tablespoon freshly squeezed lemon juice

1 teaspoon lemon zest

20 jumbo shrimp, peeled and deveined, tails on

FOR THE DRESSING

1 teaspoon honey

2 teaspoons freshly squeezed lemon juice

1 tablespoon freshly squeezed orange juice

¼ cup extra-virgin olive oil

Salt

Freshly ground black pepper

FOR THE SALAD

1 very small fennel bulb

4 cups baby arugula, washed

1 orange, peeled and cut into segments

½ small red onion, thinly sliced (about ½ cup)

¾ cup canned or cooked chickpeas, drained

Whisk the marinade ingredients together in a medium-size bowl, toss in the peeled shrimp, cover the bowl with plastic wrap, and marinate in the refrigerator for 30 minutes.

In a medium-size bowl, whisk together the ingredients for the dressing, starting with the honey and the citrus juices. Pour in the olive oil in a thin stream while you're still whisking, and season to taste with salt and pepper.

Cut the fennel bulb in half, remove the tough white core, and cut it crosswise into paper-thin slices. Set aside.

Heat the grill or a stovetop grill pan or griddle to medium-high. Take the shrimp out of the marinade, shaking off any excess liquid, and grill them for about 3 minutes on each side. The outside should be slightly browned. Transfer to a plate and reserve.

Put the arugula, orange, onion, sliced fennel, and chickpeas in a large bowl and toss with the prepared dressing. Serve the salad in individual plates topped with the grilled shrimp (five per person).

A LIGURIAN KITCHEN

Mine is a family of eaters. We love to eat—and, more importantly, we love to eat well. It helps that we've been gifted with a number of outstanding cooks through the generations. Before my mother and Silvana, there was my grandmother Teresina and my aunt Lidia, who may not have been especially creative or experimental with their cooking, but who mastered a lengthy menu of traditional Piedmontese dishes like no one else I know.

It comes as no a surprise, then, that some of my fondest memories of Bonassola are associated with the kitchen. Food is a focal point of life here, whether because Franco is a relentless gourmand with an infectious love of good food, or because, when we're here, there's not much to do but dream up the next al fresco luncheon or dinner for twenty-five. Or maybe it's because in summertime the *terreno* churns out volumes of incredible produce, so fresh it demands to be eaten within days. Whatever the reason, it seems that in Bonassola when I'm not at the beach soaking up the sun or reading a book shaded by a huge umbrella, I'm drawn to the kitchen.

Whether it was the dark, shabby room of the rental house in via Roma or, much later, the well-equipped modern workplace of Silvana and Franco's own home, in Bonassola I found the quintessential kitchen—what a kitchen should be, well beyond its physical appearance: a gathering point, a place to spend happy hours cooking in the company of people you love.

Growing up, I loved nothing more than to spend time in the kitchen with Silvana and my mother, helping to snap green beans, peel potatoes, or do whatever small chore might keep me there. Back then, I didn't cook. I just liked being in the kitchen, watching them dance around the room in what seemed like wonderfully choreographed moves, performing each task with precise, expert gestures, refrigerator to sink, sink to stovetop. It always put us in high spirits, made us chatty, lighthearted, eager to nurture our family and our guests. I didn't learn much in the way of techniques or recipes—those came later. But I did learn something perhaps more important. In this Ligurian kitchen, I learned to appreciate the comforting, soothing, uplifting power of cooking.

And it's *this* kitchen I long for and do my best to recreate wherever my journeys take me.

I have to admit that my own appreciation of good food is due in no small part to my uncle Franco's contagious passion for all things gastronomic. Franco doesn't cook himself, but no one could be more discerning when it comes to eating. He's always on the look out for the quaint neighborhood shop selling artisanal specialties and hard-to-find foodstuffs. And you know that if he recommends a restaurant, it'll be good—it doesn't matter if it's a small trattoria or a grand and fancy place with four stars. He's a bon vivant who loves to entertain and eat well in good company (and who'd clearly have a much harder time if his wife weren't such a wonderful cook—but then again, he probably wouldn't have married someone who wasn't a wonderful cook). He always keeps a few outstanding bottles of wine in his cellar to share with guests over a lavish meal. It was Franco who introduced me to the ethereal delicacy of Mediterranean white fish. It was Franco who took me out to the *scogli* (seashore rocks), to fish mussels so I could taste them fresh from the water. And it was Franco who gave me my first experience drinking espresso accompanied by thin strips of focaccia instead of a sweet *cornetto*, like everywhere else in Italy. It was on one of the many occasions when I lingered in Bonassola long after my parents. Franco offered to drive me to the train station in Genova for the return trip home and, on the way, we stopped at a *bar* for breakfast. Puzzled, I asked where the *cornetti* were. My uncle shook his head. He said nothing, only pointed to the tray filled with thin, oily focaccia bits.

Going to a restaurant with Franco always became an event. He took us to the best places in the area. Somewhere between the antipasti and the pasta, he invariably launched into a conversation with the waiter or host about the bad fishing season or the best place to get *ricciola*. By the end of the meal, he was best friends with the owner or the chef, or both, and got the royal treatment for himself and whoever came with him. That is, of course, unless he already knew everybody at the establishment. Either way, we benefited from the freshest fish, a pour of some special wine that wasn't even on the list, and a slew of complimentary *amuse-bouche* the chef dished out between courses. Every time, it was a treat.

One summer, we went to Il Gambero Rosso in Vernazza when it still was the best meal in town, unburdened by the demands of flocking foreign tourists. We sat outside under small white tents facing the tiny port abustle with fishermen preparing for a night at sea and vacationers lounging on the minuscule beach, despite the sun's setting almost an hour before. The town was vibrant and busy, yet a calmness pervaded the scene, a willful lack of urgency I only experience when I return to Bonassola and its neighboring villages. I don't remember how we started the meal. Knowing Franco, it surely was a sampler of the house antipasti: marinated anchovies, warm baby octopus salad, fried borage leaves.

"*Un po' di antipastini misti, signor Guerci?*" the waiter would intone.

"*Certo!*" Franco invariably boomed in response.

But that night what really knocked me over was a rich plate of perfect *pennette con gli scampi*. Nothing had called out to me as the waiter recited the menu items; it was Franco who recommended the *pennette*. He'd eaten at the restaurant before and claimed this dish was one of the best things on earth. He was right. A velvety tomato sauce with almost no hint of acidity enveloped tiny bits of sweet, tender scampi, with only a suggestion of spice. The flavors married so well you couldn't imagine them apart. And the sauce clung to the *pennette* in a way that happens only when pasta has been perfectly executed. I was fifteen; and I'd never quite tasted anything so complete. I closed my eyes to savor each full bite, feeling the gentle sea breeze on my skin and the sound of waves softly swaying back and forth: paradise all over again.

"Shall we continue with a *branzino* caught today, cooked gently in the oven with just a little olive oil, baby potatoes, and black olives? *Alla ligure?*" the waiter asked, with a complacency that suggested we couldn't possibly say no.

Franco looked at me. I had an ecstatic smile on my face. My father chuckled; he'd never seen me so entranced by food.

"*Of course*, we'll have the *branzino*," he said.

Branzino is a prized fish in Italy; its buttery, white flesh comes with a steep price tag. But few fish I've tasted can match its delicate, flaky texture and elegant flavor. Because of its subtlety, there's no better way to cook it than to slowly roast it with a little salt, a generous drizzle of extra-virgin olive oil, and fresh herbs. That's how Ligurians do it. To cover it with heavy sauces or mask its delicacy with spices would be a crime. Since that evening at Il Gambero Rosso, I've never wanted *branzino* any other way, and that's how I cook it whenever I'm in Italy and am lucky enough to find a good, fresh one.

"Let's go see the *terreno*," Franco said in his beguilingly energetic tone as everyone else hung lazily around the house enjoying the afternoon quiet. It was only then I realized I'd never actually seen the *terreno*. I'd eaten the tomatoes and zucchini grown on the *terreno*, drizzled the green olive oil produced from its olive trees, and made pesto with its sweet-scented basil, but I'd never set foot on the land all these goodies were coming from. I was beginning to think it might be a figment of my imagination.

In those days—and by that I mean the 1980s, not the 1880s—going to the *terreno* meant riding an almost vertical road so dusty your hair turned the color of straw and your skin developed an unhealthy light beige hue, as it became plastered with a thin layer of dirt. It didn't help that Franco drove a convertible Jeep that was not only topless but windowless, too.

This *terreno* was as far removed as you can get from the common notion of a piece of land. There were vegetable patches and fruit trees for sure, but instead of marching a field in stately rows, they grabbed precariously onto slivers of land that climbed up the hill like a giant staircase. Most of the landscape in Liguria is like this. It's a tough, arid land that's always been unkind to those farmers foolish or stubborn enough to try to tame it. The sight of it tells you all you need to know about the rugged Ligurian country folk who turned wild herbs and weeds into cuisine and made astonishingly creative use of such simple ingredients.

Silvana and Franco, with their designer clothes, sports cars, and fancy architect plans for a new home, hardly fit the image of the rustic Ligurian farmer. But they loved to care for the *terreno*—or at least to pick up the loose ends after Renzo, the gardener, had done the heavy lifting. They became exemplary weekend farmers. And their *fasce* were thriving. Silvery olive trees grew everywhere, trunks crooked and filled with ancient knots; fresh herbs—most growing wild, like *issopo* (hyssop, similar to thyme) and rosemary bushes—infused the air with their sharp woody scents. A bright green patch of basil—which Silvana picked very young when the leaves were small and pale and ideal for making pesto the Genovese way—lay on one of the terrace's far sides. They had planted fruit trees—apples, peaches, plums, and lemons—but these were still in adolescence, too young to bear fruit. Tomatoes and peppers, on the other hand, were bountiful, as were crisp lettuces, stout zucchini, and curvaceous eggplants. It was inspiring to harvest fruit and vegetables just hours before they'd be transformed into dinner through cooking's miraculous alchemy—not something a city girl gets to do very often. We picked tiny strawberries, plump tomatoes, and crispy butter lettuce. Some of that young basil made its way into our baskets, too. For dinner we could toss the greens and tomatoes into a fresh salad and marinate the strawberries in lemon juice and sugar. Or maybe we would roast the tomatoes. Dinner was rich with possibilities.

As we walked along the terraces, climbing to reach each next *fascia* above, Silvana began to pluck what looked like weeds to me. They were growing wild, and we'd stepped on them persistently while tredding along. Soon I realized they weren't weeds at all. They were quite edible, in fact. She was collecting them for *preboggion*, the foundation for *pansotti* filling and other Ligurian delights. These seemingly insignificant plants, so meek you easily crush them with your feet, are in fact one of the pillars of Ligurian cuisine.

Franco pointed to the spot they had designated for the house.

"When will it be finished?" asked my mother.

"We're stuck in small-town bureaucracy," he replied. "Ingegner Bienno isn't making it any easier for us."

Ingegner Bienno, a tall squarish man with a very small round head that could barely contain his furry mustache, had been appointed by the town of Bonassola to preside over the project. He was the senior engineer for the town of Bonassola; everyone knew him and everyone greeted him: "*Buongiorno, Ingegnere!*" with the characteristically effusive use of titles Italians cherish. (Bienno happened to be a real engineer, but citizens of the *bel paese* will often address people—particularly men—as *avvocato* (lawyer) or *dottore* (doctor), simply because they look rich or important, even if they never went near a law or medical school.)

Bienno was what many would call a *trafficone*, a "big trafficker," someone who's dedicated to deal-making and the wringing of financial advantage from any conceivable situation. After the war, Bienno had come to Bonassola from his native Tuscany and bought up countless acres of land for pennies. He ended up owning half the town and, over the decades, made piles of money reselling bits and pieces of his property at skyrocketing market values.

He was holding up the plans for Silvana and Franco's house because, he alleged, he'd never received a certain zoning permit from the regional government designed to prevent *abusi edilizi* (real estate abuses, such as building outside of zoning codes or raising houses more than permitted by law—definitely one of Italy's favorite pastimes, after soccer). They'd been waiting four years already. Little did they know, it would be four more before any ground was broken.

But this wasn't what drove Silvana and Franco absolutely bananas about Ingegner Bienno. When they bought the *terreno*, two *fasce* just above the spot they'd chosen for their future house were not part of the deal. They belonged to a local farmer. Good old Ingegner Bienno came to the rescue. In some mysterious (and undoubtedly cunning) way, he came into possession of the *fasce*, then came back to Silvana and Franco with a multi-million lire asking price for the two miserly pieces of land. My aunt and uncle had no choice, unless they wanted to be awakened early every morning by the sounds of a complete stranger's plowing and tilling.

Before we headed back to the old rental house, we paused on the spot where the new house's terrace would be. It was higher, roomier, more open than the old terrace. You could see the entire bay and endless miles of sea behind it, and around it groves of olive trees, jasmine, and oleander. The gray-blue light of nightfall made it all the more dramatic. I was suddenly aware that a new era of memorable outdoor meals and breakfasts with a view lay before me.

FROM THE LAND

dalla terra

Chef Francesco's Rossese Wine Braised Rabbit with Black Olives

Coniglio Brasato al Rossese

Our open-air dinner at Terre Bianche (see page 183), the lovely agri-tourism farm run by friendly and chatty host Paolo, had many good moments. But the high point might just have been chef Francesco's braised rabbit. Rabbit dishes are a mainstay of Ligurian cuisine—small farm animals have historically been a lot more practical to raise in the region's very vertical, terraced landscape. And this one was skillfully executed, with flavors so intense I had to ask for the recipe. So at the end of the meal, Francesco Motola came out of the kitchen and shared his secrets with me. I like to serve this rabbit with a dab of creamy polenta and some roasted winter vegetables, like squash and potatoes.

SERVES 4

1 large rabbit (about 4 pounds), cut into 8 pieces

Salt and freshly ground black pepper

¼ cup extra-virgin olive oil

2 small cloves garlic, very finely chopped (about 1 teaspoon)

1 small onion, very finely chopped (about 1 cup)

½ small carrot, very finely chopped (about ¼ cup)

½ small celery stalk, very finely chopped (a scant ¼ cup)

1 teaspoon finely chopped rosemary

1 teaspoons finely chopped thyme

1 cup Rossese wine or other dry red wine

½ cup coarsely chopped pitted black olives, preferably gaeta

2 small ripe or canned tomatoes, seeded and coarsely chopped

Season the rabbit pieces generously with salt and pepper. Heat half the olive oil in a 12- to 14-inch skillet over medium-high heat. Brown the rabbit pieces for about 5 minutes on each side. Transfer them to a dish near the stove.

Lower the heat to medium, add the remaining oil, and add the garlic, onion, carrot, celery, rosemary, and thyme. Cook, stirring frequently, for 3 to 4 minutes (be careful not to burn the garlic), then add the wine, olives, and tomatoes. Season moderately with salt and pepper, add the rabbit pieces back to the pan, and bring the wine to a boil (you may need to increase the heat a little to do this). Reduce the heat to medium-low and simmer vigorously, uncovered, for 5 to 8 minutes.

Cover the pan partially and simmer over low heat for about 30 minutes, turning the rabbit pieces once. If the sauce starts getting too dry, you can add a little water or chicken broth. By the end, the sauce should have reduced more than half and thickened quite a bit. If the sauce is too watery, you can remove the rabbit from the pan, increase the temperature and simmer the sauce vigorously to quickly reduce it. This shouldn't take more than 3 to 4 minutes. Put the rabbit back in the pan, coat with sauce and serve immediately.

Lamb Fricassee with Artichokes

Fricassea di Agnello

Fricassea is a type of stew finished with eggs and lemon juice that's common all over Italy. This hearty lamb fricassee is popular in many parts of Liguria. I enjoy making it throughout the fall and winter when I'm in the mood for something warm and soothing on a frosty day.

SERVES 4

2 medium artichokes

3 tablespoons freshly squeezed lemon juice, plus more to taste

1 tablespoon pine nuts

2½ pounds lamb shoulder or stew-lamb pieces, trimmed and cubed

Salt

Freshly ground black pepper

2 tablespoons extra-virgin olive oil

1 small onion, finely chopped (about 1 cup)

1 tomato, seeded, peeled, and coarsely chopped

1 medium clove garlic, finely chopped (about 1 teaspoon)

½ cup dry white wine

1 teaspoon finely chopped thyme

1 bay leaf

1½ cups homemade (see recipe page 210) or low-sodium canned chicken broth

2 large eggs

1 tablespoon coarsely chopped parsley

Clean the artichokes by cutting the tough stems and ½ inch to 1 inch off the top, and by removing the outer, tough leaves until you reach the tender, light green leaves near the center. Cut each artichoke in half lengthwise and remove the hairy white core inside of each. Place them immediately in a bowl of water with 2 tablespoons of the lemon juice or else they'll turn very dark. Cut each half lengthwise into eight sections. Leave the slices in the acidulated water until you're ready to cook them.

Crush the pine nuts to a paste in a mortar or small food processor and set aside.

Season the pieces of lamb generously with salt and pepper. In a large Dutch oven, heat 1 tablespoon of the olive oil over medium-high heat. When the oil is hot, add the lamb. Brown it on all sides over medium-high heat for a total of about 10 minutes. Transfer to a dish near the stove.

Add the remaining olive oil and the onion to the pan. Cook over medium-high heat for about 5 minutes, stirring occasionally, until the onions are soft. Add the tomatoes and garlic, and cook for another 2 to 3 minutes. Add the white wine and scrape any brown bits stuck to the bottom of the pan. Bring the liquid to a boil and reduce the heat to medium-low or low.

Add the lamb back to the pan along with the artichokes, thyme, bay leaf, and the broth. Season with a pinch of salt and a grind of pepper, and simmer over low heat, partially covered, for 1½ hours.

Toward the end of cooking, beat the eggs in a medium-size bowl and add the parsley, pine nuts, the remaining lemon juice, and a pinch of salt. When the lamb has finished cooking (the sauce will have reduced quite a bit and thickened a little), remove from the heat, take out the bay leaf, and add the egg mixture. Stir for a few minutes to obtain a smooth sauce, add more lemon juice to taste, and serve immediately.

Braised Guinea Hen with Grapes and Grappa

Faraona all'Uva

The Ligurian table welcomes plenty of game meat and fowl. I adapted and combined a number of traditional recipes and came up with this unusual and succulent braise that offers just the right burst of fruity sweetness to brighten up the cold months. Refrain from using flavored grappa as it will interfere with the balance of tastes.

SERVES 4

2 (2½-pound) guinea hens, quartered (legs and breasts only), skin removed

Salt

Freshly ground black pepper

5 tablespoons extra-virgin olive oil

½ small onion, very finely chopped (about ½ cup)

1 small shallot, very finely chopped (about 1½ tablespoons)

½ small celery stalk, very finely chopped (a scant ¼ cup)

½ small carrot, very finely chopped (about ¼ cup)

1 teaspoon finely chopped thyme

¾ cup grappa

1 cup homemade (see recipe page 210) or low-sodium canned chicken broth

1 cup seedless red or black grapes

1 tablespoon unsalted butter (optional)

Season the guinea hen pieces generously with salt and pepper.

Heat 3 tablespoons of the olive oil in a medium-size Dutch oven over medium-high heat. Add the guinea hen pieces and brown them over fairly high heat for about 3 minutes on each side. Transfer to a dish near the stove.

Pour the remaining 2 tablespoons of olive oil into the pan and add the onion, shallot, celery, carrot, and thyme. Season with a pinch of salt and a sprinkle of pepper, and cook, stirring frequently, over medium heat for about 5 minutes, or until the vegetables start to soften.

Remove the pan from the heat and pour in half of the grappa. Return the pan to the heat and scrape any brown pieces stuck to the bottom of the pan with a wooden spoon.

Place the guinea hen legs back in the pan, pour in the broth, add the grapes, and cook, uncovered, for about 30 minutes over medium-low heat.

Add the guinea hen breasts and cook for about 10 minutes more.

Transfer the guinea hen pieces to a plate, add the remaining grappa, and increase the heat to medium-high or high. Reduce the sauce until it has a slightly thicker texture, 3 to 5 minutes. Turn off the heat and stir in the butter, if using.

Taste the sauce for seasoning and add more salt and pepper, if needed. Add the guinea hen pieces back in the pan and coat them with the sauce. Serve immediately.

Rustic Braised Chicken with Black Olives and Rosemary

Pollo alla Ligure

Chicken cooked this way is common all over Liguria, particularly in the *entroterra*, where fish was historically less available. I like to keep it very rustic, leaving the tomato skins on and the pits in the olives. But feel free to peel and pit, if you prefer.

SERVES 4

2 (2½-pound) chickens, cut into 8 pieces, skin removed

Salt

Freshly ground black pepper

4 tablespoons extra-virgin olive oil

½ medium onion, finely chopped (about ¾ cup)

½ small carrot, finely chopped (about ¼ cup)

½ medium celery stalk, finely chopped (about ⅓ cup)

½ cup dry white wine

½ cup homemade (see recipe page 210) or low-sodium canned chicken broth

1 medium tomato, peeled, seeded, and coarsely chopped

1 tablespoon finely chopped rosemary

1 tablespoon olive paste (see recipe page 32) (optional)

18 black olives, preferably gaeta or niçoise

Season the chicken generously with salt and pepper.

Heat the olive oil in a 12- or 14-inch skillet (the skillet should be large enough to contain all the chicken pieces; if not, divide the ingredients between two smaller skillets) over medium-high heat. Brown the chicken on all sides for about 10 minutes, turning the pieces with the help of tongs or a fork and spoon.

Transfer the browned chicken to a plate near the stove and add the onions, carrot, celery, and a pinch of salt to the pan. Stir to coat them with the oil and cook for 5 minutes, stirring frequently, until the vegetables begin to soften and brown a little. Add the wine, scraping the brown bits off the bottom of the pan.

Place the chicken thighs back in the pan. Add the broth, tomato, rosemary, olive paste (if using), and olives and stir to combine the ingredients. Turn down the heat to medium-low, cover partially, and simmer for about 20 minutes. Add the breasts and simmer for another 10 to 15 minutes, until the juices are reduced by about half. Coat all the chicken pieces with the sauce, taste for seasoning, and serve immediately.

Grilled Beef and Lamb Skewers with Arugula-Basil Pesto

Stecchi alla Genovese alla Mia Maniera

There is a traditional Ligurian dish called *stecchi alla genovese*, which is somewhat heavy-duty. You pan-fry pieces of meat in butter before skewering, breading, and deep-frying them in olive oil. I decided to try something slightly different: grilled meat skewers topped by a Ligurian riff on Argentinean *chimichurri*. Sidestepping the deep-frying, the skewers are lighter and the salsa verde-style sauce helps brighten the flavors. I like to alternate meat bites with small pieces of vegetables such as onions, peppers, or cherry tomatoes. But I don't marinate them with the meat. Just toss them in olive oil, salt, and pepper before skewering.

SERVES 4

NOTE
THE MEAT SHOULD MARINATE FOR AT LEAST 4 HOURS OR OVERNIGHT.

FOR THE MARINADE

1 tablespoon finely chopped basil

1 teaspoon finely chopped marjoram

1 teaspoon finely chopped thyme

2 small cloves garlic, finely chopped (about 1 teaspoon)

1 tablespoon freshly squeezed lemon juice

½ cup extra-virgin olive oil

Freshly ground black pepper

1½ pounds beef sirloin steak

1½ pounds lamb loin

MAKE THE MARINADE In a large bowl, whisk together all the marinade ingredients. Cut the meat into bite-size cubes and add them to the bowl. With your hands, mix the meat well to coat it with the marinade, cover the bowl with plastic, and let the meat marinate in the refrigerator for at least 4 hours or overnight.

MAKE THE PESTO Place the arugula, basil, garlic, and lemon juice in the bowl of a food processor or blender and start processing. Slowly add the oil in a thin stream. Season to taste with salt and pepper and set aside.

ASSEMBLE THE DISH Heat the grill to hot.

Take the meat out of the refrigerator and remove it from marinade. Brush off the excess marinade and skewer the meat bites, making sure to alternate meat types. Season generously with salt and pepper.

Cook the skewers on the grill for about 8 minutes for medium-rare, turning the skewers every so often. Cook them a few minutes longer for medium.

FOR THE PESTO

2 cups tightly packed baby arugula

1 cup tightly packed basil leaves

2 cloves garlic

¼ teaspoon lemon juice

¼ cup extra-virgin olive oil

Salt

Freshly ground black pepper

TO ASSEMBLE

Salt

Freshly ground black pepper

Metal skewers or presoaked bamboo skewers

Serve the skewers topped with a little of the pesto or with the pesto on the side as a dip.

Sautéed Chicken Livers with Onions and Artichokes

Fegatini di Pollo con Carciofi

We have an expression in Italian that goes *"brutti ma buoni,"* which translates into something like "ugly but good." It's the perfect description for this rustic chicken liver dish. My family eats it as a main course, like *fegato all veneziana*, with a salad or braised vegetables on the side. But you can opt to serve it as an appetizer as well—in which case it will serve six to eight.

SERVES 4

3 small artichokes

3 tablespoons freshly squeezed lemon juice

5 tablespoons extra-virgin olive oil

2 large onions, thinly sliced

2 cups homemade (see recipe page 210) or low-sodium canned chicken broth

Salt

Freshly ground black pepper

1 tablespoon chopped parsley, plus more for garnish

2 ounces ham, cut into ¼-inch dice

1½ pounds chicken livers, cut into 2 × ½-inch strips

¼ cup dry white wine

Clean the artichokes by cutting the tough stems and ½ inch to 1 inch off the top, and by removing the outer, tough leaves until you reach the tender, light green leaves near the center. Cut each artichoke in half lengthwise and remove the hairy white core inside of each. Place them immediately in a bowl of water with 2 tablespoons of the lemon juice or else they'll turn very dark. Cut each half lengthwise into eight sections (cut them into four sections if the artichokes are very small). Leave the slices in the acidulated water until you're ready to cook them.

Heat 4 tablespoons of the olive oil in a 12-inch skillet over medium-high heat. Add the onions and sauté, stirring frequently, for about 20 minutes adding 1 cup of the broth in 1-tablespoon increments. You want the onions browned but not burnt. Add the broth whenever the onions start sticking to the pan (each addition should make a sizzling noise). If they start burning, turn down the heat.

Drain the artichokes and pat them dry with a paper towel. Add them to the onions with a generous pinch of salt, a few grinds of pepper, 1 cup of the broth, and bring to a simmer. Reduce the heat to medium-low, add the parsley and ham, cover partially, and cook for about 15 minutes, or until the artichokes are tender.

Meanwhile, in a different skillet big enough to hold all the livers (12 to 14 inches wide), heat the remaining tablespoon of olive oil over medium-high heat. Season the chicken livers generously with salt and pepper. When the oil is hot, add the livers and cook them for about 5 minutes over medium-high, making sure to brown them on all sides. Transfer them to a dish near the stove.

When the artichokes are done cooking, turn off the heat and add the reserved livers. With the wine, deglaze the pan used to cook the livers over medium-high heat and reduce the liquid by half, about 2 minutes. Pour the wine sauce in with the livers and artichokes, add the remaining 1 tablespoon of lemon juice, and adjust seasoning with salt and pepper. Garnish with fresh parsley and serve immediately.

Braised Pork Shoulder with Cumin, Cinnamon, and Almonds

Spezzatino di Maiale

I've adapted this braised pork from a recipe called *spezzatino di castrato*, ox stew, which Silvana makes during Liguria's few cold, windy days. It's a wonderful winter dish that will fill your house with the warming aromas of spices. And it's extremely satisfying to eat, as the meat melts in your mouth. For great results, it's important that you use the right cut of meat. I've found that a part of the shoulder called Boston butt works best, because it has lots of connective tissue that will break down as it cooks, making the meat very tender.

SERVES 4 TO 6

4 pounds pork shoulder (Boston butt)

Salt

Freshly ground black pepper

2 tablespoons extra-virgin olive oil

¾ cup finely chopped onion

¼ teaspoon ground cinnamon

¼ teaspoon ground cumin

2 whole cloves

½ cup dry red wine

1 plum tomato, peeled, seeded, and coarsely chopped

1 cup homemade (see recipe page 210) or low-sodium canned chicken broth

1 bay leaf

3 tablespoons finely ground blanched almonds

Trim the excess fat from the pork shoulder and season it generously with salt and pepper.

Heat 1 tablespoon of the olive oil in a large Dutch oven over high heat. When the oil is hot, add the pork shoulder and brown it on all sides over medium-high or high heat for 10 to 15 minutes.

Transfer the pork shoulder to a dish near the stove, pour out any fat accumulated in the pan, and add the remaining olive oil, the onion, a pinch of salt and pepper. Cook for about 3 minutes, or until the onions are soft and translucent. Add the cinnamon, cumin, and cloves, and deglaze the pan with the red wine. When the wine is almost completely absorbed, 1 to 2 minutes later, add the tomato and cook for 2 to 3 minutes more, stirring occasionally.

Place the pork back in the pan, pour in the broth (the liquid should come one-third to half way up the sides of the meat), and add the bay leaf and ground almonds. Bring to a simmer and reduce the heat to medium-low, partially cover the pan, and simmer the shoulder slowly for 2½ to 3 hours (depending on size), turning the meat every hour or so.

The sauce will have reduced and thickened a bit and will contain bits and pieces of vegetables. Transfer the shoulder to a clean cutting board, let rest for 10 minutes, and cut into equal portions. Skim the fat from the surface of the sauce. If the sauce is too watery, reduce it a little over medium-high heat (be careful not to reduce the sauce too much, as you want to have enough to accompany each portion). Adjust seasoning with salt and pepper to taste.

Serve the shoulder pieces topped with a generous amount of sauce.

Vegetable "Meat Loaf" with Green Beans and Pecorino

Polpettone di Fagiolini

Along with her legendary *verdure ripiene*, Angiolina, the owner of my aunt and uncle's old rental house in Bonassola, made a very respectable Ligurian *polpettone*, which she would bring to us at unexpected times during our stays at the house. You can serve this "meat loaf" warm or at room temperature. In either case, it's far better after a few hours, or even the next day. I often prepare it as a main course at lunchtime and eat it with a light salad, but you can opt to serve it as a side dish or, if you cut it into bite-size pieces, as an hors d'oeuvre.

SERVES 6 TO 8

1½ pounds green (string) beans

2 ounces dried porcini mushrooms (about 2 cups)

3 ounces day-old white bread, crusts removed, cut into 1-inch dice (about 3 cups)

5 ½ tablespoons extra-virgin olive oil

1 small onion, finely chopped (about 1 cup)

1 medium clove garlic, finely chopped

2 teaspoons salt

1 tablespoon finely chopped marjoram

1 tablespoon finely chopped thyme

1 tablespoon finely chopped basil

2 cups finely grated aged pecorino toscano or Parmigiano-Reggiano

Freshly ground black pepper

3 large eggs

½ cup homemade bread crumbs (see recipe page 211)

Bring a large pot of water to a boil and add the green beans. Cook them for about 8 minutes or until tender when pierced with a fork, but still al dente. Drain and shock them under cold running water or in a bowl of ice water (in this case, drain them again). Chop them finely as if you were chopping onions (you should end up with pieces that are no larger than ¼ inch).

Meanwhile, soak the dried porcini in 1 cup of warm water for 30 minutes. Drain them, squeeze out the excess water, and chop them finely. Reserve ⅔ cup of the liquid (strain it through a fine-mesh sieve, first) and soak the bread in it for about 5 minutes. Squeeze out the excess liquid from the bread and set the bread aside.

Heat 4 tablespoons of the olive oil in a 10-inch skillet over medium-high heat. When the oil is hot and shimmering, add the onions and garlic and cook, stirring frequently, for about 5 minutes, or until the onions are soft and translucent. Add the green beans and mushrooms to the pan, ½ teaspoon salt, and cook until all the water from the mushrooms is absorbed, about 3 more minutes. Add the fresh herbs and cook, stirring frequently, for 1 or 2 more minutes. Remove from the heat and let cool.

Preheat the oven to 400°F.

Transfer the cooled green bean mixture to a large bowl and add the pecorino, the squeezed-out bread, the remaining salt, and pepper. Taste for seasoning and adjust if necessary, then add the eggs, mixing well with a wooden spoon.

Oil a 9 × 13-inch baking pan with 1 tablespoon of olive oil, sprinkle half the bread crumbs on the bottom, and pour in the "meat loaf" mixture. Spread it evenly in the pan and level the top with the back of a spoon or an offset spatula. In a small bowl, mix the other half of the bread crumbs with the remaining ½ tablespoon of olive oil, sprinkle them over the loaf and pop it into the oven. Cook for 30 to 35 minutes, or until golden and slightly browned on the top. I like to drizzle a little more olive oil on top before putting it in the oven. Serve warm or at room temperature.

Roasted Zucchini Flowers with a Zesty Green Bean Stuffing

Fiori di Zucca Ripieni

When I first moved to the United States, I longed for zucchini blossoms (whether deep-fried, as on page 40, or stuffed and roasted), but they weren't easy to find. For me, zucchini flowers, with their bright orange color like the glow of the sun, have always been synonymous with summer. In Bonassola we ate them often, especially in early summer when the *terreno* churns out zucchini by the ton. You can find zucchini blossoms in summertime at farmers' markets and specialty stores. Keep in mind that they're very delicate and need to be treated with care. To clean them, cut off the green portions and remove the pistil inside. These stuffed zucchini blossoms are perfect as a side dish or as an appetizer.

SERVES 4

1 small zucchini (about 2 ounces)

2 ounces green beans (about 6)

1 ounce day-old white bread, crusts removed, cut into 1-inch dice (a scant 1 cup)

2 tablespoons whole milk

2 ounces mortadella (about 2 thin slices)

1 large clove garlic

1 cup finely grated Parmigiano-Reggiano

6 large basil leaves

2 sprigs marjoram, leaves only

Salt

Freshly ground black pepper

1 large egg

12 large zucchini blossoms

1 tablespoon extra-virgin olive oil

Preheat the oven to 450°F.

Bring a large pot of water to a boil and add the zucchini and green beans. Cook them both for about 10 minutes, or until fork tender. Drain and shock them under cold running water or in a bowl of ice water. Drain them again.

Meanwhile, soak the bread in the milk for about 5 minutes. Squeeze out the excess liquid and set the bread aside.

Place the zucchini and green beans in the bowl of a food processor, add the mortadella, garlic, Parmigiano, squeezed-out bread, basil, and marjoram leaves, and pulse seven or eight times until you obtain a smooth paste. Season to taste with salt and pepper. Add the egg and pulse a few more times.

Carefully stuff the zucchini blossoms with the filling. Arrange them in a 9 × 13-inch baking dish, sprinkle with salt, and drizzle 1 tablespoon of olive oil over them. Roast in the oven for about 15 minutes and serve immediately.

Potato Salad with Pancetta, Pickled Onions, and Mustard

Insalata di Patate alla Tedesca

I was flipping through a book of traditional Ligurian recipes when I stumbled on a peculiar potato salad called *alla tedesca*, as in "German style." Intrigued by the name, I tried it. It's quite tasty—a great alternative to regular old potato salad. My guess is that it's one of the least traditional recipes in that book—proof perhaps of the influence decades of German tourism have had on the region's cuisine. Instead of pancetta, you can use bacon, which will give it a smokier flavor. I sometimes like using fingerling potatoes instead of Yukon golds or red potatoes, just for a change.

SERVES 4

2 pounds Yukon gold or red potatoes, or a combination

⅓ cup plus 4 tablespoons extra-virgin olive oil

Salt

Freshly ground black pepper

1 cup plus 1 teaspoon red wine vinegar

½ cup granulated sugar

1 medium red onion, thinly sliced to create rings

1 cup ¼-inch dice pancetta or bacon

2 tablespoons finely chopped chives

1½ tablespoons Dijon mustard

Preheat the oven to 450°F.

Scrub the potato skins well under running water. Cut the potatoes into 1-inch dice, leaving the skins on. Toss them with 4 tablespoons of the olive oil, 1 teaspoon of salt, and a generous grind of pepper, and bake for about 30 minutes, or until they're fork tender and slightly crispy on the outside.

Meanwhile, prepare the remaining ingredients for the salad: Bring 1 cup of the vinegar and the sugar to a boil in a small saucepan. Add the onions, bring the liquid back to a boil, reduce to a simmer, and cook the onions for about 5 minutes. Turn off the heat and let the onions and liquid cool completely. Reserve the pickled onions in the liquid.

Cook the pancetta in an 8-inch skillet over medium-high heat for about 10 minutes. Strain and discard the rendered fat. Set the cooked pancetta aside.

Drain the pickled onions. In a large bowl, mix the baked potatoes with the drained onions, pancetta, and chives. In a smaller bowl, whisk the mustard with the remaining 1 teaspoon of vinegar and gently mix in the remaining ⅓ cup olive oil (don't whisk too vigorously, as you don't want to have a thick, emulsified dressing). Add the dressing to the potatoes, adjust the seasoning to taste with salt and pepper, and serve warm or at room temperature.

Heirloom Tomato Salad with Fruity Olive Oil and Basil

Insalata di Pomodori alla Moda di Bonassola

When it comes to this particular salad, I become very demanding. It relies so heavily on the perfection of the ingredients that if you're going to make it with supermarket tomatoes and run-of-the-mill olive oil, I can only say: *save yourself the trouble.* You'll be disappointed and wonder what all the fuss is about. To get worthwhile results you have to hunt down the ripest, juiciest tomatoes available and lay your hands on an excellent, fruity olive oil. Great tomatoes are abundant at the farmers' market from the middle of August through September. If you have a hard time finding heirloom tomatoes, replace them with good beefsteak tomatoes. I like heirloom tomatoes in part for their esthetic appeal: they come in a variety of colors and make the salad quite pretty. But, to be honest, in Liguria we don't have the heirloom varieties you can find in America, so farmstand beefsteaks are just fine.

SERVES 4

2 large ripe heirloom or farmstand beefsteak tomatoes

4 large basil leaves

¼ to ½ cup high-quality extra-virgin olive oil

Salt

Freshly ground black pepper

Freshly baked bread (baguette or ciabatta-style)

Cut the tomatoes into 1-inch wedges and, if too big, cut each wedge in half crosswise. You want them to be bite-size.

Cut the basil in thin strips, about ¼ inch thick.

Place the tomatoes in a large bowl, season to taste with salt and pepper, and drizzle the olive oil over them. Add the basil and toss well.

Let the ingredients marinate for 20 or 30 minutes before serving. This way, the tomatoes will give off some of their juice that, blended with the olive oil, creates pure paradise on a plate!

Serve with as many slices of bread as you want and encourage your guests to scoop up the juices with the bread.

Endive Salad with Tuna, Walnuts, and Lemon Zest

Insalata alle Noci con Indivia

This is a refreshing, brightly flavored salad that's perfect for any season when you need something sprightly to balance a heavier dish. If you can, buy celery with its leaves still attached to the stems. If you can't find it, replace the celery leaves with parsley.

SERVES 4

¾ cup shelled walnuts

3 medium-size endives, leaves separated and washed

¼ cup good extra-virgin olive oil

1 tablespoon freshly squeezed lemon juice (about ½ lemon)

1 large celery stalk, thinly sliced

1 cup celery or parsley leaves

2 oil-packed anchovies, drained and cut into ½-inch pieces

3 ounces olive oil-packed tuna, drained (about ½ cup)

¼ red onion, thinly sliced

¼ teaspoon finely grated lemon zest

Salt

Freshly ground black pepper

A very small pinch of cayenne pepper

Heat a small skillet over medium-high heat and toast the walnuts for about 5 minutes, giving the pan a few good jolts to turn the walnuts around. Remove the pan from the heat when they start browning and become fragrant, transfer to a plate, and break them in smaller pieces with your hands.

Cut the endive leaves crosswise into ¼-inch strips and reserve.

In a small bowl, whisk together the olive oil with the lemon juice, until they form a light emulsion—that is, until the oil becomes a little thicker and cloudy.

Place the endive, celery, celery leaves, anchovies, tuna, onion, and walnuts in a large bowl. Add the lemon dressing and lemon zest, and toss well. Season to taste with salt, pepper, and cayenne, and serve immediately.

Mesclun Salad with Fresh Figs and Lemon-Walnut Dressing

Insalata alle Noci con Fichi

I eat this salad almost all year round. In the winter I make it with pears or apples; in summer I use fresh ripe figs. A note on mesclun: Many grocery stores sell mesclun mixes, either prewashed and packaged, or loose. When buying mesclun, make sure the leaves are crisp and healthy, not limp and mushy. If wilted is all you find, opt for a different type of lettuce that looks healthier. Anything will do with this salad. I like butter lettuce. Better yet, get your greens at the local farmers' market; you'll be surprised by the difference in texture and taste.

SERVES 4

1 cup shelled walnuts

½ cup good extra-virgin olive oil

1½ tablespoons freshly squeezed lemon juice

1 teaspoon apple cider vinegar

1 teaspoon honey

½ to ⅔ pound mesclun greens, washed

¼ small red onion, thinly sliced

1 large celery stalk, thinly sliced

Salt

Freshly ground black pepper

4 ripe figs, quartered, or 1 thinly sliced firm-ripe pear or apple

Heat a small skillet over medium-high heat and toast the walnuts for about 5 minutes, giving the pan a few good jolts to turn the walnuts around. Remove the pan from the heat when they start browning and become fragrant, transfer to a plate and let them cool.

Place about one-third of the walnuts in the bowl of a food processor and process to a pastelike consistency, about 2 minutes (or, if you like, you can do this with a mortar and pestle). With your hands, break the remaining nuts into smaller pieces.

In a small bowl, whisk together the olive oil with the lemon juice , apple cider vinegar, and honey until they form a light emulsion—that is, until the oil becomes a little thicker and cloudy. Stir in the walnut paste.

Place the mesclun, onion, celery, and the walnut pieces in a large bowl. Toss with the dressing, season to taste with salt and pepper, and add the fruit just before serving.

Baby Zucchini Salad with Mint and Basil

Insalata di Zucchini Piccoli con Menta e Basilico

This is a lovely accompaniment for meat and fish dishes. My aunt Silvana makes a similar salad using raw baby zucchini. I've found that the zucchini I buy at the market (as opposed to the ones just picked from the *terreno*) are sometimes too bitter to be eaten completely raw, so I blanch them just a bit to take the edge off. If you can find tender, sweet baby zucchini, by all means use them raw.

SERVES 4

20 baby zucchini (about 1½ pounds)

¼ cup extra-virgin olive oil

½ tablespoon freshly squeezed
lemon juice

½ very small red onion, thinly sliced

8 large mint leaves,
cut into ⅛-inch strips

6 large basil leaves,
cut into ⅛-inch strips

½ teaspoon finely grated lemon zest

Salt

Freshly ground black pepper

With a vegetable peeler, cut the zucchini into ⅛-inch-thick ribbons lengthwise.

Bring a pot of water to a boil, add the zucchini, and cook them for about 20 seconds. Drain, and shock them under cold running water or in a bowl of ice water. Drain them again.

In a small bowl, whisk together the olive oil with the lemon juice, until they form a light emulsion—that is, until the oil becomes a little thicker and cloudy.

Put the zucchini in a large bowl and add the onion, mint, basil, and lemon zest. Toss with the dressing and season to taste with salt and pepper. Let the salad marinate for 30 minutes before serving, and serve with an extra sprinkle of pepper.

Simple Roasted Potatoes with Olive Oil, Rosemary, and Thyme

Patatine Arrosto con Rosmarino e Timo

The *terreno* in Bonassola yields abundant potatoes and this is one of our favorite ways to cook them. It's extremely easy and very tasty. Here, I like to buy baby or new potatoes in a variety of colors: some yellow, some red, even purple ones. But if you can't find them, I recommend regular Yukon golds. You can use this same technique to roast any other kinds of vegetables, such as squash or carrots or other root vegetables (although you'll have to adjust the cooking time in each case).

SERVES 4

1½ pounds baby potatoes
or Yukon golds

1 tablespoon finely chopped thyme

1 tablespoon finely chopped rosemary

¼ cup extra-virgin olive oil,
plus more for the pan

Salt

Freshly ground black pepper

Preheat the oven to 450°F.

Cut the baby potatoes in half or quarter them, depending on their size. If using Yukon golds, cut into 1-inch pieces.

In a large bowl, toss the potatoes with the herbs and ¼ cup olive oil and season generously with salt and pepper. Lightly oil a 17 × 13-inch baking pan, arrange the potatoes in a single layer in the pan, and bake for about 40 minutes, or until the potatoes are tender inside and crispy outside. Serve immediately.

Ligurian Bread Salad with Tomatoes, Tuna, and Capers

Capponadda Non Tradizionale

This recipe is a little invention of mine that borrows from the authentic Ligurian *capponadda* with a dash of Tuscan panzanella, a delicious bread salad. Tuscany is right next to Liguria and I love *panzanella* so much, it seemed worth the short reach. Another reason I fidgeted with authentic *capponadda* is that many of the ingredients required to make it are extremely difficult, if not impossible, to find in the United States. I don't know of any market that sells *mosciame di tonno* (dried tuna slices), for example; or traditional *gallette del marinaio*—the round, dry bread loaves Ligurian fishermen used to take with them on extended journeys at sea. In fact, these foods are even hard to find in Liguria nowadays. Besides, the original *capponadda*—and, even more so, its close relative *cappon magro*—is a complicated layered salad in which each ingredient forms a different layer, topped by thin slices of *mosciame*. My version is much less fussy and perfect for a weeknight meal. The recipe works best with bread that's quite hard. If your bread is on the soft side, soak it for a shorter amount of time.

SERVES 4

½ cup red wine vinegar

½ cup water

4 ounces day-old white bread, crusts removed, cut into 1-inch dice (about 4 cups)

½ cup black olives, preferably gaeta, picholine, or niçoise

2 tablespoons salted capers, rinsed

3 olive oil-packed anchovies, drained and coarsely chopped

1 cup good-quality olive oil–packed tuna, drained

Combine the water and vinegar and soak the bread in the mixture for 5 minutes. Squeeze out the liquid and transfer the bread to a large bowl.

Add the remaining ingredients to the bowl, season to taste with salt and pepper, and toss well. Make sure to break up any large chunks of tuna while mixing. If the salad appears dry, add a little more olive oil. Let the salad rest for 30 minutes before serving.

CONTINUED

Mosciame
DI TONNO

Mosciame di tonno is thinly sliced, salt-cured, and air-dried tuna. In the old days, this was the most popular way to preserve tuna in the southern Mediterranean. The method probably originated with the Moors, who called it *musama*. They brought it to the coast of Spain, during their long occupation of the region, where it's still enjoyed as *mojama*. From there it spread across the coastline all the way to Liguria. Today it's a rarity that's hard to track down even in Italy. But lately it's been staging a bit of a comeback, making increasingly frequent appearances on the antipasti menus of regional restaurants. I enjoyed it not so long ago during a dinner in Camogli with a drizzle of good olive oil and a squeeze of lemon juice—just as you would serve bresaola. In fact, it reminds me of bresaola quite a bit. Its chewiness and considerable saltiness were pleasantly mitigated by the olive oil and lemon. Ligurians use it in salads, such as the traditional *capponadda*, but it's also great torn into pieces and sprinkled on pasta in lieu of *bottarga* (salt-cured tuna or gray mullet roe).

Ligurian Bread Salad with Tomatoes, Tuna, and Capers

CONTINUED

2 ripe tomatoes, cut into ½-inch slices

½ medium onion, finely chopped (about 1 cup)

8 leaves basil, coarsely chopped

⅔ cup good extra-virgin olive oil

Salt

Freshly ground pepper

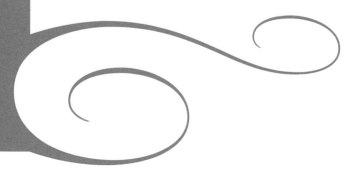

Ligurian Ratatouille with Black Olives and Toasted Pine Nuts

Ratatuia

This is the Ligurian cousin of the popular southern French dish. You'll find it uses a greater variety of vegetables than French ratatouille with a sprinkle of the ubiquitous toasted pine nuts. You can choose to serve it warm or at room temperature, but I find it tastes better if it sits a few hours before you re-heat it and serve.

SERVES 4

3 ounces green beans, cut into 1-inch pieces (about ¾ cups)

3 medium-size yellow, red, and/or orange bell peppers

⅓ cup plus 3 tablespoons good extra-virgin olive oil

2 small zucchini, cut into ½-inch dice (about 1⅓ cup)

1 small yellow squash, cut into ½-inch dice (about ⅔ cup)

Salt

1 small onion, finely chopped (about 1 tightly packed cup)

1 large clove garlic, finely chopped (about 1½ teaspoons)

1 medium eggplant or 3 baby eggplants, cut into ½-inch dice (about 2 cups)

1 large carrot, cut into ⅛ × 1-inch strips

3 plum tomatoes, peeled, seeded, and coarsely chopped

Preheat the oven to 450°F.

Bring a large pot of water to a boil and add the green beans. Cook them for about 5 minutes (they should be tender but still quite al dente). Drain, and shock them under cold running water or in a bowl of ice water. Drain them again.

Place the peppers on a baking sheet lined with an aluminum foil and roast for 30 to 40 minutes, or until soft and slightly charred on the outside. Place them in a bowl, cover it with plastic wrap, let rest for about 10 minutes, then remove the skins. Cut the peppers into ½-inch-wide strips.

In a 10-inch skillet, heat 1 tablespoon of the olive oil over medium-high heat. When the oil is hot, add the zucchini, yellow squash, and a pinch of salt, and cook, stirring frequently, for 5 to 7 minutes, or until the vegetables are soft and slightly browned. Set aside.

In a 12-inch skillet, heat ⅓ cup of the olive oil over medium-high heat. When the oil is hot, add the onion and garlic, and cook for 3 to 4 minutes, stirring frequently (be careful not to burn the garlic). Add the eggplant, carrots, and a small pinch of salt, and cook for about 5 more minutes. Add the tomatoes, olives, four of the basil leaves, and another small pinch of salt, and cook for another 10 to 15 minutes,

CONTINUED

CONTINUED

Ligurian Ratatouille with Black Olives and Toasted Pine Nuts

CONTINUED

½ cup pitted black olives, preferably a mixture of gaeta, niçoise, and oil-cured

8 basil leaves, torn roughly by hand

Freshly ground black pepper

1 tablespoon toasted pine nuts

stirring frequently and adding a few tablespoons of warm water if the ingredients in the pan seem to be too dry (but allow the veggies to brown a little and stick to the pan before adding water). By now the vegetables in the pan should be fairly tender.

Add the sautéed zucchini and squash, the roasted peppers, the blanched green beans, and the remaining basil leaves to the pan and cook for 3 to 5 minutes. Adjust the seasoning with salt, add a few generous grinds of pepper, the pine nuts, and finish with the remaining 2 tablespoons of olive oil. Don't hesitate to add more olive oil if the *ratatuia* looks dry.

Angiolina's Roasted Summer Vegetables Stuffed with Mortadella, Parmigiano, and Marojoram

Verdure Ripiene di Angiolina

Angiolina's *verdure ripiene* are a legend in Bonassola. People will go out of their way to get her to make a special batch for them. And all the small stores in town that sell focaccia, savory pies, and other prepared foods strive to imitate her recipe—to no avail. When I asked her what her secret was, she said, "It's the mortadella, no one used it in the old days because it wasn't available." I doubt that's the only thing (I suspect years and years of making *verdure ripiene* have something to do with it, too), but mortadella certainly adds a winningly flavorful note.

SERVES 4

2 small zucchini

2 small yellow squash

2 very small Italian eggplants

2 ounces day-old white bread, crusts removed, cut into 1-inch dice (about 2 cups)

½ cup whole milk

¼ pound mortadella (4 or 5 thin slices)

1 medium clove garlic

½ pound ground veal

1 cup finely grated Parmigiano-Reggiano

1 teaspoon finely chopped marjoram

1 tablespoon finely chopped basil

¼ teaspoon freshly ground nutmeg

1 teaspoon salt, plus more for seasoning

Preheat the oven to 450°F.

Bring a large pot of water to a boil. Add the whole zucchini and yellow squashes, and cook for 3 minutes. Drain and shock them under cold water running water or in a bowl of ice water. Drain them again. Cut the zucchini and yellow squash in half lengthwise and remove the seedy core with a melon baller or spoon, reserving half of the scooped-out pulp.

Line a baking sheet with aluminum foil. Cut the eggplants in half lengthwise and roast them for 15 minutes. They should be a little soft and watery in the center, but not thoroughly cooked. Scoop the pulp, leaving a good ½-inch border of pulp in the shell. Reserve the scooped-out pulp.

In a medium-size bowl, soak the bread in the milk for 15 minutes. Squeeze the milk out of the bread.

Place the mortadella, the squeezed-out bread, garlic, and reserved zucchini and eggplant pulp in the bowl of a food processor and pulse a few times until finely ground. Transfer to a large bowl and add the ground veal, Parmigiano, marjoram,

CONTINUED

CONTINUED

Angiolina's Roasted Summer Vegetables Stuffed with Mortadella, Parmigiano, and Marojoram

CONTINUED

Freshly ground black pepper

4 tablespoons homemade (see recipe page 210) or low-sodium canned chicken broth or water

2 tablespoons extra-virgin olive oil

basil, nutmeg, 1 teaspoon salt, and a few grinds of pepper. Mix well to incorporate all the ingredients, adding 4 tablespoons of broth or water.

Place the halved vegetables on a rimmed baking sheet lined with foil, season the open faces lightly with salt, and scoop a generous amount of the filling into each. Drizzle the olive oil on top of the stuffed vegetables and bake for 35 to 45 minutes, until the tops are nicely browned. Let the vegetables cool and serve at room temperature. Or cover and refrigerate them before reheating and serving warm.

Sautéed Mushrooms with Fresh Herbs and Pecorino

Ovoli in Umido

These mushrooms make a tasty side dish for meat or chicken, but I also like to serve them on warm crostini for a scrumptious appetizer.

SERVES 4

4 tablespoons extra-virgin olive oil

1 tablespoon unsalted butter

⅔ large onion, finely chopped (about ½ cup)

½ pound fresh mushrooms (cremini, shiitake, porcini, chanterelles, etc.), thinly sliced

Salt

½ cup dry white wine

1 teaspoon finely chopped marjoram

1 tablespoon finely chopped parsley

1 teaspoon finely chopped thyme

1 tablespoon finely chopped garlic (about 3 medium cloves)

Freshly ground black pepper

1 cup finely grated pecorino, preferably young toscano or sardo

In a 12-inch skillet, heat the olive oil and butter over medium-high heat. When the butter stops bubbling, add the onions. Cook them for 10 minutes, stirring frequently, or until soft and slightly golden.

Add the mushrooms and a pinch of salt, and cook, stirring frequently, for another 8 to 10 minutes, or until the mushrooms are soft and slightly browned. It's okay if a few bits stick to the pan, but if you notice any burning, lower the heat and add a few teaspoons of water.

Add the wine to the pan, scraping any browned bits. When the wine is almost entirely evaporated, add the marjoram, parsley, thyme, and garlic. Cook for 2 or 3 minutes, stirring frequently, adjust the seasoning to taste with salt and pepper, and add the pecorino. Give the content of the pan a nice stir and serve immediately.

MONTARETTO

Silvana and Franco's new house in Bonassola—the one I visit every year now—is well worth the ten-year wait. It's elegant and comfortable. A picture-perfect, pastel pink with bright green shutters surrounded by a surprisingly disciplined lawn (surprising if you consider Franco's constant struggles with the lawn mower), gushing fuchsia bougainvillea, and those beautifully knotty olive trees. But the house wouldn't have the same kind of appeal to me if it weren't for a spectacular roofed terrace, nearly equal in size to my New York City apartment, with a far-reaching view all the way to the Mediterranean. When I'm at the house, that terrace is almost certainly where you'll find me—if I'm not in the kitchen, of course.

The house's interior is decorated with a modern sensibility that allows for a few grand antiques to stand out in an altogether stripped-to-the-bare-bones design. The floors are paved with glazed ceramic tiles the color of clay. They hint at the traditional *cotto* of many Italian country villas, but their finish is anything but rustic. The strikingly white walls parade a grid of sea-themed paintings and other random objects, from a complex barometer to a weathered *lampara*. Quite a change from the plastic-wrapped chairs and mismatched faux Chippendale of the old rental.

The kitchen falls directly off the roomy, open living room, which doubles as a dining room in the winter months. (My family considers anyone who wants to eat inside in the summertime deeply disturbed.) With its clean-cut salmon-colored cabinets and white countertops, the kitchen is filled with most of the convenient appliances of modern kitchens: a dishwasher, a reliable oven, and no gas tanks to haul back and forth. A full-size French window opens over the back garden, facing the first of the *terreno*'s ascending *fasce*. Mingled with colorful wild flowers are shrubs of fresh rosemary, thyme, and myrtle, long spears of wild fennel, borage flowers with hairy leaves, and a flourishing lavender bush. When we cook, it's easy to run outside and snap off a rosemary sprig or a handful of wild fennel to add to whatever is bubbling on the stove. I remember the year I'd just come back from a trip to Provence with a mild obsession for lavender. As I was experimenting with the aromatic flowers in dozens of dishes (you'll find at least one of them, the lavender *panna cotta*, in this book), I dashed from kitchen to garden more times than I care to remember to grab sprig after sprig. Most of the dishes I tried were forgettable, but no one forgot that by the end of the day there wasn't a single flower left on the lavender bush.

It's also worth mentioning that in Silvana and Franco's new house I had a real bedroom. In the rental house, I used to sleep in a tiny room on the second floor with an aggressively sloping ceiling beneath the eave of the roof. Clearly, it had been built as an afterthought. It had a small, square window the size of a large coffee-table book with a white curtain no bigger than a handkerchief hanging loosely from its top. The only furniture in the room was a large bed with no headboard and an old chest of drawers that appeared to have been purchased at a yard sale (which don't, in fact, exist in Italy). I didn't mind the room—in fact, I liked how a cool breeze blew directly from the sea through the small window—but I dreaded having to navigate across my uncle's and aunt's master bedroom to get in. This got especially troublesome as I grew older and began to come home later at night, when everyone was already asleep, tiptoeing across the pitch dark room without waking them up, trying to ignore the terrifying sounds my uncle made when he was asleep.

It was on one of the first extended stays in the new house that I first encountered Montaretto. I'd heard about Montaretto a million times, but for all I knew it might have been the new gardener or some exotic fish. It was neither. Montaretto was a tiny hamlet of Bonassola, high up the hill in the middle of nowhere. Everything good seemed to come from Montaretto: good wild boar, good mushrooms, even good wine. And it just so happened that if you kept trekking up the road behind our house toward the hills, you got there—sooner or later. One day, Silvana, my mother, and I decided to attempt the expedition; we would have dinner in Montaretto's one and only restaurant. Armed with good walking shoes and a bottle of water, but still impeccably dressed—we were going to dinner after all, and no decent Italian woman will be caught badly dressed at a dinner table—we began the climb.

The deeper we sunk into the forest, the stronger the scents became, and the dissonant noises of crickets, cicadas, and birds grew almost deafening. The vegetation was thick and luxuriant. A small creek accompanied us part of the way. We passed an old mill that had been turned into a residence but still proudly boasted its bulky old wheel. The dimming light of dusk infused the landscape with a fablelike quality making it seem as if, for a moment, we had crossed the threshold of a different world. The feeling persisted when we arrived in Montaretto. It was as if I'd been transported back to an undefined past; it might have been the postwar years, or even earlier. One thing was certain: Montaretto was not part of this world. Perched at the very top of the high hill that divides Bonassola from Framura, the village gave way to dizzying views of the sea below. It was like floating on a hang glider except we weren't airborne—we were in somebody's backyard. Chickens scurried at our feet as free-range as they get, the clucking under-echoed screams and whistles of kids playing soccer in the nearby *piazzetta*.

We were joined by Franco and my father, who had comfortably driven themselves up the road on the other side of the hill. Together, we headed to the only "restaurant" in town (in fact, a comfortable extension of the local sports bar), a modest room brimming with craggy local folk and equally rugged visitors from nearby towns. We were overdressed.

The place had neither state-of-the-art interior design nor a breathtaking view—in fact, it had no view at all, unless you count its angle on the local communist party hangout across the street. The room was plain, furnished with big square tables and fifties-style plastic chairs. But the food was honest and delicious. Of course, there was no sign of a menu. Our waitress, a tough grandmotherly type (probably *la padrona*, the owner), delivered the carte du jour by voice. As always, Franco's savoir faire ensured we were given extra-special attention. We started off with a big plate of *ostriche ripiene*, stuffed oysters, which gave off an intense aroma of garlic and herbs, and tasted as if the sea and the earth had collided right in that dish. After the *ostriche* came a generous tasting of the restaurant's homemade ravioli. We got soft and pillowy *pansotti di zucca al burro e salvia*, squash ravioli in a butter and sage sauce, as well as rich *raviolini cu tuccu*, meat-filled ravioli with Liguria's own version of *ragù*. This dish begins with a slow roast of veal. When the meat becomes tender, part of it is shredded for the sauce and the rest is ground for the filling. The sauce is then simmered for hours with tomatoes and herbs. The result is astonishingly rich and aromatic.

We followed the excellent ravioli sampler with a gargantuan family-style seafood *fritto misto* the way they do it here. The fish—shrimp, scampi, calamari, mussels, anchovies, and other small Mediterranean white fish—is dredged lightly in flour before being thrown into hot olive oil. The result is a rather light *fritto* that's tasty and far more digestible than your average fish and chips. Syrupy baked peaches accompanied by the inevitable glass of Sciaccetrà (which probably cost more than everything else together) concluded a dinner that was inspiring precisely because it was so straightforward and unassuming—just like being with family.

WHITE LANDS

If access were the only parameter for deciding whether a trip to Paolo Rondelli's Terre Bianche is worth your while, I'd say go somewhere else—especially if you're an insecure driver. The last stretch of road to this remote hilltop country house turned eno-gastronomic inn can be quite scary: it's nothing more than a narrow tongue of asphalt (paved, at least), barely wide enough to fit one car in one direction, only inches away from a terrifyingly steep cliff with the miniaturized town of Dolceaqua lurking in plain sight several hundreds of feet below. Every time I drove that road, I prayed a car wouldn't approach from the opposite direction. *What would I do?* Back up for half a mile along the precarious strip of asphalt, in the dark perhaps? It never happened. And each time I got to the end of it and took a glimpse at the renovated stone *casolare* where our room was, I told myself it was worth it.

Terre Bianche, which means "white lands," is one of those working farms—so popular now in Italy—that take in a handful of guests, feed them great homemade cooking, (mostly from organic crops on the premises), and give poor, cement-trapped city folk the illusion that they're living the country life—at least for a few idyllic days. My husband and I visited Terre Bianche in the early summer as we explored the "other" Liguria: the infamous *ponente*—the one my uncle likes to bash.

The large window of our room on the *casolare*'s top floor opened over the entire Nervia Valley with its soaring hills—mountains, almost—every yard of which had been planted with orchards and vineyards. Close to the border with France, this area is where most of Liguria's best wine is produced, from the light and spicy Rossese di Dolceacqua to a variety of white Vermentinos and Pigatos. The *casolare*, an old stone country house that had been modernized and divided by Paolo and his family into a handful of rooms with a communal space on the ground floor, is nestled in the midst of these gorgeous vineyards. In the morning you hear the buzzing of *Ape* vehicles carting *contadini* to work the fields. After breakfast you can see them, handkerchief on their heads, pulling weeds or pruning the young vine trees. All day and night the soothing sounds of crickets and frogs trickle over the hill. They can be overwhelming at times, but soon enough you find you've grown used to it and they even become lulling and peaceful. Sirens and car horns and garbage truck engines are so normal in my everyday life they've become my white noise, and I have to reacquaint myself with nature when I go to the country.

Paolo grows more than vines on his property. He cultivates a kind of olive native to this area and extracts from it a wonderful, light olive oil. And he grows an impressive variety of organic fruits and vegetables. Paolo is passionate about the land. He has great respect and dedication for the *territorio* and for the quality of the products from his fields, be they wine, olive oil, jams, or simply fresh produce. He's a warm, charismatic, infinitely hospitable guy whose enthusiasm for what he does is heartwarming and infectious.

Paolo makes olive oil exclusively from the government-protected local variety of Taggiasca olives, which he picks when they're halfway between green and purple to ensure a balance of piquancy and fruitiness. He extracts the oil only by mechanical means, without chemicals or heat that can destroy olive oil's healthiest properties. The same is true of his grapes. He picks them when the sugar content is just right, which means that some years he may be leaving the grapes on the vine for quite a long time, subjecting them to the risks of frost and bad weather. "I want to make a good glass of wine," he says—and indeed he does. His Rossese is among the best we tasted. And his production is so limited that he often runs out, as happened with his French *barrique*-aged Rossese *riserva* we were intrigued by.

For breakfast one morning, I sat with my husband, Brad, at the long, rustic communal table on the ground floor of the *casolare*, next to the big *cucina* where Paolo's mother-in-law prepares breakfast and where chef Francesco, a family friend, creates spectacular homemade dinners out of homegrown ingredients. Our breakfast was one of the healthiest and most delicious I've had in years. Paolo offered us homemade cherry, fig, and lemon jams to spread on rustic artisanal bread. We ate incredible apricots, huge and plump with a rich, light orange hue turned darker in spots. These were the archetypal apricots, what apricots should taste like every time: sweet, dripping juice, free from the faintest hint of mealiness so common in today's disappointing supermarket varieties. Paolo's mother-in-law came in with a basket of fleshy, dark crimson cherries. "*Appena raccolte,*" she said triumphantly: *just picked*. Needless to say, they were oozing with deep cherry flavor. We quickly scoffed every last one in the basket. Paolo invited us to stay for dinner that night. It would be out in the garden among the vineyards with a view of the distant valley. Francesco was going to cook a special meal for us and a few other guests.

How could we refuse?

Paolo's other guests, we discovered as we sat at the outdoor table in the early evening, were two middle-aged couples from Sweden and two women—sisters, perhaps—accompanying an elderly lady. The Swedes were fluent in English, but the ladies only spoke Italian. Strategically, Paolo placed me in the middle so that I could translate bits of dialogue and pass conversation from one end of the table to the other. After a few awkward moments—and a couple of glasses of Vermentino—the ice was broken, and a good time was had by all.

The meal kicked off with a homemade frittata *al preboggion*, the ubiquitous Ligurian herb medley, made with fresh eggs from the farm. By way of demonstration, Paolo dashed into the kitchen and returned proudly waving a perfect oval specimen from the hen house. He cracked it into a bowl to show off the large, almost red yolk inside. It's no wonder we Italians call the yolk *rosso d'uovo* (red of the egg). It's what "real" eggs must have looked like everywhere, before industrial agriculture turned hens into egg-laying machines complete with egg-collecting conveyor belts. The showstopper of the evening, though, was chef Franceso's rabbit braised in Rossese wine with Taggiasca olives, which made its way into this book (page 152). The tender meat had a rich flavor, only slightly gamey, balanced by the vaguely bitter tanginess and slight acidity of the olives and simmered wine. It was so tasty that I sat down with Francesco after dinner to transcribe the recipe. He warned me, though: "I can give you the recipe, but if you don't have these raw materials, it won't be the same." He's right, of course.

Dinner came to a glorious end—candles were flickering in the breeze by now and wine was flowing freely—with a delightfully simple dessert, which also found its way to these pages (page 202). The sweet treat was vanilla ice cream "drowned" in Rossese-poached cherries, the same kind we'd eaten that very morning. It was the perfect finale for a rustic meal elevated to a three-star dining experience by genuine, responsibly grown, first-rate ingredients.

SWEET ENDINGS

Sweet Bread with Fennel Seeds, Dried Cherries, Pistachios, and Pine Nuts

Pandolce Genovese

Pandolce genovese is a time-honored Ligurian Christmas cake that traditional bakeries often make year-round. So when we go to Levanto to the old bakery in the *carrugi*, we always pick up a little piece. I like to use dried cherries, but if you prefer other dried fruit, or can't find dried cherries, use currants, raisins, or even cranberries instead. Orange blossom water is something you'll find in baking supply stores. If you can't find it, use orange extract—it's different but it works. Be warned: this is a rustic dessert; its texture is on the dry side and it screams for a sauce, a scoop of ice cream, or a dab of whipped cream.

SERVES 8 TO 10

NOTE
THE DOUGH NEEDS TO RISE FOR AT
LEAST 6 HOURS BEFORE IT'S BAKED.

½ cup dried cherries

¼ cup shelled pistachios

3½ cups unbleached all-purpose flour

¾ cup granulated sugar

1 (¼ ounce) package active-dry yeast

½ cup warm water or whole milk

¼ cups Marsala wine

½ teaspoon orange blossom water or orange extract

8 tablespoons (1 stick) unsalted butter, at room temperature, cut into 1-tablespoon chunks, plus more for buttering bowl and pan

1 large egg, at room temperature

1 tablespoon fennel seeds

Soak the cherries in warm water for 30 minutes. Strain and pat dry.

Bring a small saucepan of water to a boil. Add the pistachios and blanch them for 5 minutes. Strain and remove the peels by rubbing the nuts with a kitchen towel. Set aside.

Mix the flour and sugar together in a bowl.

Dissolve the yeast in the water in the bowl of a stand mixer. Add the Marsala and orange blossom water, and start mixing on medium-low speed with the dough attachment. Slowly add the flour mixture, scraping the bowl if needed, then increase the speed to medium-high. Mix for 2 or 3 minutes, or until the dough starts to form (it will still be a bit crumbly at this point). Add the butter a few chunks at a time and continue mixing until fully incorporated. Add the egg and mix until the dough takes shape, about 1 minute. Add the fennel seeds, cherries, candied peel, and nuts, and mix for 1 more minute to incorporate the ingredients. (Note that the mixer may get a little temperamental at this point. If it's having trouble mixing the ingredients, stop the motor and mix by hand.) The dough should be fairly moist.

**¼ cup candied citrus peel
or dried citrus fruit**

½ cup pine nuts

Butter a large bowl and scrape the dough into the bowl. Pat the dough into a loaf shape, cover with plastic wrap, and let it rest in a warm place for 6 hours. The loaf will rise a little, but not double in size.

Preheat the oven to 375°F about 20 minutes before baking the bread.

Butter a large rimmed baking sheet or a cookie sheet and flip the bread dough onto it. It should retain the shape of a round bread loaf. Bake, turning the pan once, for 55 minutes to 1 hour, or until a toothpick inserted at the center comes out clean. Let rest for at least 20 minutes before serving.

Sweet Focaccia with Grapes

Focaccia con l'Uva

Liguria's culinary boundaries are rather flimsy, not only with southern France, but also with neighboring Tuscany. This focaccia, for example, is awfully similar to a Tuscan treat called *schiacciata con l'uva*. I like to serve it for brunch with a sprinkle of confectioners' sugar and a dollop of whipped cream. Remember that focaccia doesn't last long after it's baked. If you're making it for brunch, bake it the same morning. You can prepare the dough the evening before and store it in the fridge until you're ready to bake.

SERVES 8 TO 10

FOR THE DOUGH

1½ cups warm water

½ cup Sciacchetrà or Vin Santo or another sweet syrupy wine, such as Passito; don't use Moscato

1 (¼-ounce) package active-dry yeast

¼ cup extra-virgin olive oil

4 cups unbleached all-purpose flour

FOR THE TOPPING

4 tablespoons extra-virgin olive oil

¼ cup granulated sugar

2 cups seedless black or red grapes, cut in half lengthwise

Pour the water and Sciacchetrà in the bowl of a stand mixer and sprinkle the yeast into it, stirring a few times until it's incorporated in the liquid. Let the mixture rest for 5 minutes, then add the olive oil.

Start mixing on low speed with a dough attachment and slowly add the flour. Increase the speed to medium and keep mixing until you obtain a smooth dough. The dough should be quite moist and stick to your fingers a bit.

Oil a large clean bowl, scrape the dough from the mixer into the bowl, cover tightly with oiled plastic wrap, and let the dough rise until doubled in size, about 30 minutes.

Oil a 13 × 17-inch rimmed baking sheet, and spread out the dough with your hands to completely cover the surface of the pan.

Preheat the oven to 425°F.

Using all the fingers of one hand, dig a few random dimples on the surface of the focaccia. Cover with oiled plastic wrap and let the dough rest in the pan for another 30 minutes, until it has risen and doubled once again.

Before baking, top the dough with 4 tablespoons of olive oil, spreading it with your hands to cover the surface evenly. In particular, make sure it gets into the dimples. Sprinkle the dough with the sugar and the grapes, pressing some of the grapes inside the dough. Bake for 30 to 35 minutes, or until the focaccia turns a nice golden brown and is cooked through. Cut and serve immediately.

Baked Peaches with Almonds and Sciacchetrà

Pesche Ripiene

In summer, I love to eat sweet, ripe peaches just as they are—simply cutting them with a paring knife over the sink to catch juices dripping down my hands. But when I find less-than-perfect peaches, I bake them this way to draw out their sweetness. Given that Sciacchetrà wine can be expensive and nearly impossible to find in the United States (a bottle going for $150 or more isn't at all unusual), you can use Vin Santo or any Passito wine instead. With a little vanilla ice cream or—why not?—a dollop of crème fraîche, these peaches are a perfect summer dessert.

SERVES 4

5 medium firm-ripe peaches

1 cup blanched almonds

½ cup plus 2 tablespoons granulated sugar

½ teaspoon finely grated lemon zest

½ tablespoon candied lemon and/or orange peel

1 tablespoon raisins

½ cup Sciacchetrà, Passito, or Vin Santo

Preheat the oven to 375°F.

Cut four of the peaches in half lengthwise, remove the pits, and set the fruit aside. Peel the fifth peach, cut it in half, remove the pit, and transfer the peach to a food processor. Add the almonds, ½ cup of the sugar, lemon zest, candied peel, and raisins, and puree until you obtain a coarse paste.

Spoon the filling evenly in the eight peach halves, sprinkle with the remaining 2 tablespoons of sugar, and drizzle evenly with the wine.

Place the stuffed peaches on a large rimmed baking sheet lined with foil and bake them for 25 to 30 minutes, or until slightly caramelized on top. To get more caramelization on top, you can broil them for the last 2 to 3 minutes of cooking. Serve warm or at room temperature.

THE PHILOSOPHER OF *sciacchetrà*

Sciacchetrà is a rare amber-colored DOC dessert wine produced in the hills surrounding Riomaggiore, Vernazza, and Monterosso—just three of the tiny Cinque Terre. To make it, local grapes, namely Bosco, Vermentino, and Albarola, are grown on *fasce* facing the sea and air-dried on trellises without direct exposure to the sun. This ensures the right concentration of sugars without compromising the overall balance of Sciacchetrà, which is pleasantly fruity but not obnoxiously syrupy, retaining a healthy level of acidity. The wine is aged for a minimum of one year, usually in oak barrels; but the longer the aging, the better it gets. There is so much concentration in the production of Sciacchetrà, that it takes 20 kilos (about 40 pounds) of grapes to make one 375 ml bottle.

On a recent visit to Liguria, I met with local producer Walter De Batte, who gives the term "meditation wine" (which Sciacchetrà is considered to be) a whole new meaning. De Batte is an oenological intellectual who makes *vini d'autore*, or artist wines, as he calls them. He spent a good ten minutes of our conversation elaborating on the use of Passito (any wine made from dried grapes, such as Sciacchetrà) as a sacrificial wine in ancient religious rituals, pointing out that *passiti* arrived on Italian shores via the Greeks, and the Phoenicians before them. His artistic approach to winemaking is even more apparent in his zeal for experimenting and pushing the limits of local grapes, so much so that some of his dry whites could easily be mistaken for wines from Burgundy, or even Bordeaux, because of their unusually full body and sumptuous mouthfeel. The results, as Walter himself readily points out, can be unpredictable (and that's half the fun), but his Sciacchetrà remains one of the most interesting and complex I've tasted, balancing dried fruit, spiciness, and honey with moderate acidity and a mineral component that's typical of these grapes.

Grappa and Raisin Potato Pudding with Lemon Whipped Crème Fraîche

Budino Dolce di Patate

This unusual "pudding" is really a soft flourless loaf made with a pureed potato base. It has a pleasant boozy flavor (thanks to the grappa) and a wonderfully moist texture that allow it to stand on its own without the whipped crème fraîche. The cream, however, adds a welcome layer of flavor and a bit of sophistication to an otherwise very simple dessert.

SERVES 6 TO 8

FOR THE LOAF

½ cup raisins

1 pound Yukon gold potatoes

8 tablespoons (1 stick) unsalted butter, softened, plus more for buttering the pan

½ cup granulated sugar

1 large egg

4 large egg yolks

½ teaspoon orange extract

1 tablespoon grappa

¼ teaspoon ground cinnamon

4 large egg whites

FOR THE WHIPPED CRÈME FRAÎCHE

16 ounces (about 2 cups) crème fraîche

¼ cup granulated sugar

1 teaspoon lemon extract

2 teaspoons finely grated lemon zest

MAKE THE LOAF Soak the raisins in warm water to cover for about 20 minutes, or until plump. Drain and blot dry.

Bring a large pot of water to a boil, and cook the potatoes until fork tender, about 30 minutes. Peel them and pass them through a ricer or food mill, as you would to make puree.

In a stand mixer fitted with the paddle attachment, beat the butter with the sugar at medium-high speed until light and fluffy, about 3 minutes. Slowly add the pureed potatoes, followed by the egg and egg yolks, one at a time. Add the orange extract, grappa, and cinnamon and mix until the ingredients are fully incorporated, about 2 minutes. Transfer to a large bowl and fold in the reserved raisins.

Preheat the oven to 400°F.

Wash and dry the mixer bowl well and beat the egg whites on high speed to a stiff peak with the whisk attachment. Carefully fold them into the potato batter.

Butter an 8 ½ × 4 ½-inch loaf pan, pour in the potato batter, and bake for about 30 minutes, or until a toothpick inserted in the center comes out clean. Let it cool in the loaf pan to room temperature. Flip the cake onto a plate and refrigerate it, if not using immediately.

Grappa and Raisin Potato Pudding with Lemon Whipped Crème Fraîche

CONTINUED

MAKE THE WHIPPED CRÈME FRAÎCHE Pour the crème fraîche and sugar in the bowl of a stand mixer. Start whipping with the whisk attachment on medium-high speed. When the cream begins to thicken, after about 2 minutes, add the lemon extract and zest. Whip for another 2 minutes to medium-stiff peaks. Cover and refrigerate if you're not using it immediately.

TO SERVE Cut 1-inch slices of the loaf and serve with a dollop of the cream.

Chocolate Gelato Parfait with Fresh Summer Fruit, Strawberry Sauce, and Whipped Cream

Paciugo

One of the main attractions of Bonassola in summertime is the Gelateria delle Rose, the only *gelateria* in town until not long ago. A quick stop at "Le Rose" for an ice-cream cone is part of my vacation routine no matter what, just like walking to the beach or rubbing on suntan lotion. But sitting on the *gelateria*'s porch in the evening with a huge *coppa di gelato* (a big bowl of ice cream) in front of me is a real treat. Their *paciugo*, which is a traditional Ligurian ice cream preparation allegedly hailing from Portofino, is one of my all-time favorites. Be creative with it—I certainly was in developing this recipe. You can use whatever fruit tickles your fancy and appetite: apricots, grapes, or even melon will do.

SERVES 4

FOR THE SAUCE

2 cups fresh strawberries, stemmed and cut into ½-inch pieces

½ cup granulated sugar

½ cup water

FOR THE WHIPPED CREAM

1 pint heavy cream

½ cup granulated sugar

½ teaspoon vanilla extract

TO ASSEMBLE

1 pint good-quality chocolate ice cream or gelato

2 firm-ripe peaches, cut into ½-inch slices

8 blackberries

½ cup raspberries

½ cup blueberries

½ cup stemmed and coarsely chopped strawberries

MAKE THE SAUCE In a small saucepan, combine the strawberries, sugar, and water, and bring to a boil. Reduce to a simmer and simmer gently for about 10 minutes, until the mixture is slightly thickened. Transfer to a blender and pulse for a few seconds, until you obtain a loose puree. Strain through a fine sieve to get rid of the seeds, forcing the puree through the mesh with the back of a ladle. Refrigerate.

MAKE THE WHIPPED CREAM Pour the heavy cream in the previously chilled bowl of a stand mixer fitted with the whisk attachment (you can use a handheld mixer instead, if you like). Start mixing over medium-high speed adding sugar and vanilla extract just as the cream starts to thicken. Whip to medium-stiff peaks (when you lift the beaters or whisk, the cream should curl just a little onto itself).

ASSEMBLE THE DESSERT Spoon a scoop of the ice cream on the bottom of four tall glasses (such as Pilsner glasses) and layer some of the fresh fruit on top of it. Continue to make layers with ice cream and fruit until you reach the rim of the glass. Top with the whipped cream and a generous spoonful of the strawberry sauce. If you have leftover sauce, you can freeze it and use it over your favorite coffee cake.

Pine Nut and Almond Meringue Brittle

Pinolate

This is my interpretation of a classic Ligurian sweet treat, *pinolate*. You can eat this brittle as a snack or add it as a garnish to ice cream. You can also use the same batter to make cookies. The flavor and texture are reminiscent of amaretti cookies, with a pine nut twist.

SERVES 6 TO 8

1½ cups (8 ounces) blanched almonds

1½ cups granulated sugar

4 large egg whites

1 cup pine nuts

¼ teaspoon baking powder

½ tablespoon unsalted butter

Parchment paper

Preheat the oven to 275°F.

In the bowl of a food processor, process the almonds and sugar together until the almonds are completely pulverized.

In the bowl of a stand mixer fitted with the whisk attachment, beat the egg whites on high speed to medium-stiff peaks.

Transfer the almond mixture to a large bowl, add the pine nuts, and mix well. Add the baking powder and carefully fold in the egg whites. Mix just enough to incorporate and blend all the ingredients, but don't overmix. You'll end up with a sort of sticky batter.

Butter a piece of parchment paper big enough to cover a 13 × 17-inch rimmed baking sheet and spread the batter evenly to form a ¼-inch-thick layer. (If you're making cookies, you'll need two 13 × 17-inch rimmed baking sheets lined with two pieces of parchment paper. Spoon a small dollop of batter—1 heaping tablespoon—over the buttered parchment paper, leaving enough space for the batter to expand while in the oven.)

Bake for 55 minutes to 1 hour, until the brittle or cookies are golden brown and firm. Let cool. If you've made a sheet of brittle, break it with your hands into smaller pieces.

Almond Cake with Fresh Figs

Torta di Mandorle con i Fichi

This is a no-frills cake with a moist texture that shows off the almonds and the fruit, if you're using it. You can serve it for breakfast or as a sweet afternoon snack—it's perfect with tea or coffee and you can jazz it up for dessert with some ice cream or a fresh berry coulis. The figs are optional: you can omit them altogether or use any other fruit that's not excessively moist, such as berries and thinly sliced apples or pears.

MAKES 1 9-INCH CAKE

16 tablespoons (2 sticks) unsalted butter, at room temperature, cut into 1-inch pieces, plus extra for buttering the pan

2 cups blanched almonds

1 cup unbleached all-purpose flour

1 teaspoon baking powder

1 cup granulated sugar

1 tablespoon sherry

1 teaspoon vanilla extract

2 teaspoons finely grated lemon zest

¼ teaspoon ground cinnamon

7 large eggs, at room temperature

8 small fresh figs (optional)

¼ cup sliced almonds (optional)

Preheat the oven to 350°F.

Butter a 9-inch round cake pan.

Place the almonds in the bowl of a food processor and grind them finely, about 1 minute.

Sift the flour and baking powder together onto a bowl.

In the bowl of a stand mixer fitted with a paddle attachment, beat the sugar and butter on medium-high speed until fluffy, about 3 minutes. Lower the speed to medium and add the ground almonds, followed by the sherry, vanilla extract, lemon zest, and cinnamon. If necessary, stop the mixer and quickly scrape down the sides of the bowl. Mix for 1 minute, then begin adding the eggs one at a time, until you obtain a loose batter. Lower the speed and slowly add the flour and baking powder. Continue to mix for about 1 minute, until you have a smooth, thickish batter.

Pour the batter in the buttered cake pan, level the top with an offset spatula, and bake for 10 minutes.

Meanwhile, if using, remove the tough stem from the figs and cut the fruit lengthwise into ¼-inch-thick slices.

Scatter the figs and, if using, the sliced almonds evenly over the semicooked batter. Bake for another 45 to 50 minutes, or until a toothpick comes out clean when inserted into the center of the cake.

Olive Oil and Basil Gelato with Chopped Toasted Pine Nuts

Gelato all'Olio d'Oliva e Basilico con Pinoli Tostati e Sbriciolati

Olive oil gelato isn't really a Ligurian specialty. But, inspired by classic Ligurian ingredients (and, admittedly, by a few successful experiments with olive oil gelato at a number of New York City restaurants), I came up with this gelato that embodies the flavors of the region in a rather unusual way. A requirement to make it is an ice-cream machine, but you don't need an expensive one. The basic churners you find in most cooking supply stores for around fifty dollars work just fine.

SERVES 4 TO 6

4 cups whole milk

1 cup heavy cream

1½ cups granulated sugar

20 large basil leaves, plus more for garnish

10 large egg yolks

2 tablespoons pine nuts

¼ cup extra-virgin olive oil

Pour the milk, cream, and sugar into a 3-quart saucepan and bring to a boil, stirring to incorporate the sugar. As soon as bubbles start forming around the edges, turn off the heat. Tear the basil leaves coarsely with your hands, add them to the pan, and let them steep for 30 minutes. Strain the mixture into a bowl and pour it back into the saucepan, making sure there are no basil leaves left.

Bring the mixture back to a boil. Meanwhile, beat the egg yolks in a medium-size bowl. When the liquid starts boiling again, turn off the heat and add ¼ cup of the milk mixture to the beaten eggs, whisking constantly to prevent curdling. Slowly add the rest of the liquid as you continue to whisk. Make sure the eggs don't curdle.

Return the custard back to the saucepan and cook over very low heat, stirring with a wooden spoon until it starts to thicken and thickly coats the back of the spoon, about 8 minutes (it may take more or less, so keep a vigilant eye on it). You should be able to trace a neat line with your finger on the back of the spoon without any dripping.

Strain the custard through a fine sieve, transfer it to a clean bowl, and chill completely over an ice bath, tightly covering the bowl with plastic wrap (let the plastic touch the surface of the cream to avoid a thin film from forming).

Meanwhile, chop the pine nuts coarsely, transfer them to an 8-inch skillet and toast them over medium-high heat for about 5 minutes, giving the pan a few jolts every so often. Transfer to a cold plate and set aside.

Add the olive oil to the cold custard and stir it in with a wooden spoon or a whisk. Freeze the mixture in an ice-cream machine according to the manual instructions. Serve the gelato in a dessert cup with a sprinkle of the toasted pine nuts and garnished with a small basil leaf, if you like.

Lavender Panna Cotta with Raspberry Puree

Panna Cotta alla Lavanda con Purea di Lamponi

The first time I made lavender panna cotta was in Bonassola after I'd just returned from a trip to Provence. Inspired by the profusion of lavender in southern France, I decided to experiment at home. All I needed to do was step out of the kitchen's French window and pick a few fresh stems from the garden. If you can't find culinary-grade lavender flowers in gourmet stores (they usually come dried, in the spice section), this panna cotta is delicious just with vanilla extract. In that case, you don't need to steep it for thirty minutes, as the vanilla extract dissolves very quickly in the cream.

SERVES 6

FOR THE PANNA COTTA
1½ teaspoons unflavored gelatin powder

½ cup whole milk

2 cups heavy cream

½ cup granulated sugar

½ teaspoon vanilla extract

⅓ cup dried (or fresh) lavender flowers

FOR THE SAUCE
2 cups fresh raspberries

½ cup granulated sugar

¼ cup water

More raspberries, for garnish

4 mint leaves, for garnish

In a small bowl, dissolve the gelatin in the milk.

Meanwhile, pour the cream, sugar, vanilla extract, and lavender into a saucepan and bring to a boil. Turn the heat off as soon as bubbles start forming around the edges of the pan and let the lavender steep in the cream for 30 minutes.

While the lavender infuses the cream with its flavor, prepare the sauce: In a small saucepan, add the raspberries, sugar and water, and bring to a boil. Reduce to a simmer and simmer gently for 10 minutes, until the mixture is slightly thickened. Transfer to a blender and pulse for a few seconds, until you obtain a loose puree. Strain through a fine sieve to get rid of the seeds, forcing the puree through the mesh with the back of a ladle. Refrigerate.

Strain the lavender out of the cream, add the gelatin mixture to the pan, and bring to a boil. Reduce to a simmer and simmer gently for 3 minutes, stirring frequently.

Pour the hot mixture in six 4-ounce ramekins until they're about two-thirds full. Let the cream mixture cool to room temperature, cover the ramekins with plastic wrap, and transfer them to the refrigerator. Chill for at least 2 hours, or until the panna cotta is completely solid.

To unmold, place the bottom of each ramekin in a saucepan of boiling water for a few seconds to loosen the panna cotta from the bottom, then flip the ramekin over, onto a plate. Serve the panna cotta topped with the reserved raspberry sauce, a few fresh raspberries, and a mint leaf.

Roasted Pears with Vanilla-Mascarpone Whipped Cream

Torta di Pere

In Liguria they call this a *torta*, but it really has nothing to do with cake. It's nothing more than thinly sliced pears baked with butter, sugar, and bread crumbs and topped with a velvety smooth mascarpone whipped cream—and it's mouthwatering. I've served it many times to people who don't like pears, and they've become instant fans.

SERVES 4

FOR THE PEARS

3 large firm-ripe Bosc pears

4 tablespoons unsalted butter, softened, plus more for the pan

1 cup coarse homemade bread crumbs (see recipe page 211)

¼ cup granulated sugar

20 seedless black grapes, cut in half lengthwise

⅛ teaspoon freshly grated nutmeg

½ teaspoon finely grated lemon zest

FOR THE WHIPPED CREAM

1 cup heavy cream

¼ cup granulated sugar

¼ teaspoon vanilla extract

½ cup mascarpone cheese

Preheat the oven to 425°F.

Cut the pears in half, core, and cut them into ¼-inch-thick slices. Butter the bottom of an 8 × 10-inch baking pan and sprinkle it with one-third of the bread crumbs.

Arrange a snug layer of pears over the bread crumbs. Sprinkle with half the sugar and another one-third of the bread crumbs, dot with half the butter, and toss on half the grapes.

Make one more layer in the same way and top with a sprinkle of nutmeg and the lemon zest.

Bake for about 25 minutes or until the pears are soft and slightly browned on the edges.

MAKE THE WHIPPED CREAM Pour the heavy cream in the previously chilled bowl of a stand mixer fitted with the whisk attachment (you can use a handheld mixer instead, if you like). Start mixing at medium-high speed adding sugar, vanilla extract, and mascarpone just as the cream starts to thicken a little. Whip to medium-stiff peaks (when you lift the beaters or whisk, the cream should curl a little onto itself).

TO SERVE Cut out some of the pears as if you were cutting a piece of cake and serve topped with a dollop of the whipped mascarpone cream.

Vanilla Ice Cream Drowned in Rossese Wine–Poached Cherries

Affogato di Ciliege Cotte nel Rossese

Affogato—ice cream that is literally "drowned" in coffee, chocolate sauce, or fruit syrup—is something you find all over Italy. But few beat the *affogato* chef Francesco Motola served us at Terre Bianche. Made with the farm's own hand-picked cherries, it had an intense cherry flavor, neither too sweet nor tart. When I asked him how he made it, he said the cherries were poached in Rossese wine with sugar and a little lemon zest—just that easy. But as simple as this dessert might be, it never fails to impress. To pit the cherries, you don't need a cherry pitter. I just cut them in half and remove the pit with my fingers. I sometimes serve this *affogato* with whipped cream, but it's delicious as well without.

SERVES 4

FOR THE SAUCE

2 cups pitted fresh cherries

¾ cup granulated sugar

**½ cup Rossese wine
(or any red wine you like)**

1 teaspoon finely grated lemon zest

1 pint good-quality vanilla ice cream

MAKE THE SAUCE In a small saucepan, combine the cherries, sugar, wine, and lemon zest, and bring to a boil. Reduce to a simmer and simmer gently for 10 to 15 minutes, until the mixture is slightly thickened and syrupy.

Remove from the heat and let it cool just a little bit. You want it to be warm but not boiling hot when you pour it over the ice cream.

ASSEMBLE THE DESSERT Scoop the ice cream in four separate ice-cream bowls (I like to use glass dessert cups) and pour the cherry syrup evenly over the ice cream.

EPILOGUE

When I'm home, in Brooklyn, I sometimes hear the distant chime of church bells on a late Sunday morning. My mind inevitably drifts to Liguria. One of the things I miss most about Bonassola is the sound of church bells tolling at all times of day and night, the echoes of their metallic clangs crisscrossing from all directions.

Now, a few rings on a lazy Sunday are unquestionably romantic and charmingly passé, but you have to understand that in Bonassola an army of bells goes on sonorous march every hour—and on the half-hour, too. And just to ensure everyone hears all three churches loud and clear, the rings are ever so slightly delayed. The main church begins at the strike of the hour. If it's two o'clock, the bells ring twice. If it's noon or midnight, they ring twelve times. Multiply this by three and you have a perpetual church-bell concerto. And on Sunday mornings, the fanatical concert masters wax particularly inventive, so that the beginning of each mass (the first is at seven in the morning) is heralded with a twenty-minute sonata that drives my agnostic, priest-bashing uncle completely berserk. Nonetheless, I've come to love the sound of those bells, even at their most annoyingly pompous Sunday preen. Bonassola without them wouldn't be the same. They represent an enchantingly old-fashioned web of history and continuity, a much welcome contrast to my fleetingly electronic urban life. This is why, when I hear bells in Brooklyn, I'm always caught by surprise.

I go back to Liguria as often as I can. During the first Italian vacation I ever took with my soon-to-be-husband, we spent a week in Bonassola. For him, too, it was love at first sight. When the time came to decide on a location for our wedding, neither of us had any doubt. We exchanged our vows in the splendid fishing village of Camogli on a perfect September evening under a sunset to die for. (That summer had been rainy and unusually cold, so my always practical mother bought dozens of colorful umbrellas to give out to guests instead of confetti. To this day, I remain convinced this is what brought out the sun in full force. In Italy, my mother's behavior is called *scaramanzia*.)

When I go back to Bonassola, there are little things I do, rituals carried out the same every time, to rekindle my ties with the town, the land, the sea, with my family and my memories. As soon as our car makes the last sharp turn out of the narrow road from Levanto, we stop and buy focaccia. We get a little of each kind: with onions, with rosemary and thyme, with cheese, or simply plain, greasy, delicious focaccia. Sometimes we buy it from Bianchetto's quaint corner store in Piazza Mazzini, with its retro signs and large green awning shading customers who nibble on focaccia at a rustic old outdoor table. Other times we'll go to La Ladrona—she knows me too well to attempt any slight of hand. Our decision is often dictated by availability. In contrast to modern-day operations with modern-day business sense, either shop is likely to run out of focaccia at any given time and leave customers waiting for the next batch. *"Mi spiace, signora"*—I'm sorry ma'am—is all they can muster in the way of customer service.

Brad and I love to savor our focaccia on a bench facing the sea along a slender path that hugs the beach for a while before curving up, past yet another church, to rejoin the *strada della madonnina*. But most times, we continue to the house to hug my family and share our delectable treasure with them on the terrace.

Our stay in Bonassola wouldn't be the same without a visit to Gianni's Bagni Sabbia d'Oro. In Italy, *spiagge libere* ("free beaches" that are open to the public), are a rarity. More commonly, beach-front property is rented by private individuals from the regional government and turned into that ubiquitous Italian coastline phenomenon called *bagni*. These are roped-off beach areas, often in close succession, with lounge chairs and umbrellas for rent by the day, the month, or an entire summer season. That in itself isn't so unusual; there are rented umbrellas and chairs on beaches all over the world. But a few attributes put Italian *bagni* in a different category. The umbrellas and chairs are much closer than I've seen anywhere else, for one thing—certainly much closer than you'll find them in the United States. This offers excellent opportunities for making new friends or, more importantly, for overhearing the details of your neighbor's kidney surgery or her sister's elopement with a Tunisian banker. I've spent many hours involuntarily sliding into other people's lives this way.

Bagni are microcosms unto themselves, miniature villages where people rest, eat, play games, read the paper, bathe, and take part in one of Italy's favorite national sport: talking. People talk politics and soccer, complain about their husbands and wives, confess infidelities, share opinions on the latest miracle drug. It's an indolent, unruffled world where leisure reigns supreme and real life is safely abandoned on the other side of the *bagni* gates.

Life at Bagni Sabbia d'Oro stays the same year after year. Each time I return, I see the same people and hear the same conversations. But far from being bored or annoyed, I'm comforted by this sameness—grateful for it. As we pass the wrought iron arch with its art deco sign and climb the stairs to the veranda in front of the bar, we greet Gianni, the owner. He's a big, smile-prone man with a thick Ligurian accent and a penchant for jokes. Like many people in Bonassola, he comes from a fishing family of modest origins. But he had great foresight in renting this piece of beach and furnishing it with bright green umbrellas and matching *cabine*. Now he works four months a year and earns about as much as a medium-weight investment banker in Manhattan. His wife, Renata, is usually on the veranda, tanned as an Amazon, bedecked with big, clunky pieces of jewelry, playing the grande dame and soaking up every single ray. (I've always wondered how she gets a uniform tan with all that clutter on her arms and neck.) She, too, is part of what makes Bonassola unique and irreplaceable in my heart. My beloved *bagni* simply wouldn't be the same without her.

At the end of a strenuous beach day, there's nothing more satisfying than a smooth *aperitivo* on the *bagni*'s veranda under the soft blue light over the calm, oily sea. Time is much more fluid in Bonassola. *Aperitivo* can stretch for a couple of hours. Before you know it, it's ten o'clock and you haven't had dinner yet. On the way back from the *bagni* a recent day, we took the long route toward home. We walked by the *campetto*, a little field where kids play soccer and where the occasional big entertainment event takes place (like the time when Johannes, the German jazz musician who's a regular vacationer, and his wife, a singer, performed for the entire town). I was surprised to see that the soccer tournament tradition pitting *villeggianti*, the vacationers, against the natives of Bonassola, the *bonassolesi*, persists to this day. Although Bonassola couldn't thrive without the *villeggianti*, natives still have a hard time accepting the self-important, puffed up city dwellers who use their village for fun and leisure a few months each year and leave all the hard work to the townspeople. This veiled hostility comes ferociously to life during the soccer tournament, when more than one player has had to get stitches or ice a badly bruised ankle.

And of course, I love to cook when I'm in Bonassola. Some days, in the early evening, as the sun disappears behind the hill, Silvana, my mother, and I change into our sneakers, spray a little Autan to fend off the blood-hungry mosquitoes, and grab wicker baskets, headed to the *fasce* above the house to gather vegetables and fresh herbs for dinner or for lunch the following day, or simply to check on the tomatoes and strawberries. Sometimes Franco and Brad come along, although my father rarely joins us—he prefers to read a book on the terrace, making the most of the gentle evening breeze.

We prepare uncomplicated meals with what's available in the garden or at the fish market. We rarely eat meat because it's less fresh, not as good here. There are no recipes, no teaspoons or measuring cups. We are guided by the smells and flavors of the garden, the type and size of the fish, and years of cooking wisdom. Despite the modernity of the kitchen in my family's warm, convivial Bonassola house, we don't have all the gadgets that I have in New York. Silvana works on a cutting board the size of a napkin, her pans are beaten up and scratched, and it's hard to find even one sharp knife in her drawers. Recipes and tools are not what make this Ligurian kitchen my favorite place on earth. It's the joy, the inspiration, the company, and the delight of cooking with the tastiest, most wholesome ingredients.

One day I'll have a kitchen like this, too.

Making Broth

Most of these broths, with the exception of vegetable broth, require the use of bones. It's often the case, however, that most supermarkets and even neighborhood butchers don't have bones readily available. Ask your butcher or the person at the meat counter to reserve bones for you next time they cut beef, veal, or chicken. Same goes with fish bones. Usually, fishmongers fillet their own fish and they'll be happy to give you the leftover bones, which they have to get rid of one way or another.

HOMEMADE FISH BROTH

Makes about 1 gallon (16 cups) broth

8 to 10 pounds fish bones and trimmings

8 ounces onion (about 1 large onion), quartered

4 ounces celery (about 2 medium stalks), cut into 2-inch pieces

4 ounces carrots (about 1 large carrot), cut into 2-inch pieces

1 bay leaf

5 sprigs parsley

2 sprigs thyme

10 black peppercorns

16 cups cold water

1 cup dry white wine (optional)

Combine the fish bones, onions, celery, carrot, bay leaf, parsley, thyme, and peppercorns in a large stockpot. Add the water, plus the wine, if using, and bring to a boil. Reduce to a slow simmer and simmer, uncovered, for 50 to 60 minutes.

Strain the broth through a fine-mesh strainer into a large bowl. Place the bowl in an ice bath and let it cool, covered with plastic wrap, before you refrigerate or freeze it. I like to freeze broth in 1-pint containers so when I need only a little bit, I don't have to defrost an entire quart.

HOMEMADE SHRIMP BROTH

Makes about 8 cups

Shells and tails from 1 pound medium-size shrimp
1 medium onion, quartered
1 medium celery stalk, cut into 2-inch pieces
2 sprigs parsley
1 sprig thyme
4 black peppercorns
8 cups cold water
1/2 cup dry white wine (optional)

Combine the shells, onions, celery, parsley, thyme, and peppercorns in a medium-size stockpot. Add the water, plus the wine if using, and bring to a boil. Reduce to a slow simmer and simmer, uncovered, for 40 to 50 minutes.

Strain the broth through a fine-mesh strainer into a large bowl. Place the bowl in an ice bath and let it cool, covered with plastic wrap, before you refrigerate or freeze it.

HOMEMADE VEGETABLE BROTH

Makes about 1 gallon (16 cups) broth

4 ounces onions (about 1 small onion), quartered
4 ounces leeks (green and white part), cleaned and cut into 2-inch pieces
2 ounces celery (about 1 small stalk), cut into 2-inch pieces
2 ounces carrots (about 1/2 large carrot), cut into 2-inch pieces
1 bay leaf
8 sprigs parsley
3 sprigs thyme
10 black peppercorns
4 quarts (16 cups) cold water

Combine the vegetables, herbs, and peppercorns in a large stockpot and add the water. Bring to a boil and reduce to a slow simmer. Simmer, uncovered, for 50 to 60 minutes.

Strain the broth through a fine-mesh strainer into a large bowl. Place the bowl in an ice bath and let it cool, covered with plastic wrap, before you refrigerate or freeze it. I like to freeze broth in 1-pint containers so when I need only a little bit, I don't have to defrost a whole quart.

VARIATION *For a deeper, more complex flavor, roast the vegetables first. Preheat the oven to 450°F. Toss the onions, leeks, celery, and carrot with 3 tablespoons of extra-virgin olive oil and transfer to a 17 × 13-inch rimmed baking sheet. Roast in the oven for 30 to 40 minutes, turning once, until nicely browned. Transfer the vegetables to the stockpot and follow the instructions above for making regular vegetable broth.*

HOMEMADE CHICKEN BROTH

Makes about 3 quarts (about 12 cups)

5 pounds chicken bones and trimmings, fat and skin removed

4 quarts (16 cups) cold water

8 ounces onion (about 1 large onion), quartered

4 ounces celery (about 2 medium stalks), cut into 2-inch pieces

4 ounces carrots (about 1 large carrot), cut into 2-inch pieces

1 bay leaf

8 sprigs parsley

3 sprigs thyme

10 black peppercorns

Place the chicken bones in a large stockpot and add the water. Bring to a boil and reduce to a slow simmer. Simmer, uncovered, for 1 hour, skimming the surface of the water with a slotted spoon. Add the onions, celery, and carrots, and simmer for another 2 hours. Add the herbs and peppercorns, and simmer for 1 more hour.

Strain the broth through a fine-mesh strainer into a large bowl. Place the bowl in an ice bath and let it cool, covered with plastic wrap, before you refrigerate or freeze it. I like to freeze broth in 1-pint containers so when I need only a little bit, I don't have to defrost a whole quart.

HOMEMADE BEEF OR VEAL BROTH

Makes about 3 quarts (about 12 cups)

5 pounds beef or veal bones and trimmings, fat removed

4 quarts (16 cups) cold water

8 ounces onion (about 1 large onion), quartered

4 ounces celery (about 2 medium stalks), cut into 2-inch pieces

4 ounces carrots (about 1 large carrot), cut into 2-inch pieces

1 bay leaf

8 sprigs parsley

3 sprigs thyme

10 black peppercorns

Place the bones in a large stockpot and add the water. Bring to a boil and reduce to a slow simmer. Simmer, uncovered, for 1 hour, skimming the surface of the water with a slotted spoon. Add the onions, celery, and carrots, and simmer for another 3 hours. Add the herbs and peppercorns and simmer for 1 more hour.

Strain the broth through a fine-mesh strainer into a large bowl. Place the bowl in an ice bath and let it cool, covered with plastic wrap, before you refrigerate or freeze it. I like to freeze broth in 1-pint containers so when I need only a little bit, I don't have to defrost a whole quart.

HOMEMADE BREAD CRUMBS

Makes about 2 cups

**3 cups day-old bread,
cut into 1-inch dice**
The bread should be pretty hard, and dry. If not, spread the cubes on a baking pan and toast in a 400°F oven for about 10 minutes. Place the bread in the bowl of a food processor and process for about 2 minutes, or until all the bread has been ground. You may need to process the bread more or less time, depending on whether you want a finer or coarser grind.

GLOSSARY

Gastronomic terms

agnolotti (*singular:* agnolotto): Traditional ravioli made in Piedmont.

aperitivo: The word refers to drinks (both alcoholic and nonalcoholic) and light snacks enjoyed before dinner or lunch, somewhat similar to "happy hour" in the United States. A classic *aperitivo* is Campari and soda, but Prosecco, white or red wine, and even beer, are common.

branzino: Mediterranean sea bass.

brodetto di pesce: A quick fish stock used as a foundation for fish stews and soups in Liguria (*brodetto* derives from *brodo*, the Italian word for "broth" or "stock").

buridda: Seafood soup or stew using a variety of different fish, traditionally leftover fish or odds and ends.

calamari (*singular:* calamaro): Squid.

ciuppin: A fish soup traditionally from Sestri Levante, where the ingredients are pureed into a smooth, creamy soup to eat with toast or leftover bread. In other areas, it is served chunky.

cornetto: The word means "small horn" and indicates most commonly the croissant-like pastry consumed in the morning by many Italians at the *bar*, along with their cappuccino.

corzetti (*singular:* corzetto): Fresh pasta shaped like coins stamped with a wooden *corzetti* stamp, typical of the eastern part of Liguria.

Crescenza: A soft-ripened, rindless cow's milk cheese that's slightly yeasty and pleasantly tart. This is the cheese most widely used on *focaccia al formaggio* from Recco.

gallette del marinaio: Literally seamen's biscuits, they are small, hardened, round, flat breads that keep for quite a long time. Ligurian fishermen used to carry them on their seafaring journeys.

maltagliati (*singular:* maltagliato): The word literally means "badly cut;" it's a type of fresh pasta usually shaped like an irregular trapezoid.

moscardini (*singular:* moscardino): Baby octopus.

mosciame di tonno: Dried tuna slices.

muscoli (*singular:* muscolo): Mussels.

orata: Mediterranean sea bream.

pansotti or pansôti (*singular:* pansotto): Traditional Ligurian ravioli shaped like triangles. The word, which is in Ligurian dialect, is the same as the Italian *panciuti*, meaning "with a belly," to indicate that these ravioli are overstuffed with filling.

peperoncino: Chile pepper; either in the form of dried red pepper flakes or of whole spicy red pepper, usually dried as well.

pesce azzurro: Small fish, such as anchovies and sardines, with silver-blue scales (*pesce azzurro* translates into blue fish). Pesce azzurro is eaten fresh in Liguria just as often as it's preserved in salt or oil.

picagge: Ligurian tagliatelle.

preboggion: a word in Ligurian dialect that indicates a medley of wild herbs (including borage, wild beet greens, nettle, sow thistle, rampion, and dog's tooth) intended to be cooked as a filling for *pansotti*, savory pies, or frittata.

Prescinseua: A dialectal term indicating a very typical eastern Ligurian dairy product that you'll find no where else in Italy (in fact, some people from the western side of the region don't even know what it is). It tastes like soft fresh cheese with sour milk in it and it's used in a variety of savory pies and ravioli fillings. It's becoming harder and harder to find fresh Prescinseua, even in Liguria.

Prosecco: Dry sparkling white wine produced in the Veneto region in the northeast of Italy.

ricciola: A large Mediterranean fish whose meat has a texture similar to swordfish.

Sciacchetrà: A prized dessert wine produced in very small quantities in the Cinque Terre area of Liguria. The relative unavailability of the wine accounts for its high price.

seppie (*singular:* seppia): Cuttlefish.

soffritto: A medley of chopped vegetables and aromatics (such as onion, garlic, celery, carrot, and parsley) that constitutes the foundation of most Italian sauces, soups, and stews.

stoccafisso: Stockfish or dried cod.

Stracchino: A soft-ripened cow's milk cheese traditionally produced in the region of Lombardy. In Italy, it's sometimes confused with Crescenza (see page 212), a similar but tangier type of cheese. People will often talk about Stracchino when what they're really referring to is Crescenza.

trenette (*singular:* trenetta): Fresh or dried eggless pasta shaped like 1/4-inch-wide linguine, but plumper and with an elliptical cross section. Traditionally, they were made with whole wheat flour.

trofie (*singular:* trofia): Typical Ligurian eggless pasta (originally from the town of Recco) shaped like tiny twisted dumplings.

Nongastronomic terms

bagni: Beach establishments where the public can rent sun umbrellas, chairs, and cabins.

bar: This word does not have the same meaning as in English. It refers to a coffee shop where people enjoy espresso and cappuccino with pastries, sandwiches, and other light fare. It's a place for breakfast or snacks. While most *bar* also serve alcoholic beverages, it's usually not the core of their business.

cabine: Beach cabins where people leave towels and swimwear; usually they're rented, with umbrellas and chairs, daily, monthly, or for the entire season.

campanile: The bell tower of a church.

carrugi: Extremely narrow, meandering streets typically found in the historical centers of many Ligurian towns, including Genova.

entroterra: Inland.

fasce (*singular:* fascia): Terracelike strips of land built from stone on hilly terrain to create a level surface for the growing of crops.

ferragosto: An Italian holiday that falls on the fifteenth of August. The name dates back to the Roman era, when Emperor Augustus decided to move all harvest celebrations from September to the month named after him. Feriae Augusti, the August festivities, became ferragosto in Italian. The Catholic Church later decided to give it a religious meaning as the day celebrating the Assumption of the Virgin Mary. Today, it marks the peak of Italians' vacation month.

festa degli incappucciati: Literally "feast of the hooded people," it's the annual festivity that happens in Bonassola on the day of *ferragosto*.

frazioni: Tiny little hamlets of a bigger town.

levante: East; more commonly called *est* in Italian.

mercato: A neighborhood farmers' market; there are daily *mercati* in big cities and towns and weekly ones in smaller towns such as Bonassola.

panetteria: A bread bakery and/or retail store; most *panetterie* bake the bread they sell, whereas others are only resellers.

peschereccio: A fishing boat; refers both to smaller boats as well as big commercial fishing vessels.

ponente: West; more commonly called *ovest* in Italian.

scogli: Seashore rocks common in some coastal areas of Italy where there are no natural beaches.

strada: Road.

terreno: A piece of land.

trattoria: Small restaurant, generally in the countryside, serving traditional, homemade food with no frills.

SOURCES

A. G. FERRARI FOODS

14234 Catalina Street

San Leandro, CA 94577

PHONE: (877) 878-2783

WEB: www.agferrari.com

For artisanal trenette, Ligurian olive oils, truffle oils, salted anchovies, oil-packed tuna, and pecorino sardo. You'll even find corzetti stamps!

CORTI BROTHERS

5810 Folsom Boulevard

Sacramento, CA 95819

PHONE: (800) 509-3663

WEB: www.cortibros.biz

Here you can find stockfish (and salt cod), Ligurian olive oils, and salted anchovies.

D'ARTAGNAN

280 Wilson Avenue

Newark, NJ 07105

PHONE: (800) 327-8246

WEB: www.dartagnan.com

If you can't find guinea hen and rabbit at a store near you, order it from D'Artagnan.

CHEFSHOP

PHONE: (877) 337-2491

WEB: www.chefshop.com

You'll find packaged trofie (if you don't feel like spending an afternoon making them), salted anchovies and salted capers, and various types of rice, including arborio, carnaroli, and vialone nano.

iGOURMET

508 Delaware Avenue

West Pittston, PA 18643

PHONE: (877) 446-8763

WEB: www.igourmet.com

A good resource for a few specialty items for the Ligurian kitchen, from Crescenza to oil-packed tuna and mortadella.

BOB'S RED MILL

5902 S.E. International Way

Milwaukie, OR 97222

PHONE: (800) 349-2173

WEB: www.bobsredmill.com

Here you can order the chickpea flour (they call it garbanzo bean flour) you need for farinata.

KATY'S SMOKE HOUSE

P.O. Box 621

Trinidad, CA 95570

PHONE: (707) 677-0151

WEB: www.katyssmokehouse.com

Good source, if a bit pricey, for smoked swordfish and other smoked fish.

ITALIAN WINE MERCHANTS

108 East 16th Street (between Park Avenue South & Irving Place)

New York, NY 10003

PHONE: (212) 473-2323

WEB: www.italianwinemerchant.com

Great source of Ligurian wines, from Rossese and Vermentino to Sciacchetrà.

THE COOK'S GARDEN

P.O. Box C5030

Warminster, PA 18974

PHONE: 800-457-9703

WEB: www.cooksgarden.com

If you want to grow your own Genovese basil, you can order seeds from this website.

If you decided to take the leap and buy a mortar and pestle, here are a couple of resources:

www.williams-sonoma.com

www.chefscatalog.com

INDEX

indice

a

b

d

Butter Lettuce Rolls in Warm Veal Broth (*Lattughe in Brodo*), 106–107

Roasted Zucchini Flowers with a Zesty Green Bean Stuffing (*Fiori di Zucca Ripieni*), 164

mortar and pestle, 16

mushrooms

Chickpea Soup with Swiss Chard and Mushrooms (*Zimino di Ceci*), 108

Hearty Baked Risotto with Sausage, Artichokes, and Mushrooms (*Riso del Campagnolo di Ponente*), 81–82

Sautéed Mushrooms with Fresh Herbs and Pecorino (*Ovoli in Umido*), 177

Seared Tuna Steaks with Quick Porcini Mushroom Ragù (*Tonno alla Genovese*), 130

Vegetable "Meat Loaf" with Green Beans and Pecorino (*Polpettone di Fagiolini*), 162–163

mussels

Seafood *Fritto Misto* (*Fritto Misto di Mare*), 132

Seafood Risotto with Clams, Mussels, and Shrimp (*Risotto ai Frutti di Mare*), 79–80

Silvana's Chunky Seafood Soup (*Buridda come la fa Silvana*), 105

mustard, Potato Salad with Pancetta, Pickled Onions, and Mustard (*Insalata di Patate alla Tedesca*), 165

n

nile perch

Ligurian Seafood Bisque with Paprika Crostoni (*Ciuppin con Crostoni di Paprika*), 101–102

Silvana's Chunky Seafood Soup (*Buridda come la fa Silvana*), 105

o

octopus

Baby Octopus Drowned in White Wine and Tomato Sauce (*Moscardini Affogati*), 50

Warm Squid and Baby Octopus Salad with Potatoes, Garlic, and Olive Oil (*Insalata di Mare Tiepida del Pescatore*), 48–49

olive oil, 16

Focaccia with Extra-Virgin Olive Oil and Sea Salt (*Focaccia*), 52–54

Heirloom Tomato Salad with Fruity Olive Oil and Basil (*Insalata di Pomodori alla Moda di Bonassola*), 166

Olive Oil and Basil Gelato with Chopped Toasted Pine Nuts (*Gelato all'Olio d'Oliva e Basilico con Pinoli Tostati e Sbriciolati*), 198–199

Simple Roasted Potatoes with Olive Oil, Rosemary, and Thyme (*Patatine Arrosto con Rosmarino e Timo*), 170

olives, black

Bruschetta with Cherry Tomatoes, Black Olives, and Basil (*Bruschetta con Ciliegine, Olive Nere, e Basilico*), 33

Chef Francesco's Rossese Wine Braised Rabbit with Black Olives (*Coniglio Brasato al Rossese*), 152

Crostini with Lemon-Scented Olive Paste (*Crostini con la Pasta di Olive*), 32

Focaccia with Tomatoes, Onions, and Olives (*Pizza all'Andrea*), 59

Ligurian Bread Salad with Tomatoes, Tuna, and Capers (*Capponadda Non Tradizionale*), 171–172

Ligurian Ratatouille with Black Olives and Toasted Pine Nuts (*Ratatuia*), 173–174

Pan-Seared Swordfish with Capers, Olives, and Toasted Pine Nuts (*Pesce Spada con Capperi, Olive, e Pinoli*), 136

Rigatoni with Swordfish, Olives, Rosemary, and Sage (*Rigatoni col Pesce Spada*), 94

Roasted Orata with Black Olives and Baby Potatoes (*Orata al Forno con Olive Nere e Patatine Arrosto*), 122

Rustic Braised Chicken with Black Olives and Rosemary (*Pollo alla Ligure*), 155

Salt Cod Stew with Olives, Tomatoes, and Pine Nuts (*Stoccafisso Accomodato*), 124

Shrimp-Stuffed Cuttlefish in Vermentino Wine Sauce (*Seppie Ripiene*), 138

Warm Squid and Baby Octopus Salad with Potatoes, Garlic, and Olive Oil (*Insalata di Mare Tiepida del Pescatore*), 48–49

olives, green

Pan-Seared Swordfish with Capers, Olives, and Toasted Pine Nuts (*Pesce Spada con Capperi, Olive, e Pinoli*), 136

Rigatoni with Swordfish, Olives, Rosemary, and Sage (*Rigatoni col Pesce Spada*), 94

onions

Crostini with Crescenza Cheese, Caramelized Onions, and White Truffle Oil (*Crostini con Crescenza, Cipolle Caramellizzate, e Olio al Tartufo Bianco*), 35

Focaccia with Sweet Onions (*Focaccia con le Cipolle*), 55

Focaccia with Tomatoes, Onions, and Olives (*Pizza all'Andrea*), 59

Frittata with Baby Zucchini, Caramelized Onions, Goat Cheese, and Fresh Herbs (*Frittata di Bonassola*), 41–42

Sautéed Chicken Livers with Onions and Artichokes (*Fegatini di Pollo con Carciofi*), 158–159

q

r

INDEX

LIGURIAN KITCHEN

...mio. guarci e fostreb m...

...on affetto e ve...

...lla Poste.

Ciao Silvana

From Hippocrene's Regional Italian Cookbook Library

"Hippocrene—a fount of ethnic cookbooks."
—PUBLISHERS WEEKLY

TASTES FROM A TUSCAN KITCHEN

MADELINE ARMILLOTTA AND DIANE NOCENTINI

Located in central Italy, Tuscany is one of the most beautiful parts of the country. In *Tastes from a Tuscan Kitchen*, the authors, a Canadian woman and her British friend, depict the culinary specialties of this scenic region in more than 100 healthful recipes. Dishes range from such staples as *Pasta e Lenticchie* (Pasta and Lentils) and *Cacciucco* (Fish Soup) to the delightfully titled *Bongo Bongo* (Chocolate Profiteroles). Sauces, pestos, and crostini add to this collection of foods which defy the myth that Italian food is bad for the waistline. Together with an informative section on Tuscan wines this books presents an accessible and thoroughly enjoyable selection of Tuscan treats.

200 pages • 6 × 9 • $24.95 hc • 0-7818-1145-7 • (5)

CUCINA PIEMONTESE

MARIA GRAZIA ASSELLE AND BRIAN YARVIN

Cucina Piemontese provides an opportunity to explore Piedmont, known for its use of butter, cream, beef and truffles, as well as humbler ingredients such as pasta, polenta and root vegetables. More than 95 recipes have been rendered in this lovely volume, written with the American home cook in mind. Beginning with antipasti of *Cipolline in Agro Dolce* (Sweet-and-Sour Onions) or *Acciughe al Verde* (Anchovies in Green Sauce), journey though the region with *Tajarin con Sugo Burro e Salvia* (Egg Pasta with Butter and Sage Sauce) and *Brasato al Vino Rosso* (Beef Cooked in Red Wine), concluding with one of Piedmont's famous desserts, *Zuppa Inglese* (Ladyfinger Cake). A beautiful color insert, historical and cultural information, seasonal menus and a chapter on regional wines, including the famous Barolo, are all included in this insider's perspective into a fascinating cuisine.

159 pages • 6 × 9 • $27.50 hc • 0-7818-1123-6 • (303)

CUCINA DI CALABRIA: TREASURED RECIPES AND FAMILY TRADITIONS FROM SOUTHERN ITALY

MARY AMABILE PALMER

"[This volume] delivers fully on its promise of an authentic Southern Italian culinary experience."
—PUBLISHERS WEEKLY

For centuries Calabrian food has remained relatively undiscovered because few recipes were divulged outside of the region's tightly knit villages or even family circles. However, Mary Amabile Palmer has gathered a comprehensive collection of exciting, robust recipes from the home of her ancestors. *Cucina di Calabria* is a celebration of the cuisine she knows intimately and loves, a cuisine that is more adventurous and creative than that of most other parts of Italy. Nearly 200 recipes offer something for every cook, whether a novice or experienced. Anecdotes about Calabrian culture and history, traditions, festivals, folklore, and of course, the primary role that food plays in all aspects of Italian life complete this wonderful piece of culinary anthropology.

320 pages • 8 × 10 • $18.95pb • 0-7818-1050-7 • (660)

SICILIAN FEASTS

GIOVANNA BELLIA LA MARCA

Sicilian Feasts was born out of Giovanna La Marca's love for her native Sicily. She shares the history, customs, folklore, and the flavorful and varied cuisine of her beautiful Mediterranean island in these recipes, stories, and anecdotes. *Sicilian Feasts* offers more than 160 recipes, along with menus for holidays, notes on ingredients, list of suppliers, an introduction to the Sicilian language, and a glossary of food terms in Sicilian, Italian, and English.

Dishes such as *Mpanata*, a lamb pie from Ragusa, are sure to please one's most exacting guests. Simple methods and readily available ingredients allow even novices to create feasts in their kitchens. La Marca features examples of elaborate dishes created by the monzu, a class of eighteenth- and nineteenth-century professional cooks—ones you can now effortlessly recreate with modern appliances. She also introduces her readers to the practice of transforming almond paste into beautiful and realistic marzipan fruits, a traditional Sicilian art form. Illustrations demonstrate special techniques used to prepare these dishes in this delightful Italian cookbook.

240 pages • 6 × 9 • $24.95hc (Can $39.95) • 0-7818-0967-3 • W • (539) • June

CUISINES OF THE ALPS: RECIPES, DRINKS, AND LORE FROM FRANCE, SWITZERLAND, LIECHTENSTEIN, ITALY, GERMANY, AUSTRIA, AND SLOVENIA

KAY SHAW NELSON

A majestic mountain system of south-central Europe, forming about a 750-mile arc from the Gulf of Genoa in the Mediterranean Sea to Albania, the Alps have dozens of peaks taller than 10,000 feet. They are divided into the Western Alps (southeastern France, northwestern Italy), the Central Alps (north-central Italy, southern Switzerland, Liechtenstein), and the Eastern Alps (parts of Germany, Austria, and Slovenia), each of which contains several separate ranges.

In *All Along the Alps*, Kay Shaw Nelson offers more than 140 recipes that range from classic Italian pasta dishes to the wonderful fish preparations found in each of the regions. A section on beverages examines the wine production of these countries, from the well-known French and Italian wines to the more unfamiliar offerings of Slovenia and Liechtenstein, and an extensive historical and geographical introduction complements the comprehensive headnotes. The cuisine of the Alpine regions is ample evidence that the people who live there share a fondness for fine food, regardless of their regional or cultural differences.

220 pages • 6 × 9 • $24.95hc • 0-7818-1058-2 • W • (59)

TRAVEL

LANGUAGE AND TRAVEL GUIDE TO SICILY

GIOVANNA BELLIA LA MARCA

A native of Ragusa, Sicily, and the author of Hippocrene's *Sicilian Feasts*, Giovanna La Marca takes us through the beauties of her home country's landscapes, architecture, and people, who are so devoted to their world famous cuisine that the highest compliment they could pay to a book like the *Language and Travel Guide to Sicily* is that it is "as good as bread." This book comes with an eighty minute audio CD that guides the reader through the language as well as the land, providing invaluable assistance to anyone who hopes to explore Sicily.

200 pages • 5 ½ × 8 ½ • 0-7818-1149-X • $21.95 pb w. audio CD • (38)

SICILY: AN ILLUSTRATED HISTORY

JOSEPH F. PRIVITERA

This concise history relates how Sicily rose to become the first independent, civilized nation of greater Italy, as well as home to many of the world's most distinguished philosophers, mathematicians, scientists, and artists. The narrative subsequently recounts the region's millennium-long decline at the hands of foreign invaders, its hard-won battle for freedom in 1860 under the leadership of Giuseppe Garibaldi, and its current status as a center of art and tourism.

152 pages • 5 × 7 • 0-7818-0909-6 • $12.95 pb • (301)

ITALY: AN ILLUSTRATED HISTORY

JOSEPH F. PRIVITERA

Written in an accessible style this illustrated history covers the full panoply of Italy's history — from Roman days to the present times.

150 pages • 5 × 7 • 0-7818-0819-7 • $14.95 pb • (436)

LANGUAGE

BEGINNER'S ITALIAN

JOSEPH F. PRIVITERA

The essential rules of Italian grammar are clearly explained in a series of ten lessons, each composed of a conversational dialogue, vocabulary, and exercises to accompany the grammar explanations. In addition, a chapter focusing on the Italian verb system, an Italian-English vocabulary, and a key to the exercises complement the text.

192 pages • 5½ × 8½ W • 0-7818-0839-1 • $14.95 pb • (208)

ITALIAN-ENGLISH/ ENGLISH-ITALIAN DICTIONARY AND PHRASEBOOK

FEDERICA L. CLEMENTI

Getting around in Italy becomes easy with this handy language guide. Featuring 2500 entries and an easily accessible format, it provides basic grammar and the vocabulary and phrases essential to any traveler.

213 pages • 3¾ × 7 • 0-7818-0812-X • $11.95 pb • (137)

ITALIAN-ENGLISH/ ENGLISH ITALIAN PRACTICAL DICTIONARY, NEW EDITION

PETER F. ROSS

This practical dictionary features over 35,000 entries for students and travelers. A phonetic guide in both languages and a handy glossary of menu terms is included, as well as a bilingual instruction on how to use the dictionary. Also included — a bilingual list of irregular verbs and abbreviations.

433 pages • 5½ × 8¼ • 0-7818-0354-3 • $12.95 pb • (201)

INSTANT ITALIAN VOCABULARY BUILDER, REV. WITH AUDIO CD

TOM MEANS

This useful learning supplement is the only Italian language acquisition book that uses word-ending patterns. The words introduced in each lesson are accompanied by exercises that are fun and edify. Perfect as a classroom supplement or self-study tool, it is appropriate for all ages and levels of study.

200 pages • 6 × 9 • 0-7818-0980-0 • $ 19.95 pb w. audio CD • (152)

SICILIAN-ENGLISH/ENGLISH-SICILIAN DICTIONARY & PHRASEBOOK

JOSEPH F. PRIVITERA

The speech of the Sicilian people bears the imprint of the island's remarkable history. Primarily based on Latin and Italian, it contains traces of Greek, Arabic, French, Old Provençal, and Spanish. This book features a concise Sicilian grammar and a bilingual dictionary with pronunciation guide. The comprehensive phrasebook offers guidance for situations including dining out, accommodations, and obtaining medical care.

200 pages • 3¾ × 7½ • 0-7818-0984-3 • $11.95 pb • (494)

BEGINNER'S SICILIAN

JOSEPH F. PRIVITERA

This introductory guide teaches the structure of the Sicilian language, covering essential grammar in 10 lessons, along with practice dialogues, vocabulary and expressions, and review exercises. An introduction to the Sicilian culture also includes information for travelers.

159 pages • 5½ × 8½ • 0-7818-0640-2 • $11.95 pb • (716)

HIPPOCRENE CHILDREN'S ILLUSTRATED ITALIAN DICTIONARY

Children are blessed with infinite curiosity and a truly extraordinary capacity for learning. Now little ones have this enticing dictionary to help prepare for Italian classes in school – 500 entries and illustrations provide them with basic vocabulary.

94 pages • 8½ × 11 • 0-7818-0771-9 • $14.95 • (355)x

Prices subject to change without prior notice. To purchase Hippocrene Books contact your local bookstore, visit www.hippocrenebooks.com, call (718) 454-2366, or write to: HIPPOCRENE BOOKS, 171 Madison Avenue, New York, NY 10016. Please enclose check or money order, adding $5.00 shipping (UPS) for the first book, and $.50 for each additional book.